LATINO PROTESTANTS IN AMERICA

Also by Mark T. Mulder

Shades of White Flight: Evangelical Congregations and Urban Departure

Also by Gerardo Martí

A Mosaic of Believers: Diversity and Innovation in a Multiethnic Church

Hollywood Faith: Holiness, Prosperity, and Ambition in a Los Angeles Church

Worship across the Racial Divide: Religious Music and the Multiracial Church

The Deconstructed Church: Understanding Emerging Christianity (with Gladys Ganiel)

LATINO PROTESTANTS IN AMERICA

Growing and Diverse

Mark T. Mulder, Aida I. Ramos, and Gerardo Martí

ROWMAN & LITTLEFIELD
Lanham • Boulder • New York • London

Published by Rowman & Littlefield
An imprint of The Rowman & Littlefield Publishing Group, Inc.
4501 Forbes Boulevard, Suite 200, Lanham, Maryland 20706
https://rowman.com

6 Tinworth Street, London SE11 5AL, United Kingdom

British Library Cataloguing in Publication Information Available

Library of Congress Cataloging-in-Publication Data
Names: Mulder, Mark T., 1973– author. | Ramos, Aida, author. | Martí, Gerardo, 1965– author.
Title: Latino Protestants in America : growing and diverse / Mark T. Mulder, Aida I. Ramos, and Gerardo Martí.
Description: Lanham, Maryland : Rowman & Littlefield Publishers, 2017. | Includes bibliographical references and index.
Identifiers: LCCN 2016048443 (print) | LCCN 2016053616 (ebook) | ISBN 9781442256545 (hardback) | ISBN 9781538153147 (paperback) | ISBN 9781442256552 (electronic)
Subjects: LCSH: Hispanic American Protestants—United States. | United States—Church history. | BISAC: RELIGION / Christianity / Protestant. | SOCIAL SCIENCE / Ethnic Studies / Hispanic American Studies. | SOCIAL SCIENCE / Sociology of Religion.
Classification: LCC BR563.H57 M85 2017 (print) | LCC BR563.H57 (ebook) | DDC 280/ .408968073—dc23
LC record available at https://lccn.loc.gov/2016048443

CONTENTS

PREFACE

Latino Protestantism stands as a vigorous outlier of religious *growth* in this country. Overall, the percentage of Christians in the United States has been in steady decline, and the share of adults who claim no religious affiliation continues to expand. Focusing on Protestantism, we see that both mainline and evangelical churches have suffered losses in recent years. Focusing on Catholicism, the percentage of Latinos who identify as Roman Catholics has slumped from 68 percent to 55 percent in less than a decade. Yet, within the larger milieu of seeming religious malaise in America, Latino Protestantism has demonstrated a remarkable vitality as surveys report that more and more Latinos identify as Protestant. Latino Protestant churches are growing, and Latino Protestant parachurch organizations are expanding. Despite this vibrancy, we know very little about Latino Protestants.

Latino Protestants in America addresses the lack of understanding and information by collating the best existing scholarship on this fascinating group alongside reporting some of our own original, social scientific observations. We find an increasing interest in Latino Protestants among scholars, among journalists, and among church leaders and Christians in general. Based on the increase of magazine articles and conferences related to Latino Protestants, we believe that this volume fills a synergistic niche of academic, journalistic, and ecclesial audiences. The information, evidence, and arguments distilled in the following pages are provided in the hope that they will provoke even greater attention on this burgeoning wing of Christianity in the United States.

In the end, our intention is to substantiate and further stimulate more careful and more intensive lines of inquiry on Latino Protestants and their churches.

Thanks first and foremost to friends, new and old, who shared with us varied aspects of Latino Protestantism. Words cannot convey the levels of appreciation to all the leaders and members of the congregations who took time in their busy lives to welcome us. By opening their lives, their churches, and their communities, these men and women allow researchers like us privileged access to this dynamically growing and evolving group in the United States. Without them, this book would not be possible. Any errors committed in our sincere attempt to accurately describe the multiple, layered aspects of Latino Protestant Christianity are solely our own.

Toward collecting ethnographic data for this research, Gerardo Martí and Mark Mulder received grant support funded by Lilly Endowment to form the Latino Protestant Congregations (LPC) Project.[1] Aida Ramos is a primary contributor to the project as an LPC Project research fellow. Together, along with a team of colleagues across the American continent, we have been gathering interviews and observations from churches large and small, urban and rural, mainline and evangelical, whether located in homes, church basements, rented facilities, or large megachurches. We thank all the research fellows involved in the LPC project—Debbie Berho, Ricardo Franco, Peter Marina, Jonathan Calvillo, Melissa Guzman, Karen Hooge Michalka, Jeanette "Lil Milagro" Henriquez, and Mandy Rodgers-Gates—for their consultation and vital role in collecting data from Latino churches across the country. Chris Coble and John Wimmer at Lilly Endowment enabled funding for our ambitious project. Our up-close and intimate participation with Latino Protestant churches (LPC's) have greatly expanded our perspectives, offering both affirmation and surprises about this fascinating and important segment of the U.S. population. Special thanks go to John Witvliet, director of the Institute for the Study of Christian Worship, and to Neil Carlson, director of the Calvin Center for Social Research, for the considerable support received during our data collection. Gratitude is also extended to Jenna Hunt and Karen Van Drunen for their hospitality in hosting three consecutive years of LPC Project meetings under the Seminars @ Calvin umbrella in Grand Rapids, Michigan. Davidson College provided additional funding to Gerardo

2015–2016 through the Boswell Family Sabbatical Fellowship. Portions of the article titled "Latino Protestants and Their Churches: Establishing an Agenda for Sociological Research" published in *Sociology of Religion* are used in chapter 7 with permission from the journal.[2]

Mark would like to thank the colleagues within his department for fostering a robust atmosphere of collegiality at Calvin College. Much is owed to Todd Vanden Berg, Lissa Schwander, Roman Williams, Elisha Marr, Jon Hill, Rachel Venema, Kristen Alford, Joe Kuilema, and Stacia Hoeksema. Outside the hallway, colleagues John Witvliet, Don De-Graaf, Jeff Bouman, Gail Heffner, Cheryl Brandsen, Michelle Loyd-Paige, and Todd Cioffi deserve thanks as well. Gratitude is also extended to good friends Jamie and Deanna Smith and Dan and Bethany Slane, who help to make Grand Rapids home. A special thanks as well to Jeremy Hekhuis, a dear friend and fellow traveler who helped to establish a foundation for this work years ago. A significant portion of this volume was written across the table from Peter Boumgarden at Ferris Coffee; he provided valuable and winsome company throughout. Mark also continues to owe much to the formative Seminars @ Calvin designed and facilitated by Michael Emerson and Steve Warner. Finally, a most profound note of gratitude to Dawn Mulder for her loving support, keen insight, and profound grace.

Aida would like to foremost thank Gerardo Martí and Mark Mulder for the opportunity to be a part of the LPC Project—a life-changing and critical point in her life and growth as a scholar of Latino religion. Their friendship and support along with the rest of the fellows has been a gift. A special thanks to LPC Project research fellow Melissa Guzman, who was always willing to take the time to provide feedback at the drop of a hat and whose expertise has been invaluable. Also thanks to LPC Project research fellow Debbie Berho for her encouragement and camaraderie and to Lloyd Barba for his keen insights and feedback. Aida would also like to thank colleagues at the University of Texas at San Antonio, particularly, Melinda Denton, for her unwavering care and mentorship, as well as John Bartkowski, Christopher Ellison, Gabriel Acevedo, and Heather Edelblute for their guidance, friendship, and support. I am so grateful for my dear comadres, Molly Dondero and Mieke Beth Thomeer, who provided critical feedback and writing support throughout the whole project. Another special thank you to current and former students for their assistance in this project at the University of Texas at San Antonio: Tara Fletcher, Socorro Montañez, Christina Helm, Keila Taylor, and Reed DeAngelis. Many thanks also for the care and support by many at Grace Northridge in San Antonio.

Gerardo again thanks the LPC Project research fellows for their contributions through data collection and collaborative discussion in furthering social scientific research on Latino Protestants. The LPC Project's codirector, Mark Mulder, has proven to be a wonderful partner and collaborator. Davidson College provided a productive setting for the management of the larger research project and for the preliminary analysis of the information collected so far. LuAnne Sledge in the Grants and Contracts office deserves high praise for her invaluable work in managing grant accounts for the LPC Project. Gerardo also thanks Gayle Kaufman (Davidson College), Samuel Sanchez y Sanchez (Davidson College), and Kevin D. Dougherty (Baylor University) for their friendship, feedback, and camaraderie.

Sarah Stanton, senior editor at Rowman and Littlefield, was always efficient and gracious in working through all stages of the project, and Karie Simpson managed the complex processes largely invisible to authors yet essential for their published work.

I

LATINO PROTESTANTS ARE MORE THAN "NOT CATHOLIC"

WHAT DO WE KNOW ABOUT LATINO PROTESTANTS?

On a Sunday morning, a Pentecostal congregation in the Pacific Northwest worships in a disciplined manner: no dancing, limited bodily movement, every segment of the service to run a rigidly designated amount of time. At the same time, a nondenominational megachurch in Texas worships in an expansive dance-club atmosphere: throbbing bass, strobe lights, and a beautiful cast of worship leaders. Another two thousand miles to the east, in North Carolina, an Episcopal church begins its service following a solemn, traditional Anglican liturgy: hymns, intercession, ministry of the sacrament—all are included. These disparate scenes of worship seemingly have little in common. They sing different songs. They speak various languages. They hear different sermons. The edifices range in size and aesthetics. The order of ritual varies from congregation to congregation to congregation. And yet, a common thread weaves the three aforementioned churches into the same complex tapestry: all three represent a diverse and thriving segment of American Christianity—*Latino Protestantism*.

Our simple—yet significant—reason for writing this book is that Latino Protestantism is growing rapidly in the United States. In a religious landscape where disaffiliation and the rise of the "nones" seems to be the driving trend and the narrative of numerous studies, Latino Protestantism stands as an outlier of remarkable religious growth.[1]

Overall, the Latino population in the United States continues to increase: reaching over fifty-five million in 2014—accounting for over 17 percent of the population.[2] Within that larger trend of population growth, 22 percent of Latinos identified as Protestant in 2014—up from 19 percent Protestant in 2007.[3] Beyond that, it is estimated that by 2030 half of all Latinos in America will be Protestant.[4] Already in 2015 Latino Protestants in the United States outnumbered Episcopalians by a factor of three to one.[5] This dramatic surge, though, is not just about numbers. The rise of Latino Protestants will impact the changing nature of American politics, economics, and (obviously) religion. It remains surprising that the growth and impact of Latino Protestants has not been more widely recognized by the general public. On the cover of the April 4, 2013 issue, *Time* magazine proclaimed that the United States was experiencing "The Latino Reformation." The cover story noted the rise of Latino Protestants, "one of the fastest growing segments of America's churchgoing millions." However, writer Elizabeth Dias also highlighted the necessity for her story because this emergent population of Latino Protestants has remained largely invisible to both mainstream American culture and to many of their fellow Protestants. Dias asserted that the unobtrusive location of many of their churches (including storefronts, church basements, and living rooms) as well as the dominance of their worshipping in a foreign language (Spanish, including many region-specific dialects) confounds research efforts and therefore contributes to lack of attention.[6]

Beyond language and location difficulties, we also know that researchers have discovered unique challenges in conducting surveys on U.S. Latinos. No less than the Pew Research Center has related complications that include "language barriers, sampling issues, and cultural differences."[7] Pew reports that, for instance, Latinos tend to be more likely than other racial/ethnic groups to refuse to participate in surveys or, having agreed to take the survey, to not answer specific questions. Beyond that, studies also indicate that Latinos are the racial/ethnic group most likely to live in cellphone-only households. Why would that matter? Cellphone surveys remain less used than landline surveys because they have considerably higher implementation costs. For these reasons, we have relatively limited data about Latinos—including the Protestants in their midst.

Thus, even as many indicators point to the groundswell of this segment of Protestantism, our understanding of Latino Protestants—and Latinos in general—remains limited because obtaining reliable information is difficult. While there have been issues of low response rates with some of the Pew surveys we cite, other studies demonstrate similar conclusions, and we can be certain of this shift to/growth of Latino Protestantism.[8] These survey issues also signal the necessity of qualitative work to substantiate the patterns in the quantitative data. Beyond that, however, our qualitative work attempts to better understand local context, worship patterns, expressions of identity, and civic engagement. *Latino Protestants in America* seeks to address the lack of understanding and information by collating the best existing scholarship on this group alongside reporting our own original, social scientific observations. Our ethnographic glimpses rely on the field notes and interviews collected by the LPC Project Research Fellows from 20 Latino Protestant congregations across the continental United States.[9] In the end, we intend to synthesize, clarify, and further stimulate an intensive line of inquiry regarding Latino Protestants and their churches.

PAYING ATTENTION TO LATINO PROTESTANTS

One of U.S. Christianity's Few Growth Markets

We contend that it is past time to begin paying attention: this burgeoning wing of Protestantism has been gaining momentum and will only continue to expand in significance in the coming decades. It is estimated that by 2050 almost one-third of the U.S. population will be Latino.[10] Moreover, some scholars predict that because of high fertility rates, conversion from Roman Catholicism, and immigration from Protestant majority source countries (such as Guatemala and El Salvador), more and more of these U.S. Latinos will profess a Protestant faith. As the numbers of Latino Protestants increase, their presence will continue to have greater consequence in the larger culture. We make the case that the rise of Latino Protestantism will be one of the most important trends in U.S. religion in the coming decades.

Latino Protestants and their congregational life matter because we *do* know that religious devotion and practice has deep salience for Latino Protestants. That is, the sparse existing research available demonstrates that their religion really matters to them. Robert Putnam and David Campbell noted in *American Grace: How Religion Divides and Unites Us* that 85 percent of Latino evangelicals indicate that religion is *very important* in daily life.[11] That high percentage is seen in even starker relief when compared with their coreligionists (white evangelicals: 75 percent) and their co-ethnics (Latino Catholics: 72 percent).[12] In other words, faith holds more significance for Latino Protestants than it does for white evangelicals or Latino Catholics. For Latino Protestants, their faith matters and, thus, permeates other aspects of their lives. We know, for instance, that Latino Protestants (whether coming from evangelical, Pentecostal, or mainline orientations) tend to be more religiously active than their Catholic counterparts. And it is more than personal devotion that is significant; Latino Protestant congregations capture and channel their religiosity. They attend church services and small groups more often than Roman Catholics.[13] In short, much of social life for Protestant Latinos centers on the local congregation. With that in mind, their churches are strategic arenas for understanding this growing but neglected religious segment.

As we explore Latino Protestantism, we wish to avoid bland generalizations or knee-jerk categorizations. Our goal in writing this book is to present a textured, thick portrait of and introduction to Latino Protestant churches and their attenders by taking advantage of our newly gathered ethnographic data and synthesizing it with survey data. In fact, we will demonstrate that Latino Protestants engage in widely divergent worship practices: some staid and rigidly ordered, others exuberant and charismatic, and still others somewhere between on the continuum. We will also see differences in issues of identity and neighborhood/community engagement. Our research allows us to explicitly confront the tendency toward homogenizing "Latino Protestants" as a singular racial-ethnic group or religious milieu, and we will use our data to further illustrate and explain careful distinctions and their significance.

Not Just a "Fiesta"

As we conduct our own qualitative research on Latino Protestants and their churches in the United States we are struck by the number of times we have heard and read sweeping statements from pastors, church consultants, denominational leaders, and seminary professors that assume a modicum of uniformity among this group. We see *Latino Protestants in America* as an initial interrogation of that seemingly widely held assumption. In our synthesis and explanation of relevant scholarship, we demonstrate a complexity and diversity among Latino Protestants that will be both provocative and generative. We also make the case that the significant diversity and complexity of this developing subset of Protestantism in the United States demands more attention from both church leaders and academics.

Although there are currently more Latino Roman Catholics than Protestants in the United States, we focus on Protestants primarily because there is a surge of population growth among Protestants—consequently Latino Protestant churches—yet they are so poorly understood. By emphasizing the types of diversity found among Latino Protestants and illustrating them from our own research we wish to both recognize and further accentuate the multiplicity of dimensions to discover. These are aspects of Latino Protestantism that are left ignored, unexamined, or unexplained. For example, we have been surprised by recent research examining Latino Protestants in which the authors seemingly craft contradictory claims.[14] While emphasizing the variety of the Latino experience early in their writings (e.g., "we see ourselves as a 'heterogeneous and complex' minority" and "diversity is [the Latino] trademark"[15]), later in the *same publication* they will highlight deep commonalities (e.g., that Hispanics are "passionate"[16] people, who nearly always live "in the same types of neighborhoods and communities,"[17] and desire to attend churches with mostly Latinos[18]). Indeed, after first asserting Latino diversity, multiple writers end up later assuming a level of homogeneity: "most of us [Latinos] share a common religious worldview and spirituality"[19] and are "characterized by a distinctive Hispanic orientation."[20]

Not only do we find contradictory claims of diversity alongside homogeneity, we also find that contemporary writers confidently assert essentialist stereotypes as analytical statements. For example, we have been surprised in reading books on Latino Protestants—among the only sources published on Latino Protestantism available today—by the frequency of vague assessments that confidently assert Latino Protestants have "worship services with a Latino flavor"[21] and engage in "passionate worship."[22] As social scientists, we are left scratching our heads. What does it mean for a *Latino* church to have a "*Latino* flavor"? Moreover, these authors claim that Latino churches are said to have "worship services that look like a fiesta" and are characterized by "the spirit of fiesta."[23] In our assessment, such categorizations play on racialized stereotypes of Latinos that fail to describe—even less explain—any concrete dynamics or mechanisms operating in these churches.[24]

As a constructive response, we attempt to avoid such front-loaded, racialized assumptions and use careful synthesis and explanation to better understand the dynamics and nuance of congregational practices among Latino Protestant Congregations. Rather than reduce complex dynamics to vague generalities, we draw on available scholarship alongside our own original research to follow up on avenues of distinction that point to the substantive social structures affecting these congregations. For example, looking at Pew Hispanic Center's studies more carefully, we note the diversity of religious orientations among the 20 percent of Latinos they report as being Protestant: 15 percent are "evangelical" ("born again"), and within that percentage half of them are more specifically "Pentecostal." The other 5 percent of Latinos are mainline (e.g., Presbyterian, Methodist, Lutheran, Episcopalian).[25] Generally, this means that one-third of Latino Protestants are Non-Pentecostal (Baptistic) evangelicals, one-third are Pentecostal evangelical, and one-third are mainline Protestant—important information for considering, again, the distinctiveness of Latino Protestants in terms of religious belief and practice.

Pew studies also reveal other types of diversity. Specifically, we know the diversity of Latino congregations extends to members of these churches. Evangelical and mainline Latino Protestants are more likely to have English rather than Spanish as their primary language compared to Latino Catholics.[26] Evangelical and mainline Latinos are also more likely to have higher household incomes and higher levels of education.[27] While the trends found in these figures are not so strong as to conclude that all evangelicals and mainline Latinos who speak English are both wealthier and better educated, for social scientists who wish to conduct qualitative studies, these trends sensitize them to pay attention to such diversity and how such variations may affect the liturgical structure of Latino congregations.

Defining "Latino Protestant Congregations"

Reliable data from current research also demonstrates other distinctions. Nearly 75 percent of Latino Protestants attend congregations that are majority Latino; 80 percent report the presence of Latino leaders in their congregation, and 90 percent report worship services are available in Spanish. With that data in mind, we feel prompted to consider more dimensions:

- Latino congregational membership: Are they the few or the majority?
- Latino church leadership: Is it absent or present?
- Language in services: Do we find English, Spanish, and/or Bilingual services?

In response to these questions, it might be tempting to suggest that "truly Latino" congregations are (1) majority Latino, (2) have Latino faith leaders, and (3) use Spanish as the primary language. Yet, a closer look at Pew data reveals that this categorization would capture *only 62 percent* of Latino evangelical churchgoers and *only 48 percent* of mainline Protestants. In short, such an operationalization of Latino churches ignores the breadth of difference that exists among Latino Protestants—the type of distinctions that qualitative researchers like us most want to explore. More importantly, such categorization removes the opportunity to investigate how social forces affect the context of specific congregations and what determines the choice of liturgy, ministry programming, and other ecclesial activities.

DIVERSE AND WIDELY DIFFUSED

While we can successfully tease out aspects of diversity in the quantitative research made recently available, the numbers fail to capture much of what is actually occurring within these congregations. Building on the few qualitative sources available, our ethnographic research provides yet more intriguing directions for future lines of inquiry. For example, we know that the ethnic makeup of Latino Protestant congregations can vary. Manuel Vasquez compared a Salvadoran and a Peruvian Protestant church in an insightful study of two congregations.[28]

However, Vasquez reveals that the character of these two churches was not necessarily reduced to their national origins. He found that the Salvadoran church maintained strong transnational ties to El Salvador, making the members of this church ethnically committed to a specific Hispanic culture. In contrast, the Peruvian congregation was far more diverse, containing members with origins across a broader spectrum of Latin America. Even more, the Peruvian congregation defined themselves as broadly "Hispanic" and saw themselves as more connected to the United States as "Americans." When we grasp the contrasting dynamics of these churches (ethnic-specific versus pan-ethnic Latino ethnicities), both of the churches examined by Vasquez contrast further with the Latino members of the multiethnic Protestant church called Mosaic examined by Gerardo Martí.[29] Latinos made up about one-third of this Los Angeles church, but Mosaic members did not prioritize either their ethnic connections or their ethnic roots. The church did not emphasize ethnic affiliations, preferring members to see themselves as highlighting the commonality of their religious identity as "Christians" with other races such that ethnic groups "transcended" their ethnic differences. Overall, we suggest that by looking at both Vasquez and Martí's studies we see how the nature of being "Latino" can change. The ethnic composition of a congregation and the social and theological imperatives that impinge on members affect the understanding of what it means to be a proper member of these churches—which impacts the nature of Latino Protestantism among various churches.

In recent years, ethnographic studies have brought out even more interesting dynamics among Latino Protestants. Jane Juffer examined a Reformed church in northwest Iowa that sought to become a hybrid religious site of Anglo-Latino worship.[30] The congregation had become an unexpected synthesis of Dutch and Latino cultures. Our guess is that most observers would be stunned by such a case. Juffer asserts that the site of her ethnography, Amistad Cristiana church, functioned not as an institution of Latino assimilation to the United States but rather as a place where attenders with different ethnic backgrounds found unity in their reliance on a Protestant work ethic. In another case study, Laura López-Sanders examined Latino immigrants in the Greenville-Spartanburg-Anderson region of South Carolina.[31] López-Sanders spent time as a participant observer at Latino Protestant worship services and Bible studies and argued that the religious orientations of these congregations affected their experience of mainstream assimilation. Latinos who attended more liberal Protestant churches tended to integrate into the "new South" more quickly than those who worshipped in more conservative Protestant churches. Both Juffer's and López-Sanders's studies are further examples of ethnographic research that offer textured, qualitative insights concerning Latino Protestants in two disparate regions of the country. This volume attempts to integrate the best of both quantitative *and* qualitative research into a coherent distillation of the heterogeneity of Latino Protestants in personal identity, church life, and social engagement.[32]

Our own research, which involves collecting qualitative data from Latino Protestant congregations across America (including Oregon, California, Indiana, Texas, North Carolina, New York, Massachusetts, Rhode Island, and Wisconsin), provides further intriguing complexity and highlights dynamics that productively expand our sensitivities to Latino Protestantism. Latino churches included in our ethnographies include Pentecostal, Baptist, Episcopal, Presbyterian, Assemblies of God, and nondenominational. Thus our sites of inquiry span both geography and theology. In the end, we see this book as offering a broad-based exploration of Latino Protestants in the United States in the early twenty-first century.

RELATIONSHIP TO ROMAN CATHOLICISM

A Waning Affiliation

A major component of this story involves the correlated decline in the percentage of Latinos who identify as Catholic. Historically, many observers in the United States have equated Latinos with the Roman Catholic faith. Much of that assumption, of course, finds basis in the dominance of Catholicism within many Latino countries. Indeed, at one point in time, the vast majority of Latinos in the United States did practice a Catholic faith. The residue of that history wove the Catholic faith deeply into the fabric of Latino identity in this country. With the significant shift away from Catholicism, though, there have arisen accompanying questions about what it means to be a Latino without the Catholic faith.

As already noted, Latino Protestantism growth has been catalyzed by high fertility rates,[33] immigration from significantly Protestant source countries, and conversion from Catholicism. Regarding conversion, Latinos have been leaving the Catholic Church at high rates. Gastón Espinosa estimated about six hundred thousand[34] defections annually in the late 2000s and asserted "that for every one [Latino] who comes back to the Catholic church, four leave it."[35] A scholarly consensus for explaining Catholic-to-Protestant conversion, however, has not been established.

Explaining Protestant Attraction for Latinos

As early as the 1960s and 1970s, a few scholars took note of Latino conversions to Protestantism.[36] These early studies tended to view the religious change as a symptom of the Durkheimian concept of *anomie*.[37] That is, that the process of migration and resettlement left these Latinos socially anchorless and casting about for a new religion onto which they could fasten themselves. Within that tumult, Pentecostalism functioned as a new refuge. In a bit of contrast, sociologist Andrew Greeley posited that the appeal for Latinos in evangelical Protestant groups centered around the assumption that membership in those types of churches stood as signifiers of middle class respectability in the United States.[38]

Espinosa attributes the decided shift toward Protestantism, in part, to ethnic identity: While many Catholic parishes might be spilling over with Latinos, the priests might still be ethnically Irish- or Polish-American. Beyond that, the hierarchical apparatus of the Catholic Church inhibits its ability to be more responsive to an influx of Latino attenders. On the other hand, Espinosa contends that Latino Protestant congregations remain more likely to have a Spanish-speaking pastor who might resonate more effectively with attenders. Moreover, the relative freedom of many strains of Protestantism allows for liturgy to be shaped in a way that might better echo the rhythms and cadences of the mother country. Beyond that, Latinos trekking to Protestant congregations frequently find a church polity that allows for increased and appealing opportunities to participate in the leadership of the church.[39] For a population that remains socioeconomically marginalized and even vilified by certain politicians, congregational leadership mitigates social dislocation and offers opportunities to build social capital.

Beyond that, though, others have indicated the heightened religious experience may also explain the Protestant lure in some cases. Samuel Rodriguez, president of the National Hispanic Christian Leadership Conference (NHCLC) and a Pentecostal pastor, argues that part of the Protestant appeal centers on a less mediated and more "experiential" worship experience.[40] That is, at least part of attraction of Latino Protestant congregations rests in the claim of "direct access to Jesus."[41]

The Latino losses being absorbed by the Catholic Church has not gone unnoticed. A 2007 article in the *National Catholic Reporter* indicated that the church would do well to recognize that it had allowed a serious marketing problem with Latinos to fester. In many ways, Catholic parishes had failed to present themselves as resources of help and information:

> The Catholic church is too physically and emotionally distant to help [Latinos] cope with the pressures and uncertainties of their new life in the United States. To be sure, the Catholic church has many social services available, but these are typically presented in a bureaucratized fashion, through special offices and agencies. They are not parish-centered in a way that makes Hispanics feel welcome and at home. This is where Protestant evangelicals have gained the advantage.[42]

From the Catholic perspective, then, the decentralized agility of Protestant churches allows them to respond to both the physical and spiritual needs of Latinos in ways that make conversion more appealing.

Identity Issues for Converts

Though these conversions out of Catholicism occur in high numbers, the phenomenon should not be misconstrued as an easy decision or smooth process. Studies have demonstrated that an intertwining of ethnic and religious identities tends to manifest in high social costs for those who convert. Congregational and family/friend networks tend to be so overlapping that a rupture within the church affiliation reverberates throughout an individual's social matrix. Because the Catholic Church serves as a venue for social life participation in various Latino cultural traditions, a switch out of the tradition has significant cultural costs. For instance, it could be interpreted that conversion to Protestantism represents a step toward assimilation into a U.S. religious mainstream where distinctive Latino identities might be abandoned. Indeed, there exists some evidence for a movement away from "Latinoism" within the switch to Protestantism. First, English-dominant Latinos remain more likely to convert. Second, for those who switch, the religious identity tends to supersede racial/ethnic identity. In other words, conversion to Protestantism may become a primary identity that weakens the significance of all other components of identity. [43]

Interviews with former Latino Catholics demonstrate that those who convert feel a great amount of tension among family members who have remained Catholic. Informants indicated that they worried that they had betrayed their families and their communities by abandoning long-standing traditions and rituals. One twenty-two-year-old women told us: "With my family that is still in Mexico and the one that is here [Texas], I have never been able to connect with them or have a close relationship because of my [Protestant] faith. That's part of my Mexican culture, I don't think I will be fully in touch because they marked us as traitors."[44] Clearly, for some converts the switch to Protestantism has painful costs that rupture familial and community bonds.

Moreover, some—but not all—of our informants also related the feeling that conversion to Protestantism signaled a process of becoming less Latino and more "white." When Ana, a nineteen-year-old women joined a Pentecostal congregation, she discussed her "new ideas, new beliefs, actions" that resulted in being "definitely thought of as more white." When pressed how such a racial transition could work as she still attended a Latino church, she responded that she had stopped making "Hispanic decisions." Statements such as these lead us to conclude that, for many, their Latino identity remains deeply intertwined with religion and faith.

At the other end of the spectrum, though, we also heard from Latino Protestants who felt their conversion allowed them to remain in perfect harmony with their racial/ethnic identity. In one instance, the congregation offered regular classes that engaged issues of identity and nurtured deepening senses of what it means to be a Latino. Thus, Latinos have myriad experiences of what it means to be a Protestant within an ethnoracial group that remains predominantly Roman Catholic.

With these complexities in mind, it remains crucial to remember that although Latino Protestantism thrives in the United States, it does so in the shadow of the Catholic Church. That is, Catholicism remains a significant force within many Latino lives—even for many Protestants. Moreover, we see Latino Protestants nurturing unique identities and practices within their congregations. For some, these mimic Catholic practices. For others, though, they directly repudiate Catholic elements of worship. In short, the relationship between Latino Protestants and the Catholic Church remains complex and variegated.

LATINOS, ETHNICITY, AND LANGUAGE

Along with a religious complexity, we should also note an intra-group ethno-racial diversity among Latinos. That is, we acknowledge that "Latino" as a category fails to capture the subdivisions and boundaries that exist within this ethno-racial group. Part of the failure resides in the fact that "Latino," though useful as a type for analysis, remains socially constructed and contested. The term, "Latino," assumes a pan-ethnic identity that simply does not exist. In fact, "Latino" functions only as a tool of convenience to bind together members of multiple ethno-racial and national-origin groups.[45] Part of the distinctiveness within Latino Protestantism follows from the fact that Latino cultural, historical, and national backgrounds vary widely.

An aspect of the construction of ethnoreligious categories involves labels. Typically, "Hispanic" and "Latino" tend to be used interchangeably.[46] We, however, will use "Latino" throughout the book. While we acknowledge the extensive use of "Hispanic," we find "Latino" to be somewhat more inclusive. Since it functions as a singular language category, "Hispanic" necessarily—but not always intentionally—excludes South and Central American nations that have official languages that range from Portuguese to French. With that in mind, we utilize "Latino" in an effort to capture *groups* of people who trace a national background to Latin America (Mexico, Cuba, the Dominican Republic, Haiti, Puerto Rico, Central America, and South America). At the same time, we acknowledge arguments for the use of terms like "Latin@" and "Latinx" as a method for establishing gender neutrality. While we find validity in employing these terms, the issue of labeling remains contested. Because of such little use in Spanish-speaking countries and the inherently gendered structure of the Spanish language, some scholars have wondered about the utility of "Latinx." Moreover, the case has also been made that "Latino" already serves as a gender-neutral descriptor: "In Spanish, when referencing groups, we only use the feminine ending when referring to an exclusively female group."[47] In addition, we use "Latino" out of deference to the vast majority of the informants with whom we conversed as part of the LPC Project—it functioned as their term of preference. In the end, these robust discussions regarding identity also serve to demonstrate its fluidity within the Latino communities in the United States.

Other recent studies also undermine assumptions regarding Latinos and language proficiency. First, the majority of Latino adults (71 percent) in the United States indicate that fluency in Spanish is not a necessary component of Latino identity.[48] Beyond that, a growing majority of Latinos speak English proficiently: from 59 percent in 2000 up to 68 percent in 2013. During that same juncture, the percentage of Latinos who indicated that they spoke Spanish at home declined from 78 to 73. The shift in language usage is symptomatic of the fact that U.S.-born Latinos continue to increase in share of the population while immigration from Latin America stagnates. In fact, 89 percent of U.S.-born Latinos spoke English proficiently in 2013. In sum, U.S.-born Latinos increasingly live in households where *only* English is spoken (40 percent). Moreover, the U.S. Census Bureau projects that English will become more popular in Latino homes while Spanish usage will see a corresponding decline.[49]

Even as Latinos demonstrate acculturation through growing English proficiency, the United States remains both a racially stratified and a polarized nation where prejudiced views continue, sadly, to be abundant. A 2014 study revealed that native-born whites in the United States have distinctive opinions regarding native and foreign-born racial minorities (including blacks, Latinos, and Asians). For example, native-born whites tend to have significantly more negative views of Latino and Asian immigrants than their native-born counterparts. Moreover, native-born whites reserve their most negative stereotypes for immigrant Latinos.[50] Combined with systems and structures of racial injustice, such antipathy certainly has consequences for the lives of Latino Protestants in the United States.

LATINO PROTESTANT INFLUENCE ON U.S. SOCIETY

Attempting to Attract Latinos

As Latino Protestantism continues to grow in the United States it will be influenced by the larger religious milieu of the country. Nevertheless, Latino Protestants have demonstrated indications that they will also be shapers of religious life. Both mainline and evangelical denominations have initiated intensive outreach efforts to woo Latinos. Researcher Larry Ortiz recounts the transformation of an upper-class Presbyterian congregation in a large southwestern city. In an effort to be welcoming to Latinos, the former Anglo-only congregation has been transformed into a "fully bilingual, multicultural church" that frequently includes healing services during weekly worship (a fairly unusual occurrence within the Presbyterian liturgy).[51] Religious studies scholar Marie Friedmann Marquardt describes a similar attempt to appeal to Latinos at an Evangelical Lutheran Church in America congregation in Houston that implemented materials and liturgy "that would provide continuities with the Catholic traditions with which the church's [Mexican-American] members were familiar."[52] In some instances, then, local churches demonstrate initiative to present a more winsome worship style for area Latino populations.

In addition to these congregational transformations, conferences about integrating Latino Protestants into denominations occur frequently throughout the year and from coast to coast. These meetings include plenaries that discuss the growth of Latino Protestants and how traditionally white denominations and congregations might strategize to make their churches more hospitable. As studies demonstrate a clear trend of religious disaffiliation within Protestant Christianity (especially among mainline denominations), these denominations and congregations have begun to consider what they might be willing to consider to attract Latinos.[53] Some have begun to earnestly study demographic trends and engage in marketing strategies that utilize Spanish-language media.[54]

Political and Community Engagement

Beyond influencing traditionally white churches, some Latino Protestant congregations have also begun to demonstrate a willingness to shape local, regional, and national discourse on a range of topics. One researcher has noted that even small Latino Protestant congregations may be "bustling centers of activities which are open and operating most days of the week that not only include worship, praise, and Bible study, but offer other services catering to community needs."[55] Another report notes that the social outreach of Latino Protestant churches frequently outstrips "any government program, with pastors snatching young men away from gang life and fighting to uphold the rights of immigrants."[56] One ethnographic study of a Latino Pentecostal congregation in a southwestern U.S. city recounts how the church's Sunday school offered language and literacy education for teenage attenders who had been marginalized in overcrowded remedial and ESL classes at the local public high school. While the Latino students in the study found the high school isolating, alienating, and hostile, they describe the church as a place that felt supportive and caring. In fact, the Sunday school instruction at the church allowed students to achieve state-established literacy goals for high school graduates.[57] In this way, Latino Protestant congregations serve as educational refuges.

Another ethnographic study finds, in certain contexts, Latino Protestant congregations offer an alternative to gangs. Sociologist Edward Flores argues that Latino Protestant congregations mitigate against downward mobility for former gang members. That is, the churches act as an arena where social capital is built through "religious optimism." The congregation offered community, belonging, and accountability. More than that, though, churches also functioned as sites for training and development of employment skills.[58]

High Profile Networks and Organizations

Though it remains true that many Latino Protestant congregations operate below the radar, some sustain a rather high profile. In fact, some would be classified as "megachurches" that worship in conspicuous multimillion-dollar sanctuaries. For example, Templo Calvario in Santa Ana, California, counts six thousand members and in 2009 opened an

$11 million facility. In addition, the congregation founded a charter school, the Edward B. Cole Academy.[59] And Templo Calvario has company: Latino Protestant megachurches exist across the country in places like Texas, Florida, New York, and Illinois. These congregations tend to not limit themselves to weekend worship services. In sum, then, Latino Protestant congregations span a wide range of activities and organizational acumen—from intimate living room gatherings to massive congregations with highly developed educational and social service delivery programs.

Beyond the megachurches, there has also been growth in faith-based Latino Protestant nonprofits and community-oriented organizations. These associations exercise power at local, regional, and national levels. With Latino Protestants representing a growth demographic in the United States, politicians have started to take notice. Gabriel Salguero, a Latino Protestant pastor in Orlando and president of the National Latino Evangelical Coalition (NaLEC), sat on President Barack Obama's Advisory Council on Faith-Based and Neighborhood Partnerships and regularly writes for the *Huffington Post*'s religion page. NaLEC represents a consortium of over three thousand Latino Protestant congregations. In early 2015, the organization followed Pope Francis' condemnation of the death penalty with their own statement demanding the repeal of capital punishment.[60] Salguero argued that capital punishment continues to be "plagued by racial and economic disparities." In addition, the aforementioned Samuel Rodriguez and the NHCLC (which claims to represent 40,000 congregations) tend to be prominent voices on issues that range from social service delivery to education to immigration reform.[61] Rodriguez argues that congregations have a central socioeconomic role: "In the Latino community, the church is still the most influential institution." With that in mind, Rodriguez contends, "Our faith empowers us to deal with the daily minutiae."[62] At all levels, we see Latino Protestants leveraging a growing influence throughout the United States.

A MAP OF THE BOOK

Here is a brief summary of the following chapters. Having delineated the growing significance of Latino Protestants, chapter 2 offers a brief history of Latinos in the United States. We make the case, first of all, that Latinos are not newcomers. In fact, they have been here a long time. The complexity of Latino history in the United States demands that the larger narrative regarding immigration not simply subsume the story told about their religious lives. Recent studies demonstrate the numerical significance of Latinos in the United States. We now find almost six million Latinos in the Los Angeles metro area, over four million in New York, and over two million in Houston. Even in seemingly out-of-the-way places like Salt Lake City, there are now 250,000 Latinos accounting for 15.7 percent of the population there.[63] In short, data reveals the demographic growth and dispersion of Latinos *throughout* the United States as a significant social trend.

This second chapter combines an understanding of both indigenous and migration patterns. The significance of within-country Latinos for their religious orientation continues to be important. Perhaps contrary to popular perception, in 2013 less than half of Latino adults in the United States were born in another country (35 percent).[64] The decline in Latino foreign-born population has complex foundations. Much of it can be traced to the decline in Mexican migration to the United States because of the economic recession, intensified border enforcement, and demographic and economic transformations in Mexico. However, we also note that the decline in immigration has been met by an oppositional trend in rising numbers of U.S.-born Latinos. Within increasing birthrates, we expect to see more than a million Latinos entering adulthood every year. Beyond history, this chapter will also include a discussion of the current statuses of Latinos in the United States: marriage and living arrangements, population by geography and region, language usage, socioeconomic status, and health-related issues.

Chapter 3 describes what we currently know about Latino Protestants. That is, we provide the state of current research and identify the significant contours of Latino Protestant churches and cultures. We note that as many as 35 percent of Latinos identify as Protestant. Reports ranging from the Pew Hispanic Center's *Changing Faiths: Latinos and the Transformation of American Religion* to Trinity College's *U.S. Latino Religious Identification, 1990–2008: Growth, Diversity, and Transformation* allow us to discern that several factors—immigration, birth rates, and religious conversion—cause us to expect the number of Protestant Latinos to grow. While the majority of Latinos in the

United States are still currently Catholic, the proportion of ex-Catholic Latinos is rising, and most of them are switching to Protestantism—a pattern that is expected to continue well into the coming decades. Included in our discussion are comparisons of language usage, socioeconomic status, place of birth, and educational levels within the varying religious traditions of Latino Protestantism and compared to Latino Catholics. In addition, we highlight a basic conclusion: The longer their families have been in the United States, the more likely Latinos are to be Protestant. The overall movement toward Protestantism by Latinos has been described as a "revolution."[65]

Building on that discussion, chapter 4 focuses on the complexity of identity among Latino Protestants. We work to further sophisticate notions regarding Latino Protestants' religious, national, ethnic, and political identities. Alongside the more recent shift to Protestantism and away from Catholicism among Latinos have come questions regarding the future of "Latino identity." What is a Latino without the Catholic faith? The significance of this question is exemplified in a common saying among people of Mexican origin: "To be Mexican is to be Catholic." Among Catholics, church and kinship groups can be so mutually reinforcing such that Catholicism can occupy a central place within Latino identity. Spheres of family, language, and tradition are often sociologically intertwined. Moreover, because the Catholic Church serves as a medium for social participation in various Latino cultural traditions (e.g., infant baptism, *quinceañeras*, marriage, *las Posadas*, and other social and life-cycle events), switching out of Catholicism carries significant cultural costs.[66] Thus the conversion to Protestantism is often characterized as a step toward assimilation into American religious mainstream in which their distinctive Latino identity is abandoned. Of course, a competing line of thought argues that the bastion of Latino identity is not dependent on an active Catholic practice. Nor is switching to Protestantism a sign of the "whitenization" of U.S. Latinos. Our own ethnographic data reveal that Latino Protestants appear to be able to preserve their cultural distinctiveness apart from their white Protestant counterparts. These Latinos redefine what it means to be Latino outside of their Catholic faith through the development of new cultural practices, new definitions, and newly modified yet Catholic-associated practices (i.e., Protestant churches holding a service in celebration of a *quinceañera*). Additionally, Latino Protestants regularly distinguish their unique position in the mostly white-run Protestant denominations to which they belong by holding Latino-centered conferences, developing Latino-authored theological streams, and discussing the challenges of Latino-inflected racism in their daily religious lives.

Chapter 5 builds on the individual level of personal identity of Latino Protestants and examines the congregational life of their churches. In this chapter we unpack the richness of our understanding of Latino Protestant church communities. As noted above, Latino Protestants, living in a religious country to begin with, demonstrate even more intensity than most Americans in both what they believe and how they practice those beliefs. Because of that fervor, it is important to understand how congregational life shapes and outlines the practice of Latino Protestantism.

The consistent trend of diversity among Latino Protestants continues to bear out when looking at congregational behaviors. For instance, an aspect of Latino Protestant diversity demonstrated in the Pew survey data is church attendance. Attending church weekly is a much greater priority among Latino evangelicals than Latino Catholics; however, weekly attendance is slightly lower among mainline Protestants. Evangelicals are also associated with the higher proportions that practice daily prayer and weekly reading of the Bible. We also see distinctiveness in the percentage of Latino Protestants who participate in prayer groups: 75 percent of evangelicals compared to 47 percent of mainline Protestants.[67] We describe these patterns of congregational involvement and their significance to reveal how Latino Protestantism is embedded within larger social and religious structures.

The diversity of religious orientation among Latino Protestants also leads to describing the considerable range of liturgical styles found in their churches, which includes an awareness of varying theological priorities and alternate congregational practices. In this chapter we pay careful attention to the Pentecostal/renewalist movement and its influence on Protestant Latinos. Latinos identify with the Pentecostal/renewalist movement at a much higher rate than the rest of the U.S. population, and that affiliation has had significant influence within many Latino churches that are not themselves Pentecostal in their orientations. Indeed, we find that Latino Pentecostalism threatens to overshadow all other forms of Protestantism.

In this chapter we also stress the significance of space, location, and context for Latino Protestant churches and their ministries. The built environments in which they find themselves have substantial implications for congregational practice and church constituency. From the rural plains of the agricultural economy of Central California to the density of core city neighborhoods in New England, we see all manner of Latino Protestants working, residing, recreating, and worshipping in all sorts of venues and circumstances. Still, this can be difficult to discern, so we demonstrate how Latino churches affect and are affected by modern demographic and socioeconomic issues using our ethnographic data.

Chapter 6 expands on the previous chapter by discussing the social engagement of Latino Protestant congregations with their communities and with American society as a whole. We see heterogeneity in how Latino Protestants and their churches approach social and political engagement. To be sure, we note a social conservatism: In contrast to Latino Catholics, a higher percentage of Latino Protestants are opposed to abortion and same-sex marriage.[68] Yet, we also note, once again, that *among* Latino Protestants there also exists diversity in social views and political affiliations. For instance, there remain wide discrepancies between evangelical Latinos, Pentecostal Latinos, and mainline Latinos in their opinions on politics, abortion, same-sex marriage, and gender roles. To that end, a Chicago-based study of Latinos found that when examining contemporary issues that ranged from U.S. intervention in Iraq to the U.S. embargo against Cuba, mainline Latinos tended to express opposition almost as much as Latino Catholics, while a distinct minority of both Pentecostals and evangelicals expressed negative views regarding such foreign policy issues.[69] Beyond political viewpoints, we also find differences among Latino Protestants in terms of community activities and engagement. We also discuss how the lack of citizenship status should be remembered as a variable that might inhibit some from participating in overt political action.

In our understanding of Latino Protestantism, social engagement means more than politics. Congregations of all religious orientations and racial backgrounds have entered into social service delivery, and Latino Protestants are no different in that regard. However, Latino Protestants tend to offer interventions like health services less frequently than their Catholic counterparts. The percentages among Latino

Protestant churches also vary among the mainline, evangelicals, and Pentecostals depending on the health service being delivered. For instance, evangelicals are more likely to offer sex education, while mainline churches offer more opportunities for blood pressure screenings. Pentecostals, in turn, are the least likely to offer either of those health services. In short, the strand of religious tradition within Protestantism has significant influence on how these Latinos engage the larger community. We also note that Latino Protestants demonstrate different expectations for certain social behaviors such as sexual behaviors and alcohol and tobacco use.[70] Our text illustrates sometimes vast discrepancies in the social norms among Latino Protestants.

Finally, in chapter 7 we note the complexity and richness of Latino Protestant churches. The chapter synthesizes important findings, considers significant issues yet to be addressed, and speculates about potentially rich and generative avenues of inquiry related to Latino Protestant churches. In fact, the compelling heterogeneity and complexity of Latino Protestants demands disciplined, systematic, and rigorous research and analysis. This chapter provides a proposal for framing questions toward understanding the future of Latino Protestantism, raises issues to be pursued (like legalization and citizenship), and speculates about personal, organizational, and cultural issues that will be most pressing for Latino Protestants in the coming decades. In the end, because we intend for this volume to be a *social scientific* introduction to Latino Protestants and their churches, we will use this final chapter to suggest an agenda for further research.

2

THE EARLY HISTORY OF INDIGENOUS AND IMMIGRANT LATINO PROTESTANTS

WHAT ARE THE ORIGINS OF LATINO PROTESTANTS IN AMERICA?

Recent studies clearly establish the numerical significance of Latinos in the United States. At the turn of the twenty-first century, Latinos have now surpassed African Americans to become the largest racial minority in the country. Scholars have described Latinos as the "engine" of population growth in the United States.[1] Whereas in 1970 they represented less than five percent of the U.S. population, Latinos today account for 17 percent of the population. Moreover, that population growth has been accompanied by a geographic dispersal. Higher concentrations of Latinos are now found in new locales that include the Deep South, the Midwest, and the Great Lakes—frequently to the benefit of stagnant or declining nonmetropolitan communities.[2] In short, data reveal not only the *quantitative growth*, but also the *geographic diffusion* of Latinos in the United States as a significant demographic trend. In this second chapter, we discuss the complex history of Latinos in the United States.[3] In this second chapter, we discuss the complex history of Latinos in the United States.

The U.S. takeover of formerly Mexican territories remains a fairly obscure historical event in the American imagination. In an instant, Latinos suddenly *found* themselves in a new country without having migrated. With this new population to target for evangelism, white missionaries moved to the new Southwest. Early Protestant growth among Latinos in the United States occurred through the efforts of these transplanted missionaries. We explore the rise of homebred Latino Protestantism in the nineteenth and twentieth centuries and discuss the ways their proselytizing was simultaneously successful and unsuccessful. We also consider how seemingly temporary patterns in history contribute to the growth of U.S. Latino Protestantism now. A significant portion of Latino history in the United States, of course, has deep resonance with immigration patterns as well.[4] While some scholars have argued that immigration has been a powerful engine of religious renewal for newly "American" Latino Protestants, the growth of Latino Protestantism is not simply a result of immigration. Instead, Latino Protestantism is a heterogeneous phenomenon that has roots both in the expansion of United States territory as well as migration from numerous Latin American nations.

This chapter highlights both indigenous and migration patterns. The significance of the development of religious orientation for within-country Latinos is largely ignored in contemporary scholarship. Contrary to popular perception, Latino immigration has declined such that by 2012, less than half of Latino adults in the United States were born in another country. When considering all Latinos (not just adults), the percent of foreign-born drops to just 35.5 percent.[5] The decline in Latino foreign-born population has complex foundations, but much of the decrease can be traced to the drop in Mexican migration because of economic recession, intensified border enforcement, and various demographic and economic transformations in Mexico. The decline in immigration is countered by an oppositional trend in rising numbers of U.S.-born Latinos. With increasing U.S. birthrates, we expect to see more than a million Latinos entering adulthood every year for the foreseeable future. Thus, despite declines in immigration, Latinos stand as a growing percentage of the U.S. population.

LATINO PROTESTANTS IN THE NINETEENTH CENTURY

United States' Conquest of the Southwest

While the significant rise of Latino Protestantism in the United States is a contemporary phenomenon, it should be stressed that communities of Latino Protestantism have been present in the country for at least 150 years.[6] Historical factors such as war, conquest, power conflicts, and race/ethnic tensions have shaped the present contours of Latino Protestantism. As has been noted, one of the most prominent Latin American nations within that history has been Mexico. Up until 1848, Mexico's border extended up to modern day Canada and encompassed most of the southwestern United States—a geography that includes the states of Idaho, California, Nevada, Arizona, Utah, Colorado, New Mexico, Wyoming, and Texas.

In 1821, Mexico won its independence in a hard-fought and costly war with Spain, making it unable to devote resources or time to its northern territories. In these regions, small, rural communities proliferated, land remained affordably available, and government oversight was low.[7] Mexico enacted the General Law of Colonization in 1824 in an attempt to make the areas prosperous and establish protection from raids from Comanche and Apache as well as help Christianize indigenous groups.[8] This law allowed Mexican citizens, Christian Native Americans, and white Americans to claim land in Mexico's northern territories.[9] Droves of white American settlers immigrated, especially to Texas, and with those settlers came Protestantism.[10]

By 1830, white settlers largely outnumbered Mexican citizens. Mexico halted further immigration due to whites' refusal to adhere to Mexico's antislavery laws and out of sheer fear of the power their growing population would garner.[11] These concerns resulted in stronger limitations on white immigration to the region by the Mexican government and passage of legislation that required whites to release their slaves. Texas rebels, motivated by the desire for both more autonomy as well as assumptions regarding their racial and religious superiority over Mexican Catholics, sought to be free of Mexican rule.[12] With the aid of Tejanos (i.e., Mexican Texans), white Texans instigated a civil war against Mexico. Texas became an independent nation in 1836 and the United States formally annexed the territory in 1845. Eventually, the

United States gained control of Mexico's capital, forcing a Mexican surrender that led to negotiations. In 1848, the Treaty of Guadalupe Hidalgo resulted in Mexico relinquishing parts of or entire territories of New Mexico, California, Arizona, Utah, Wyoming, Nevada, and Colorado to the United States.[13]

In one fell-swoop, 100,000 Mexican citizens in these territories experienced becoming strangers in their own native lands.[14] Article X of the Treaty of Guadalupe Hidalgo ensured Mexicans the full rights and privileges of citizens of the United States as well as retention of all land grants given to them by the Mexican government at the time—so long as the grant owner had filled the conditions of their contract.[15] However, many Mexicans in the new seceded territories had not received an official title yet due to bureaucratic slowdown in Mexico. In U.S. courts, Mexicans frequently lost land litigation lawsuits to white Americans.[16] It became an ongoing struggle for Latinos in the area to maintain their land and ranching lifestyles. Over time, lawsuits, competition with white settlers, economic hardships, weather, and disadvantages in getting loans led to the loss of wealth and property.[17] These accumulating costs, along with the new American racial hierarchy in which they now found themselves, contributed to the relegation of Tejanos as second-class citizens. In this lower social status, Mexicans experienced segregation from whites in their neighborhoods and schools. Moreover, being barred from political participation left them with little recourse in addressing their socioeconomic standing. Mexicans often found themselves subject to threats, racial violence, and state sanctioned killings by the Texas Rangers.[18] Racist arguments about their racial inferiority based on skin color were used to justify their treatment.[19] These attitudes toward Mexicans in the Southwest are important to note, as they played an influential role in strategies employed by Protestant missionaries.

White Protestant Missionary Activity to Latinos in the Southwest

Missionary activity has been present in the American Southwest since Spanish conquest of the region in the late 1500s.[20] Spanish Catholics built mission settlements throughout the Southwest and focused on the conversion of Native Americans.[21] Revivalism and evangelistic outreach characterized much of the religious ethos of the United States during the mid- to late nineteenth century. However, for many Protestant denominations' missionary boards who worked in the Southwest, Spanish-speaking communities remained a marginal priority.[22] Eventually, proselytizing efforts toward Mexicans in Texas, Northern Mexico, and other parts of the Southwest took root.[23] In Texas, white missionaries from all the major Protestant denominations began their work to convert Mexican and other non-white populations beginning in 1830, sixteen years before the beginning of the Mexican American War.[24] In northern New Mexico and Colorado, white missionary Protestant activity did not appear until later in 1920. In California, missionary efforts began at the end of the nineteenth century but were not as extensive as in other parts of the Southwest.[25] Many of the early missionaries to these communities were women from the Presbyterian Church who began their ministries by teaching English.[26]

White missionaries came into these communities ill prepared to understand the local people, lacking both the Spanish-speaking skills to communicate and the historical and cultural knowledge of Mexican Americans.[27] Many experienced culture shock and described Mexican American communities in the Southwest as alien and foreign. Efforts toward assimilation went hand-in-hand with evangelization. Along with spreading the gospel, white missionaries emphasized the need to "Americanize" the Mexican American.[28] Goals of assimilation were not just important but central to their ministries.[29] At the crux of assimilation efforts, racial tensions influenced relationships between Mexicans and their white missionaries. Indeed, it is nearly impossible to disentangle the prejudiced attitudes that fueled tensions with Mexico during the Texas Revolution and Mexican American War from white evangelization efforts to Mexican people in the Southwest. Deeply embedded in these prejudices were beliefs about whites' racial superiority and Mexicans' corresponding inferiority.[30]

In fact, white missionaries commonly referred to their potential Mexican converts as childlike, pitiful, "unmotivated," unsanitary, and a "slumbering people."[31] Missionaries described Mexican Catholics as lacking self-initiation and future planning.[32] They compared Mexican Catholic communities to "Sodom and Gomorrah," cities in the Bible that God destroyed for their reprehensible vices.[33] Mexicans' mixed racial backgrounds (European and Native American ancestries), combined with their Catholic faith, formed the basis of prejudiced explanations for perceived cultural inadequacies.[34] White missionaries idealized white American culture and saw the establishment of loyalty to American values as the key to progress that Mexican communities needed.[35] These values shaped missional strategies, and some Mexican Americans (although not the majority) sought to assimilate as best as they could.

Protestant evangelization efforts implemented a strong anti-Catholicism as well. In sermons and revivals by Methodists, Presbyterians, Disciples of Christ, and Baptists in Texas, religious leaders portrayed Mexicans as captives of Catholicism who needed to be rescued.[36] Missionaries in New Mexico and Colorado constructed similar narratives. They framed Catholicism as anti-American and a symbol of the disturbing remnant of colonial rule in the Americas. These narratives often alienated the Mexican communities, isolated white missionaries, and weakened conversion efforts.[37] Because family and social life centered on Catholic holidays and traditions, Protestant missionaries substituted those with new ceremonies such as the Fourth of July and Thanksgiving. These efforts proved futile as they sought to replace the symbolic unity that Catholicism gave Mexican Americans with activities that had no historical or cultural meaning for them.[38]

Latino Protestant congregations started by white missionaries were also characterized by inequity in leadership positions. Whites held the primary positions of power in the congregations and exercised their clout by designating lay leaders and making unilateral decisions about finances. For example, among Presbyterian ministers, few Mexican congregants had the opportunity to be ordained. Whites controlled almost all published materials, both English and Spanish. Spanish Presbyterian congregations found themselves relegated to second-class status and referred to as "Second Presbyterian" churches as opposed to white congregations who retained the "First Presbyterian" nomenclature.[39] Among these southwestern Presbyterians and other religious groups, fear of a Mexican American takeover of Protestant church structures resulted in their being marginalized in their churches despite efforts to Americanize them.

Often, missionary newsletters lamented the lack of large numbers of converts.[40] Numerically, denominational leaders expressed dismay at the meager conversions from white Protestants among Mexican communities in the Southwest region. Indeed, in Northern Mexico, Colorado, and parts of Texas, their efforts largely failed.[41] Two primary reasons explain the stagnant level of conversions. First, Protestant missionary denominations competed with each other for converts with scarce resources. Second, and most importantly, the prevailing ethnocentrism by white missionaries in the Southwest prevented them from garnering converts.[42] As previously mentioned, the central goals of these efforts included making Mexican Americans more "American," which translated into being more individualistic, more capitalistic, and less communal. Missionaries oriented their efforts at behavior and attitude change in the context of prejudicial beliefs of what they thought "Mexicans" were like. Mexican communities often sensed the missionaries' attitudes of condescension, thereby undermining conversion efforts. Contemporary notions of cross-cultural partnership were not found in missionary strategies, and missionaries failed to see the strength of Latino Catholic culture.[43] The missionaries underestimated the traditional power of Catholicism as a source of bonding and as an important organizing social institution in rural Mexican communities. In fact, for some Mexicans, the Protestant emphasis on individual Bible reading just made them more fervent in their Catholic faith.[44]

It should be noted that missionary efforts did provide desperately needed education opportunities and medical care that the U.S. government had failed to provide. For example, free schooling gave Mexican children new prospects. It was in these educational contexts that negative, preconceived notions about Mexicans were challenged. Often teachers described the children as being "bright," "capable," and eager to learn. Missionaries also praised the willingness and sacrifice of Mexican parents for the education of their children. In these settings, conversion efforts often gained the most ground. Children of Mexicans sent to Protestant boarding schools more readily adopted the white American Protestant ethos.[45] Schools also provided a venue for Catholic parents to be exposed to Protestantism directly as they received encouragement to attend Protestant meetings and services. Medical services focused on sanitation efforts, caring for small children, and the elderly. Later, the Catholic response to the provision of social services by Protestants consisted of establishing their own schools and recruiting more clergy for the area.[46] This mirrored what has historically occurred across the globe: When Protestants established missions in Catholic areas, Catholics respond in kind, spurring religious competition.[47] While historical records of white missionary efforts provide indications of deep-rooted ethnocentrism, the evidence also demonstrates that some had great affection for and emotional attachment to the Mexican American communities they served. Some reevaluated their preconceived notions about Mexican Americans[48] and felt challenged by the kindness, hospitality, and politeness the communities showed toward them.[49] Many exercised a deeply sacrificial ministry. Work in these communities came at high costs in personal health, and many missionaries died as they experienced the same lack of health care and sanitation that the Mexican community suffered from and endured.[50]

While missionaries underestimated the social power that Catholicism held for these communities, there also existed widespread dissatisfaction among Mexican Americans with the Catholic Church. Despite an overall loyalty to the church, many laypeople reported not feeling cared for and believed that the Catholic Church did not effectively address the people's needs.[51] Particularly in New Mexico, reports implicate abusive priests who charged high fees for spiritual rituals and long neglected their Mexican American congregants who felt starved for spiritual guidance. This spiritual hunger, combined with the harsh treatment that the Catholic Church exhibited toward Latino Protestants (including excommunication and refusal of burial in church cemeteries), made any social services provided by Protestants all the more appealing. Besides validating concerns of poor Mexican American Catholics who had some experience of exploitation, Protestantism also allowed more access for women to serve in the church.[52] Despite these advantages, Protestant missionaries still struggled to amass a large body of Latino converts. Overall, Mexican Americans in these communities benefited from the social services brought by Protestantism—education, healthcare, and/or biblical literacy—yet the great majority did not leave aside their commitment to the Catholic Church.[53]

LATINO PROTESTANTS IN THE TWENTIETH CENTURY

Latinos and Protestant Denominations

While the ninetieth century was marked by the failure of white missionaries to garner many converts, the twentieth century saw a flourishing of autonomous, Latino-led Protestant organizations and congregations. By 1900, denominations had established enduring Latino Baptist, Congregational, Disciples of Christ, Methodist, and Presbyterian organizations.[54] In 1900, there were 5,632 adult Mexican origin church members in 150 Spanish-speaking congregations, mostly in Texas and New Mexico.[55] In Texas, Protestant denominations reported 2,378 Mexican American adult members of which almost 60 percent belonged to the Methodist Episcopal Church, followed by Presbyterians at about 23 percent, Baptist at 15 percent, Methodist Episcopal Church at 2.1 percent, and Disciples of Christ at 0.3 percent. Near the end of the nineteenth century, California had a mere 115 Mexican American Protestants in three congregations located in Southern California.[56]

It is important to stress that even while nascent, these earlier Latino Protestant congregations in the Southwest were not homogeneous. Their differences stemmed from unique cultural, geographic, and denominational contexts. Communities in northern New Mexico and Southern Colorado had weaker ties to Mexico in the Southwest. In Texas, some Spanish-speaking congregations often had leaders that they recruited from denominationally affiliated congregations in Mexico.[57] Also in Texas, Latino Baptists quickly drew lines of distinction from Catholicism in their evangelization efforts, increasing their numbers more rapidly compared to Latino Presbyterians and Methodists.[58] Maintaining a clear distinction from Catholics and a strong proselytizing focus helped Baptists to grow, while congregations from more Catholic-friendly denominations, such as Presbyterian and Methodist, did not increase as quickly.

In contrast to the experience in Texas, Baptists experienced the least amount of success in northern New Mexico and Colorado compared to other denominations. Episcopalians and United Brethren in Christ also reported frustration in their attempts to grow in the region.[59] Church organizational structure and polity, more than theological stances, predicted denominational survival.[60] For example, Latino Presbyterian congregations had the advantage of established financial resources; they created schools before churches and did not segregate Latino and white congregations.

California Protestant congregations remained small due to the small population of people at the time of the American takeover of the region,[61] and evangelical Protestant Christianity grew slowly in California in the nineteenth century.[62] Nevertheless, California would assume a much larger role in Latino Protestantism in the twentieth century when immigration turned the sparsely populated state into one of the most Latino-dominant regions in the country.

Alienation and Acculturation

Some scholars argue that Protestantism represented one of the many adaptations that Mexican Americans had to make as a conquered people.[63] Early on, white denominational leaders separated Latino Protestants from their white counterparts in congregations. Because of the ties to Mexico and prevalence of Spanish in these congregants, white Protestants saw them as foreign and un-American (despite being comprised of Mexican Americans). Within the Mexican American population, converts to Protestantism also endured alienation from Catholic communities as well as disownment by their Catholic family members. Converts characterized the alienation as a worthy sacrifice for the sake of faith. However, they endured more than just rejection from Catholics. They also experienced a double marginalization—from Mexican American Catholic communities they came from and from white Protestant denominations to which they belonged.[64]

Latino Protestant congregations became central because they functioned as important centers of social participation and support for converts.[65] While socially isolated in several ways, their churches provided the space for the first indigenous Latino Protestants to develop their own identity and subculture, which continues today in modern Latino Protestant congregations in the United States.[66] Newfound religious expression included elements of Catholicism, Mexican, and southwestern culture—a mix that provided means to resist some forms of assimilation. Latino Protestants also nurtured the prevalence of Spanish in their congregations and the adoption of culturally Catholic practices such as *quinceañeras* and *las Posadas*.[67] Protestantism also provided a means for Latinos to access dominant white American culture, education, and medical care to which most Mexican Americans had limited access.[68] Finally, Latino Protestant identity further emphasized a believer's direct access to God, especially through prayer, worship, and personal Bible reading.

Pentecostalism and the Azusa Street Revival

One of the most important historical moments for indigenous Latino Protestantism in the United States occurred at the beginning of the twentieth century during the Pentecostal Azusa Street Revival in Los Angeles in 1906. The movement began with a Bible study held by African American Holiness evangelist William J. Seymour. Expanding beyond the Bible study, the movement (along with the Welsh Revival of 1904) gave rise to the modern Pentecostal church and its Latino variants.[69] The movement spread like wildfire throughout the neighborhood, then the city, and eventually the whole country. On April 9, 1906, followers claimed a second outpouring of the Holy Spirit through a second Pentecost similar to that found in the biblical Book of Acts.[70] The religious awakening led to mass conversions, speaking in tongues, and accounts of miracles.[71]

A unique aspect of the Pentecostal movement included challenging strict segregation based on race. Segregation and racial violence against African Americans and Latinos had dominated the early twentieth century.[72] Despite this history, Latinos, whites, and African Americans worshiped together in an unparalleled manner during the Azusa Street revival.[73] Latinos participated heavily, and Latino Catholics converted to Protestantism at the meetings in large numbers. The revival stands as a key event in the birth of the modern day Latino Pentecostal church.[74] Latinos went on to play an important role in spreading the movement into the Southwest and launched the ministries of many influential Mexican American evangelists, including Abundio L. López and Juan Navarro Martínez, argued to be the first official U.S. Latinos ordained in the Pentecostal Church.[75]

LATINO PROTESTANTISM BEYOND
BORDERLAND MEXICANS

While the history of Latino Protestantism in the United States has primarily centered in the American Southwest, the subsequent development of "Borderland" Latino Protestantism also has significant resonance. Borderland *Latinidad* defines much of what Latino Protestantism currently is throughout the United States.[76] The early establishment of Mexican American Protestantism in the United States created a
powerful culture, and it is within that milieu that Latino immigrants
often find themselves. Even when Latinos arrived from other parts of
the world, Borderland culture largely defined their understanding of
American Protestantism.

Although Borderland Latino Protestantism deserves much more
scholarly attention, it also remains important to not neglect the history
of Protestantism among other prominent Latino groups in America
such as Puerto Ricans.[77] Not long after the end of the Spanish-
American War, Protestant denominations sought to evangelize Puerto
Ricans on the island. Records reveal Puerto Rican–led Pentecostal congregations flourishing on the island from 1916 to 1928.[78] Scholarly work
regarding the history of Puerto Rican Protestant churches remains limited, but some accounts cite Pastor Juan Lugo, an early Puerto Rican
convert to Protestantism, as founding the first Pentecostal Church in
New York City.[79] Protestant congregations, particularly established
Pentecostal churches, held an appeal for Puerto Ricans living in New
York—due to the lack of Spanish services in Catholic Church congregations in Brooklyn in the 1920s and the availability of social services
offered by Protestant groups.[80]

Several distinct waves of Latino immigration in the twentieth century played key roles in homegrown Latino Protestantism. At least since
1848, there has always been a significant population of Mexican people
in the United States, and large-scale immigration from Mexico began in
earnest in 1910 due to people fleeing the Revolution.[81] During the
1930s, economic hardship during the Great Depression led to a largely
negative national sentiment toward Latinos entering the United States
(often referred to as "The Mexican Problem"). In this era, many Mexican immigrants and Mexican Americans returned of their own accord
to Mexico, while others experienced mass forced repatriation by the

U.S. government—even those with U.S. citizenship. The situation soon reversed. By 1942, the United States once again needed Mexican workers due to labor shortages during World War II. The Bracero Program (1942–1962) was developed as a solution. Through this program, thousands of Mexican immigrants were brought by both the United States and Mexican governments with worker visas for agricultural jobs onto American soil.[82]

Starting several decades after Mexican immigration, Puerto Rican immigration to the United States began to rise steadily at the conclusion of the Spanish-American War in 1898.[83] In 1917, the Jones Act granted Puerto Rican migrants U.S. citizenship.[84] In contrast to Mexican immigrant patterns, which ebbed and flowed depending on the policy needs of the United States, the Jones Act created long-lasting and permanent migration rhythms between the island and the mainland United States. Puerto Rican migration numbers continued to rise pre-WWI (with only a slight dip during the Depression) and peaked in the 1950s and 1960s.[85] Most Puerto Ricans migrated to New York, often moving back and forth between the U.S. continent and the island.

With an even later advent, Cuban immigration began in the 1960s with refugees fleeing from the turmoil of Fidel Castro's Cuban Revolution. Cubans initially concentrated in south Florida, but then quickly diffused throughout the United States following economic opportunities. A second wave of Cubans came to the United States between 1965 and 1970 when immigration sanctions in Cuba were lifted and families were allowed to be reunited,[86] and a third wave began during the 1980s.[87] Scholarly work on the history of early Cuban Protestant congregations remains scarce. However, research on contemporary Cuban Protestant congregations in Miami demonstrates that they established transnational ties with churches in Cuba,[88] which more than likely were important in their history. While Cuban immigration has slowed, the recent lifting of the embargo with Cuba may stimulate yet another increase of immigrants, with many of them bringing a native Protestantism now more widely practiced in Cuba.

The history of Central American congregations, especially Guatemalan and Salvadorian Protestant churches, is more recent—beginning with upsurges of Central American immigration post-1980s.[89] Central Americans have immigrated to the United States in small numbers since the nineteenth century, and large-scale immigration to the United

States did not begin until the 1980s.[90] Widespread political unrest and violence between totalitarian regimes and left-wing rebels in the region forced many to flee their homelands, particularly Honduras, El Salvador, Guatemala, and Nicaragua.[91] The numbers of Central Americans have continued to increase over the years from 1.32 million in 1990 to approximately 3.2 million in 2013.[92] Since 2010, Central American immigration (particularly among women and children) rose due to increasing gang violence in the area before dropping again in 2015 due to Mexican deportation.[93] Central Americans have also diffused throughout the United States.

CONTEMPORARY GROWTH OF LATINO PROTESTANTISM AND IMMIGRATION

Certainly the timing and origin of immigration flows from different regions of Latin America affect Latino religious identity and participation.[94] Twenty-eight percent of the foreign born in the United States are from Mexico, the largest sending source of immigration into the United States (followed by the continent of Asia).[95] We also know that the religious identities of immigrants become more important once they enter the United States because keeping ties to religious traditions helps preserve meaningful connections to their home countries. Latino religious practices diversify the religious landscape of America by introducing new religions or, as in our case, "Latinoizing" [96] denominations and Christian groups that have been traditionally non-Latino. Likewise, immigrant flows provide a surge in attendance for certain denominations with struggling numbers. For example, Catholic affiliation within the white population of the United States in the last decades has been dwindling, yet overall Catholic adherence is sustained primarily through replacement of white members by immigrants from Latin America.[97]

Findings from the General Social Survey demonstrate that the decline in Latino Catholics from the 1970s to 1990s and the exodus from Catholicism bolstered mainline Protestantism more than conservative Protestantism.[98] However, the destinations of ex-Catholic Latinos are changing. Similar to what is happening in the general U.S. population,[99] evidence suggests that Latinos are also becoming "nones," that is, have no religious affiliation.[100] In terms of movement *within* Christianity, though, the most recent evidence indicates that Latinos are filling evangelical streams more readily than mainline ones, particularly Pentecostalism and related Charismatic movements.[101] The proportion of Latino Catholics has been steadily diminishing since the 2000s, while the proportions of Latino Protestants (both evangelical and mainline) have increased. The recent growth of Latino Protestants is especially attributed to higher levels of contemporary immigration in the United States, which has been increasing steadily with the initial passage of the Immigration and Naturalization Act in 1965 and continuing into the early twenty-first century. Indeed, examining data on the percent change in religious affiliation over the lifetimes of foreign-born Latinos reveals that Catholicism has had a net loss of 19 percent, while Protestantism has had net gains of 8 percent.[102] These patterns provide evidence that Latino Protestant growth stems primarily from immigrants switching from Catholicism to Protestantism once they arrive to the United States as well as Latinos bringing their homegrown forms of Protestantism into the United States (which is especially true for Central Americans).[103] Immigrants have higher rates of religious participation and fertility, and they socialize their children into their faith. They therefore may strongly influence future generations to be Protestant as well.

Some have argued that the immigration factors that spurred Latino Protestant growth will be short lived. These scholars insist that steady immigration from Latin America will bring an increase of Catholics, partly at the expense of Latino Protestants.[104] However, we know that Latino immigration, particularly unauthorized immigration, declined during the Great Recession from 2007 to 2009 and has continued to decline since then.[105] For example, Mexican immigration, which has been the leading immigrant source for the United States (16 million from 1965 to 2015), has decreased.[106] More Mexican immigrants are leaving the United States than coming, with a net loss of 140,000 from 2009 to 2014.[107] In like manner, the number of foreign-born Latinos is projected to decrease by 2050.[108] While not as dramatic as the case with Mexico, Central American (mostly made up of women and children) and South American immigration has also declined since 1964. For the first time, Asian immigration is expected to surpass Latino immigration by 2055.[109] Despite a decline in Latino immigration in recent years,

reports indicate that the growth of Latino Protestants has either garnered net gains or has remained steady (between 22 and 23 percent
from 2005 to 2013) while the proportion of Latino Catholics continues
to decline.[110]

About 20 percent of those Latinos raised as Catholic leave the Catholic Church as adults.[111] Such a trend signals that the recent shift into
Protestantism, despite immigration decline, is related to switching
among Latino immigrants' U.S-born (or just raised) children and
among Latinos who have been in the United States for many generations. In addition, Protestant in-roads among Latinos consist of a complex mix of connections to Protestant-sending communities, mission
churches, and networks that remain intact despite the slowdown of
immigration. Also, compared to Catholicism, Protestantism places
greater emphasis on proselytizing, particularly among its lay members,
a pattern that has been consistent among U.S. Latino Protestants since
the nineteenth century. Their evangelistic emphasis positions Protestantism to withstand potential losses from diminished Latino immigration. Church leaders cite the commands of Jesus Christ in Matthew
chapter 28 (often termed "The Great Commission"), encouraging
members to "make disciples"[112] by inviting nonbelievers to church, per-
sonally investing in "nonbeliever's" lives, and creating opportunities for
engagement with the community (i.e., free community dinners, free oil
changes, farmer's markets), all with the hope that people will get exposed and eventually accept "the gospel." In several of the Latino Protestant congregations we ethnographically observed, leadership often
encouraged members to bring people from their families and workplaces to church, to share the gospel with them, and to pray for their
salvation. A tool in its evangelizing mission is apologetics, or learning
how to defend Christianity against intellectual arguments. Opportunities to learn apologetics and how to share the gospel are often formal-
ized in church programs. For example, at Alabanza Baptist, a small
congregation in the Southwest, local seminary professors and graduate
students teach weekly classes to church members that provide specific
responses for the most prominent critiques of Christianity. Such robust
doctrinal training at the lay level can influence the switching to Protestantism within church members' extensive Latino relational networks.

Without a doubt, the rapid growth of Latino Protestants in the United States is a recent historical phenomenon, and it is important to more

accurately determine the contemporary factors driving this growth. While the proportions of Latino Protestants have registered at the highest points ever observed in survey data, we also know that Latino Protestantism has homegrown roots in the United States characterized by a rich historical depth in the nineteenth and twentieth centuries. It remains important to remember that the roots of Latino Protestantism run long and deep.

HOW HISTORY INFORMS LATINO PROTESTANTISM TODAY

As the United States becomes more diverse and multiethnic, Latino Protestant congregations will be an important component of these changes. Familiarity with the historical origins of indigenous U.S. Latino Protestantism is integral for understanding and illuminating contemporary religious dynamics and the growing significance of Latinos.

First, nineteenth-century conversions of Mexican Americans to Protestantism were small in number, but those who did convert did so, in large part, because they felt neglected by the Catholic Church. Likewise, modern-day converts to Protestantism among Latinos express similar frustrations and feelings of disconnection from the Catholic Church that were commonly expressed among earlier generations of converts (discussed in depth in chapter 3). Like their historical counterparts, contemporary Latino Protestants reported that they found Protestantism's emphasis on direct access to God through prayer, worship, and individual Bible reading attractive. These long-standing historical patterns (a lack of feeling cared for by the Catholic Church and the access to individual, authoritative interpretation of the Bible), demonstrate that dissatisfaction with the Catholic Church and a form of "spiritual hunger" have been important catalysts for the growth of Latino Protestants for at least 150 years.

In contrast to modern-day Latino Protestantism, converts during the nineteenth century were few in number. What explains this difference between nineteenth and twenty-first century evangelization efforts? Differences in the messages offer a potential answer. In the past, white missionaries encouraged Latino conversion to Protestantism in the Southwest with arguments about Anglo superiority. Moreover, palpable

feelings of disapproval of Latino communities and strategies focused on
changing Latino culture to be more like the dominant white American
culture tended to taint evangelism efforts. Over time and into the twentieth century, Latinos gained autonomy in their congregations, created
their own organizations and missional aims, and became primary agents
of evangelization. With control of the narratives and increased congregational autonomy, racist messages about white superiority lessened
and the Protestant message became more appealing, helping spur the
growth of Latino Protestantism. Our own ethnographic data indicate
that some Latino Protestant congregations continue to use arguments
against Catholicism as a tool of evangelism. However, unlike the past,
critiques of Catholicism tend to be crafted much more carefully and
with restraint. While this is not the case in all of the congregations we
have observed, many recognize the need to not offend potential converts who have Catholic backgrounds. Any assessments of Catholicism
tend to be gentler and less hostile than early missionary efforts. For
example, Catholic priests received invitations to pray during the centen-
nial celebration of the Protestant Azusa Street Revival in 2016.[113]

Additionally, many contemporary white-dominated Protestant denominations express more sensitivity to issues of diversity and inclusion.
There have been sustained efforts to encourage and support minority
leadership in Protestant denominations and congregational networks.
Several mainstream denominations host Latino-focused conferences
every year, including the Southern Baptist Convention, the Reformed
Church in America, the Apostolic Pentecostal Church, and the Anglican
Church in North America. Parachurch organizations like The Leadership Network and Asociación para la Educación Teológica intentionally
gather and resource Latino Protestant leaders. The priority of assimilation was important in the early days of Latino Protestantism, and it
remains a complex consideration in contemporary congregations and
denominations as well. From our observations, some congregations
readily embrace their Latino heritage, while others find such emphasis
to be unbiblical.[114] Finally, we find historical precedent in maintaining
caution in using all-encompassing definitions to strictly determine the
boundaries of Latino Protestantism (discussed in chapter 4).

Latino Protestant congregations have been diverse from their birth
in the nineteenth century, and they continue to be so (and even more
so) with the increase in different types of Latino groups in the United

States. One of the most important aspects of this growth is the conversion of Latino Catholics to Protestantism. Understanding who Latino Protestant converts are and why they leave the Catholic Church remain critical questions.

3

THE LATINO REFORMATION TODAY

WHO ARE LATINO PROTESTANT CONVERTS?

The rapid growth of Latino Protestantism across the Americas (North, Central, and South) is one of the most significant shifts on the religious scene. Latin America has abundant evidence of Protestant expansion.[1] We focus on the Protestant expansion within the United States.[2] Findings from the 2005 Hispanic Churches in American Public Life (HCAPL) Survey, a national random-sample telephone survey of 2,310 Latinos across the United States and Puerto Rico, found that approximately 70 percent of U.S. Latinos identified with Catholicism and 23 percent identified as Protestant—with the majority of these Protestants belonging to fundamentalist, evangelical, and charismatic groups.[3] In 2008, the Pew Hispanic Center reported that as many as 35 percent of Latinos identified as Protestant. Then, in 2013, the Pew Research Center reported that the proportion of U.S. Latinos who identify as Catholic dropped from 67 percent in 2010 to 55 percent in 2013,[4] with evangelical Protestantism making the most gains from this shift. Overall, the proportion of Latino Catholics has consistently decreased, while the proportion of Latino Protestants (mainline, Baptist, Pentecostal, and nondenominational Christian combined) has increased.[5] Without a doubt, Latino Americans are switching to Protestantism, although it's important to recall that the profound developments of Protestant growth in Latin American (especially Pentecostal growth) in the last thirty years means that Latino immigrants, particularly from Central America, are coming to the United States already *as* Protestants.

DISCONNECTION WITH THE ROMAN CATHOLIC CHURCH

Face-to-face interviews conducted as part of the LPC Project[6] indicate that Latino Protestants leave the Catholic Church primarily due to a sense of disconnection from their previous Catholic faith. In an interview about her conversion from Catholicism to Protestantism, Martha, a forty-eight-year old Latina in El Paso, Texas, described the night she decided to attend a Protestant service on her own. Martha, a high school math teacher, arrived home from a terrible day at work to moody family members. She quickly left the house and turned back to her car to drive off the stress. Drawn by how full a church parking lot looked on a Wednesday night, she found herself sitting in her car outside of a Latino Protestant congregation. She looked for the furthest spot possible from the church building and parked, waiting for her stress to dissipate. She had no intention to go inside, but eventually, she felt compelled to enter. Finding a seat in the back of the sanctuary, Martha listened to the pastor speak and soon asked herself, "Who told this guy about me?" Tears began to pour from her eyes as she finally felt she was receiving answers to spiritual questions she had held for a long time. Martha returned home, prayed the "prayer of salvation" by her bed, reading from the back of a book from the *Left Behind* series. Martha had been a committed Catholic her entire life and came from a family that remained deeply attached to their Catholic heritage. However, in her later adult years, Martha began to feel disconnected from her Catholic faith due to questions and challenges she had about the Church. In an attempt to save her faith, she had searched for answers to questions from Catholic clergy and family members, but none of their responses satisfied her. It was not until she encountered a Protestant church that she felt she really could connect to God again. That night, Martha decided she was no longer Catholic but "Christian"—a term she and many other Latinos use to declare themselves as Protestant.[7]

Martha's story is an example of the growing shift away from Catholicism and toward Protestantism among Latinos in the United States.

While the majority of Latinos in the United States are still currently Catholic, the proportion of ex-Catholic Latinos is rising, and most of them are switching to Protestantism—a pattern that is expected to continue well into the coming century.[8] In this chapter we detail the antecedents of this shift. Included in our discussion are comparisons of language usage, socioeconomic status, country of origin, and educational levels within the varying religious traditions of Latino Protestantism. While the contexts and mechanisms of these former Catholics vary, ethnographic findings reveal one of the main motivations for conversion among Latinos: feeling disconnected and alienated from the Catholic Church.

These feelings of detachment manifest through two main avenues, first, a lack of understanding of the Catholic practices in which they participate; and second, a perceived lack of access and knowledge of scripture, which converts feel Protestantism is able to provide for them as they navigate their daily lives. Our interviews consistently noted a lack of resonance with their previous Catholic faith as an important catalyst to Protestant conversion. Their Catholic faith had become an obligatory practice without tangible implications for their life. Former Catholic faith and practices—such as attendance of Mass and prayer—lacked deeper meaning for them. Engracia (age fifty, female) described her former Catholic practice as ordinary and mundane:

> The Catholic Church really has nothing to offer me in terms of edifying or building my life with God. To me it's just [as] if I were to go to the store. It really would be very empty for me.

Similar to Engracia, informants compared going to mass or being Catholic as an "add-on" to their schedule to be merely checked off. They described their Catholicism as being rote and lacking substantial or authoritative meaning in their lives. Manny (age forty-five, male), described his Catholic practice and day-to-day living as separate: "I was like, 'Gotta go to church Sunday because, man, I partied hard this weekend,' you know? That was my Catholic faith." Alicia (age forty-six, female) described her Catholic faith as obligatory: "Going to Catholic Church, I only felt I went there for the sake of tradition, [but] at Iglesia Mundial, I started to have a personal relationship with God. You feel it, you live it, and you can see the difference between one and the other." Alicia and many other former Latino Catholics noted the stark difference they felt in terms of connection and feelings of relationship with a higher being when they were Catholic and after they became Protestant.

Camilla, a twenty-nine-year-old, single, Mexican American woman, describes herself as heavily involved at Word of Life, a mega-church in the Southwest. Since her conversion from Catholicism in 2011, Camilla volunteers almost every Sunday as a greeter and in the children's ministry. She stays for all three services the congregation offers, making sure to attend the small Spanish service the church hosts in order to improve her Spanish. Like many informants, Camilla said that her move away from Catholicism began with a lack of understanding the rationale for ritual and practices that felt at times forced. She describes her frustration:

> I didn't understand why I had to get confirmation. . . . Why is there a Bible, but we don't read it in the church? Why is that man, Jesus, still on the cross—didn't he go to heaven? I had questions about the Virgin Mary. Why is she idolized so much? Is she a god? Why do you spend a whole month about her? And those questions were never answered. Why are there statues of saints everywhere? Why are they important, and why are they saints?"

Camilla sought answers to her questions as a teenager from her Catholic family at first, then from extended family who belonged to a strict, fundamentalist Protestant denomination. When neither could answer Camilla's questions to her satisfaction, her mother arranged meetings with Catholic clergy. Camilla played basketball for her high school and previously had clashes with clergy for missing youth group for tournaments, so she expressed nervousness about how her questions would be received. Her fears were not unfounded, and she described the inability of the leadership in her Catholic congregation to seriously consider her questions without calling her motives into question. Completely disillusioned by the experience, Camilla stopped going to mass altogether. Camilla's frustration characterized many informants' experiences while Catholic: They felt blocked by those in power in the church from asking questions—further alienating them from the Catholic faith.

Camilla had difficult times during her twenties battling alcohol and drug addiction and attempting to escape an abusive relationship. Eventually, Camilla met friends, owners of a gym she attended, who invited her to Word of Life, and her conversion process began. She described her first experience at Word of Life, which had lively, concert-like praise and worship:

> We walk in, and my friend [gym owner] told me "There are no crosses here. There's no saints. There's no statues. This is different, but just be open." And I was like, "I am; that's why I'm here." He was like, "Okay, well if you want to sing, the words are on the screen. Just sing. If you want to lift your hands up, go for it. If you want to clap, do whatever you want." I was like, whatever, I'm not going to do any of that. So I was reading the words, and something happened to me. I know it was the Holy Spirit now, but at the time I felt my heart literally . . . like something tickling me, moving me. I wanted to cry, and I was, like, no way! I'm not going to cry! I remember this clearly. I'm not going to cry; I'm not going to cry!

Camilla's description of the emotional experience during her first visit to Word of Life contrasted with her experience in the Catholic Church, where she felt completely disconnected and alienated from the Catholic practices and questioned the very nature of the faith.

Like Camilla, Valeria, found it difficult to connect with rituals that felt perfunctory and repetitive:

> When I went to Catholic Church . . . I heard the father saying the same things. The prayers from the Catholic Church . . . are always the same and repeat themselves. Now it is different. I feel that I am talking with God [and] that I am telling him my stuff . . . like a conversation.

Informants felt that their Catholic congregations did not encourage them to read their Bible for themselves, nor did they feel they had the freedom to evaluate scripture or question it. Kenny (thirty-four, male) described being kicked out of a class at his Catholic congregation for continuing to ask questions about the biblical evidence for dinosaurs. Converts like Valeria described the ability to connect to scripture as one of most important spiritual practices in deepening their connections with their Christian faith:

> I do not see that [the Catholic Church] motivates people to read the Bible. . . . [But] we [as Christians] are motivated to go to the Bible

and verify everything that is said to us. For us to have a greater
relationship with God, we should read the Bible because it is [how]
we will get to know the life of Jesus.

Numerous informants indicated that the inaccessibility of scripture
when they were Catholics functioned as an important turning point in
their decision to convert. In contrast, Protestantism appeared to be
easily accessible, welcoming difficult theological questioning, and providing guidance for informants' lives.

Converts also conveyed dissatisfaction with the worship style of
Catholics, with which they found little connection. Martha (whose conversion was featured at the beginning of this chapter), demonstrates
this perspective:

> [Mass] just seemed pointless. It seemed dry. I thought, "If this mes-
> sage that they're preaching, the message of salvation, the message of
> mercy, the message of grace, why aren't they more excited about it?
> Why aren't they happy about it? Why are they just droning on and
> why are they not just shouting it from the rooftops with all joy and
> with all freedom?"

Ofelia (age fifty-one, female), along with other informants, described the lack of freedom in worship as a Catholic and, in contrast,
relished the freedom that worship in her Protestant congregation allowed:

> In the Catholic Church you cannot applaud. You cannot lift your
> hands. In the Catholic Church you do not have that; it is more re-
> served, very reserved. There is no freedom. But what I experienced
> at Iglesia Mundial was freedom. The worship was my freedom.

Informants characterized Catholic worship as rigid and limiting, while
they perceived Protestant worship practices as flexible and engaging. It
is important to note that not all Latino Protestant congregations allow
such freedom in worship, particularly those associated with fundamentalist groups. Ultimately, however, the pull to Protestant worship felt by
converts was due to the perceived absence of a restrictive tradition,
allowing for freedom of expression.

In contrast to the feelings of disconnect that Latino converts said
they felt with the Catholic Church, they found the intimacy with God

offered in Protestant theology appealing. Indeed, statistical analysis of related items in the 2006 Hispanic Survey data indicates that out of all the categories to cite for reasons for conversion, "to get closer to God" has the highest proportion of responses (91 percent) among Latino Protestant converts. God was not articulated as distant but as personal and similar to a close friend. Celeste (age forty-six, female) compares her prayer life before her conversion and then after: "I thought only priests and other Catholic leaders prayed, so I didn't really pray to God. I didn't have a communication with him at all. But once I became a Christian I learned how to talk to God and how to discern some of the things Jesus was saying in the Bible."

The ability to pray and be heard by God without intercessors (i.e., priests) allowed Celeste to make her faith more personal and meaningful. Informants often cast Catholicism as "religion": a formal, man-made institution concerned primarily with following rules. Protestantism, on the other hand, provided them a "relationship" with God. Camilla exemplifies this perspective, "Jesus didn't die for a religion. I have a relationship with God. It's not a religion, I'm not religious." These narratives are significant given there is no former theological stance in Catholicism that articulates God as inaccessible or distant. In fact, Catholicism highly regards and promotes a close, personal relationship with God through reading scripture.[9] These findings reveal that a disconnect exists between the formal theological standings about God's accessibility in Catholicism and how informants experience those Catholic intercessory practices.

THE DEMOGRAPHICS OF LATINO PROTESTANTS

Socioeconomic Status and Religious Affiliation

In order to understand Latino Protestants and Latino converts to Protestantism, we turn to a discussion on the demographic characteristics of this population. We summarize the central variables that explain patterns in religious affiliation among U.S. Latino converts such as socioeconomic status, nativity/language status, and national origin status.

Socioeconomic status (SES) has long been established as significant for examining the tapestry of religious affiliation in the United States—

although these patterns change and sometimes reverse over time. For example, Catholics were among the poorest segments of the American religious population (i.e., immigrant Italian Catholics in the 1920s). Now, some Catholics (particularly white Catholics) enjoy an SES comparable to "high church" populations that include mainline Presbyterians, and Episcopalians.[10] Currently, religious groups with the lowest SES status tend to be Protestant groups such as Southern Baptists, Pentecostals, and other conservative Protestant denominations.[11] The link between education (an important measure of SES) and religiosity may help explain the lower status among these Protestant groups.[12] Generally, fundamentalist and conservative Protestants have lower educational attainment;[13] particularly for women in these denominations.[14] Therefore, there is reason to believe that there are significant socioeconomic distinctions between Latino Protestants and Latino Catholics.

Among all Latinos in the United States in 2012, the median household income was $39,005 (compared to whites at $57,009). In the same year, 64 percent had at least a high school degree and 13.8 percent had a least a bachelor's degree or higher.[15] Overall, the SES of Latino Protestants seems to be similar to that of the general Latino population in the United States, with caveats along denominational lines as found in previous research. Some evidence suggests that Latino mainline Protestants and some evangelical Protestants have a higher SES than Latino Catholics, although these findings vary slightly from study to study.

For example, findings from the General Social Survey, one of the oldest, largest, and best-established surveys of American life, suggest that Latino Protestant converts tend to have higher education, income, and occupational prestige.[16] Pew Hispanic Center's *Changing Faiths: Latinos and the Transformation of American Religion* survey of 4,016 U.S. Latinos indicates that 42 percent of Latino Catholics did not graduate from high school and 46 percent had household incomes of less than $30,000.[17] This is lower than the national average for Latinos in general. In contrast, 64 percent of Latino evangelicals have at least a high school diploma and only 39 percent have an income below $30,000. The majority of Latino mainline Protestants have at least a high school degree (64 percent) and a smaller proportion (29 percent) of them compared to other groups have a household income less than $30,000. Another study by Trinity College in 2008 confirms that Latino mainline Protestants have the highest level of education and 63 percent have an income above $50,000. Also, Baptists and nondenominational Christians have higher levels of college completion compared to Latino Catholics.[18] The Protestant income advantage is explained by "nativity status," that is, whether they are native born U.S. citizens. A higher proportion of Latino Catholics are immigrants compared to Latino Protestants, who tend to be English dominant and are, presumably, non-immigrants. Therefore, the lower SES among Latino Catholics may be due to these factors, with Latino Protestants having income-raising advantages.

Other studies have demonstrated that Latino Catholics have advantages over their Protestant counterparts. For example, Catholics have slightly higher levels of high school completion compared to conservative Protestant groups.[19] Data from the National Survey of Youth has found that Latino Catholic and mainline Protestants gain assets at a faster pace and are more likely to be in the upper- and middle-income levels compared to African Americans, while Latino conservative Protestants demonstrate no such advantage.[20] Latino Catholics seem to have the most socioeconomic advantages when compared to Pentecostals, who have the lowest levels of college-going and college completion. Pentecostals tend to be the poorest in the Protestant religious tradition, which in turn impacts educational levels.[21] Also there is anecdotal evidence to suggest that some fundamentalist leaning Latino Pentecostal congregations may deter their members from seeking higher education,[22] however our ongoing ethnographic research and other reports suggest that there are some Pentecostal congregations that in fact support their youth going to college. This is particularly impactful for the Latino population, who are disadvantaged educationally compared to whites in the United States.

Strangely, in the same dataset, Pentecostals have the highest income, second only to mainline Protestants. Age composition (e.g., an older population and therefore chance for income accumulation) and geography (Latino mainline Protestants tend to live in the North rather than the South) may account for this income-level difference.

Some of these conflicting findings in regard to which group is more advantaged SES-wise, Latino Protestant or Catholics, is probably due to differences in methods (i.e., descriptive versus predictive analyses), measures (i.e., income/education versus wealth/mobility), and other unmeasured differences in sample characteristics of Latino Protestants in each study. However, the majority of the evidence suggests that Latino Protestants (especially mainline Protestants) are socioeconomically advantaged over their Catholic counterparts. This evidence has catalyzed discussions as to whether conversion to Protestantism functions as a sign of increased social mobility.[23] It is important to note that *advantaged* does not mean *wealthy*. Indeed, many Latino Protestant converts find themselves entering into some of the least wealthy denominations, including those in the Pentecostal and Charismatic vein.

Language Use among Latino Protestants and Converts

The loss of Spanish and a preference for English among Latinos in the later generations stands as a marker of cultural assimilation.[24] Some argue that assimilation into U.S. society (where Protestants are the majority) explains Latino disaffiliation from the Catholic Church and the shift toward Protestantism.[25] Statistics support this. For example, the majority (55 percent) of Catholic Latinos indicate Spanish as their dominant language, while 63 percent of evangelicals and 73 percent of Latino mainline Protestants indicate either that English is their primarily language or that they are bilingual.[26] Overall, Catholic Latinos have larger proportions of Spanish speakers compared to Latino Protestants.

Studies demonstrate that Latino Protestant converts are more likely to say they are English dominant compared to their Catholic counterparts.[27] Nativity differences between Catholics and Protestants may explain why Latino Catholics tend to be Spanish dominant as they remain disproportionally more likely to be foreign born compared to Protestants.[28] Another similar study using the same data found that Latino Catholics are also more likely to use Spanish at home. Some scholars speculate that the Protestant practice in Latin American sending countries tends to break with local culture and tradition. Therefore, Latino Protestantism in the United States embraces a reorienting religious identity that reduces ethic identification more than Catholics, who show greater institutional acceptance of their ancestral ethnic culture in their churches—including continued support of Spanish usage among Latino Catholics.[29]

Countries of Origin among Latino Protestants

Among all Latin American countries of origin, Mexicans were more likely to report being Catholic. In terms of conversion, those Latinos who identity their family origin as Puerto Rican and Central American are more likely to be converts compared to Mexicans; while those Latinos who have Puerto Rican, Cuban, Salvadorian, Central American, or South American ancestry are more likely to be lifelong Protestants compared to those Latinos with Mexican ancestry.[30] These numbers mimic the rate of Protestant adherence in Latin America as well.[31] These patterns are explained by the fact that many of these origin groups have a long history with lay-led Protestant movements such as in Central America. Similarly, the large number of Puerto Rican Protestants connects with the long history that Puerto Rico has with the United States due to the Spanish-American War in 1898, where Protestant missionaries made gains in conversion.[32] In contrast, Mexico has had a strong connection to Catholicism and Catholic adherence that has not waned like it has for other Latin American countries. Other analyses report distinctive patterns of Protestant adherence according to country of origin. Puerto Ricans and Central Americans (Guatemalan, Salvadorian, Honduran, Nicaraguan, Costa Rican) have the highest proportions of Protestants compared to other groups, particularly Mexicans.[33]

MOTIVATIONS FOR CONVERSION

Based on research discussed above, we know that there are demographic patterns associated with conversion to Protestantism by Latino Catholics. These can lend a clue but do not fully explain the process of conversion, which remains multifaceted. Rational choice theory has offered prominent explanations for religious switching.[34] Rational choice theory assumes that people approach all decisions by evaluating costs and benefits and then act in ways that maximize benefits and minimize costs.[35] The theory concludes that when people attempt to maximize their religious return on investment, they spur on a religious marketplace and religions compete for adherents by promising benefits of "religious goods" (i.e., assurance of salvation, internal peace, or emotional uplift). In other words, the individual performs as a rational actor, always calculating their actions in accordance to their best interests.

Beyond individualistic motives, community norms and expectations will constrain individual choice if an individual believes the community is able and willing to punish them for violating community norms.[36] Sociologists have used this sanctioned-based and community-focused perspective in explaining religiosity through a theory called the "semi-involuntary institution," a theory that scholars originally developed to explain African American religious attendance differences between the North and South.[37] Among African Americans, church membership offered a key to social respectability and a gateway to opportunities for full participation in the civic life of black communities. Consequently, overall church participation levels were somewhat higher in the rural South than elsewhere because black churches imposed social sanctions for noncompliance, making complete withdrawal from church more costly.

The semi-involuntary institution theory also helps explain the conversion of Latino Catholics to Protestantism.[38] Because Catholicism often occupies a central place within Latino communities and because the Catholic Church serves as a medium for social participation in Latino cultural traditions (e.g., *quinceañeras, las Posadas*, first communion, marriage, and other social and life cycle events), switching to Protestantism can have significant social and emotional costs.[39] Overall, persons with deeper embeddedness within Latino communities may have fewer incentives to switch from Catholicism to Protestantism. To test this theory, researchers used Latinos living in the same telephone exchange as a proxy for Latino concentration. Areas of greater Latino concentration may have more consolidated social ties, as residents tend to share not only ethnicity but also religion, cultural practices and folkways, and membership in community organizations. In areas with greater concentration of Latinos, the expectation is that there would be less likelihood of conversion. Similarly, because Latino concentration is also dependent on geographic location in the United States—with Latinos being mostly concentrated in the Southwest (Texas, New Mexico, Arizona), Pacific (California), and specific areas on the East Coast (New York, New Jersey, and Florida)—conversion would be unevenly distributed. Latinos in these areas will be less likely to leave Catholicism and become Protestants.

Other scholarly work imagines conversion to Protestantism as reflecting other crucial dynamics. For example, becoming Protestant may be a means of gaining power, challenging the status quo, or rechanneling political anxieties into religion in order to cope with political discord.[40] Some scholars, taking a Marxist approach, explain the transformation of Latin America's religious landscape to Protestantism as a means in which those in power are able to create more docile and submissive low-wage workers.[41] Yet others view conversion as a form of exercising individual agency, an individual willfulness seen among Latin American women, whose conversion to Protestantism gained them cultural power to usurp a damaging machismo they faced in their domestic lives.[42]

Other research has sought to challenge both the purely rational choice and Marxist leaning explanations for Latino Catholic conversion to Protestantism. For example, research about conversion among Mexican immigrants and Chicanos in Los Angeles finds that conversion and religious communities for this group provided *both* a means for people to gain agency *and* a means of subordination: Pentecostalism provided religion-based "escapist" conceptual tools for coping with oppression while at the same time providing tools to overcome social problems in poor, Latino communities.[43] People who converted from Catholicism to Protestantism fell into two general categories. The first included those who found themselves battling serious crises in their lives (such as drug addiction and gang related problems). Protestantism offered them the comfort and resources they needed to overcome their addictions. That finding resonates with other research on the growth of evangelicalism in Latin America that highlights the ability of evangelicalism to give people conceptual tools to deal with challenges. In a study about conversion among poor men in Venezuela, the switch to Protestantism offered the spiritual tools necessary to reinvent themselves and their orientation toward dealing with their problems.[44] Similarly, data from the Pew study in 2006 found that facing a crisis was the second-most-cited reason for conversion among U.S. Latinos, next to converting in order to be closer to God.

The second category included lapsed Catholics or those who lacked a strong connection to Catholicism in the first place. For these Latinos, their former Catholic practice was generally shallow, and individual investment in the faith was minimal. Among lapsed Latino Catholics, their move into Protestantism was due to the appeal of the church's social life. The Pentecostal church appeared inviting and friendly and provided opportunities for intimacy and belonging. Such a positioning proves particularly significant for new immigrants who lacked a social support network. Overall, Luis Leon states, "For Mexican Americans and immigrants who lack social skills, the congregation functions as a mechanism of cultural brokerage . . . where they remake self, community, and nation."[45]

Another more recent study on conversion among Latinos in the Southeast focused on churches that lacked resources and included large populations of unauthorized Latino migrants.[46] Marie Friedmann Marquardt describes the conversion of Catholic Latinos into the Evangelical Lutheran Churches of America (ELCA) as not a strategic move based entirely on gaining benefits but as unexpected and unintended. Surprisingly, Marquardt found that many Latinos who faithfully attended the Lutheran congregation went years without realizing it was actually not a Catholic church. The leadership of the church at the time obfuscated the church's denominational identity by adding elements to the church worship they believed to be "culturally sensitive," such as displaying crucifixes and Stations of the Cross in order to make Latino Catholics more comfortable. Over time, congregants learned that the church was not Catholic yet stayed anyway because they had already become deeply invested in the church, some even still identifying as Catholic even though they actually attended a Protestant congregation. The Protestantism of this Lutheran congregation provided the opportunity to practice their religious life in a way that allowed them, as immigrants, to be more connected with others, gain friends, and have a more hands-on role in the congregation compared to their experience in the Catholic Church. The intimacy of the Lutheran church proved appealing and prompted some to disaffiliate from their Catholic roots.

Interviews with Latino converts found that they emphasized supernatural experiences with a higher being more often than they discussed the social benefits they received from their conversions.[47] However, a challenge for understanding Latino conversion is the fact that causes for conversion based primarily on spiritual experience or personal circumstance are difficult to measure through "paper and pencil" survey research. Likewise, it is important to note that converting for the sake of accruing social benefits and converting for spiritual reasons are not mutually exclusive. Because of the complexity undergirding the shift to Protestantism among Latinos, it is important to use multiple methods, including interviews and observations, in order to fully understand the cause of the Latino Protestant reformation taking place in the United States.

FROM CATHOLICISM TO PROTESTANTISM

The shift away from Catholicism to Protestantism among Latinos functions as a key component in the recent growth of Latino Protestantism in the United States. However, no singular reason explains the momentum of conversion of Latinos to Protestantism. The journey of Latino converts to Protestantism is diverse and influenced simultaneously by social characteristics (i.e., socioeconomic status, family heritage), personal circumstances (i.e., challenges and crises), and opportunity (i.e., exposure to Protestantism). One conclusion that can be made with confidence is that many Latino converts either had a nonexistent or limited relationship with Catholicism before their conversions (although they still thought of themselves as such) or had some level of dissatisfaction with the Church that pushed them to seek other spiritual alternatives. In our own data, informants expressed pointed criticism of Catholicism. Part of this may be due to the nature of disaffiliation, which as has been described as akin to divorce.[48] On the other hand, evidence suggests that some Latino Protestant congregations have adherents who still religiously identify as Catholics.[49] In the spectrum of Latino Protestant identities, where do these Latinos locate themselves? Further theoretical development is needed to confront the complexity of the multiple and layered experiences of Latino Protestants converts.

Most quantitative data indicate that socio-demographic factors characterize converts as being primarily English dominant or bilingual and more upwardly mobile, particularly if they are mainline Protestants. The advantage is not as strong among Pentecostal and fundamentalist Baptist groups. Data also indicate that Central Americans and Puerto Ricans are more likely to be converts, although clearly the majority of Latino Protestants in the United States are of Mexican origin. Clearly, the complicated nature of Latino Protestant conversion requires further inquiry in an effort to disentangle the knot of SES, language, national

origin, social benefits, and spirituality. As we consider the Latino Reformation today, we also know that Latino Protestant identity involves
more than simply issues of conversion. For instance, our interviews
reveal that for many Latino Protestants, their identity has a dynamic
interaction with congregational life. These issues of identity within congregational contexts will be addressed in the next chapter.

4

ETHNIC IDENTITY AND VARIETIES OF LATINO PROTESTANT CHURCHES

WHAT ARE THE ETHNO-RACIAL DYNAMICS IN LATINO PROTESTANT CONGREGATIONS?

At Alabanza Hispanic Church,[1] a small Latino Baptist congregation in the Southwest, Pastor Carlos Flores enthusiastically began his Sunday sermon. Normally, the church has separate English and Spanish services, but today was a special combined service for both congregations. Pastor Carlos came as a toddler from Guanajuato, Mexico, with his family in the 1980s. The thirty-five-year-old pastor stood on the platform in front of the congregation and told the congregation (first in English then in Spanish) that he had news to share. He announced that God had laid it on his heart to change the church's name, specifically dropping the word "Hispanic" from the title. Pastor Carlos spoke fluently and quickly to the church in both languages without the aid of a separate translator. He explained that the name stood as a barrier to the church's goal of "reaching all people," and it needed to be more inclusive. He noted the many occasions when visitors to the church inquired if only Latinos could attend. He pointed out that when people drive by, they look at the sign and think, "Maybe they just speak Spanish there," and decide not to come. He assured the church several times that he had no intentions of asking them to change who they were or their culture. The church's new name would be spelled and pronounced in the same way in both Spanish and English—ensuring that the church would still value the Spanish-speaking congregants. He emphasized that he was not in denial about his heritage and reminded the church of his Mexican birth and that he remained proud of that fact—he joked that no matter how hard he scrubbed his skin he would never be able to remove its brown pigment, garnering chuckles from the congregation—but his Latino identity did not hold the status of his first "calling." Instead, his first calling in life is to be a Christian.

Another church, Poderoso Amor, a large nondenominational mega-church in the southwestern United States, is located just twenty minutes from the Mexican border. The church is exclusively Spanish speaking and has no English service. The congregation was planted as a satellite campus in 2001 as a missionary effort by members of the original church Poderoso Amor México located right across the border in Mexico. Over time, the attendance in the American church surpassed that of the original Mexican congregation. Transnational ties remain strong at this church, and Spanish is the dominant language in all dealings there. However, unlike Alabanza Hispanic Church, none of the leadership or members expressed particular worry that their focus on the Latino population would be detrimental to their church's mission.

As these cases demonstrate, there is variation in the way that Latino Protestant congregations come to understand their identity as *Latino* churches. In this chapter, we delve into Latino identity formation and explore the role that Latino Protestant congregations play in this process. Churches are spaces in which U.S. Latino *identidad* is ironed out, expressed, and augmented. The more recent shift away from Catholicism toward Protestantism among Latinos has prompted questions regarding the future of "Latino identity." What is a Latino without the Catholic faith? As mentioned earlier, the significance of this question is exemplified in a common saying among people of Mexican origin: "To be Mexican is to be Catholic," therefore the switch to Protestantism may indicate assimilation into the American religious mainstream. We offer an overview of the complexities of Latino identity. To begin, we summarize the theoretical implications for Latino identity separate from Catholicism and provide a synopsis of empirical support in this topic. We then present ways in which Latinos process their identity in a context outside of Catholicism and within Latino Protestant congregations by distilling newfound ethnographic data.

COMPLEXITY OF LATINO IDENTITIES

Many social scientists argue that race and ethnicity are social constructs.[2] An individual's race/ethnic category is not based on biology, but rather on the intersection of "individual social identity and the very structure of society."[3] Unlike European immigrants in the United States (e.g., Italian, Polish), Latinos are more likely to identify with their ethnic identity more readily in later generations.[4] The issues involved in disentangling ethno-racial dynamics are far from being just black or white. The terms "Latino" and "Hispanic" tend to be used interchangeably in the United States to describe people who have origins or historical connection to Spanish-speaking countries, particularly those countries in Latin America that experienced colonization by Spain. The meanings of these and other terms have varied over time and context. For example, middle-class activist groups such as the League of United Latin American Citizens (LULAC) in the 1920s often used "Latin American" as a term to create distance between themselves and recent immigrants (who had lower socioeconomic statuses) and even African Americans.[5] The creation of the panethnic term *Hispanic* was due to efforts of Mexican American and Puerto Rican advocacy groups such as The National Council of La Raza (NCLR).[6] Until 1970, the U.S. Census Bureau categorized Latinos as "white" (except for a onetime inclusion of a "Mexican" category in 1930), making it impossible to track patterns of social inequality within the U.S. Latino population.[7] More recently, some argue that the term *Hispanic* privileges a connection to European roots in Spain and has classist undertones.[8] For that reason, scholarly circles have demonstrated a recent tendency to use *Hispanic* less frequently in favor of *Latino*. That trend indicates an overall sense that *Latino* better represents the indigenous and African roots in the population.

The political recognition and access to job programs hoped for by Latino advocacy groups in the United States demanded accurate information on the Latino population. Eventually, disparate ethnic groups negotiated and settled on a new "Hispanic" panethnic category. Advocacy groups, government officials, and Spanish-language media companies promoted the new category of Hispanic collective identity.[9] While a collective notion of panethnicity helped secure access to funding to ameliorate inequalities and brought camaraderie between Latinos of different national origins, it has also homogenized Latinos in the minds of Americans. Subsequently, the diversity of the people who fall under this category, which entails twenty different countries and numerous indigenous groups in Latin American, continues to be lost. In other words, the creation of *Hispanic* allowed wider recognition at the cost of watering down differences between groups. Understanding the experiences of Latino Protestant congregations in the United States today requires recovering and considering these differences. Moreover, Latinos have divergent and various experiences of racialization in the United States and more than likely are situated in a *racial ideology continuum*,[10] that is, a spectrum by which Latinos identify as white and colorblind on one end, and on the other end, see themselves as racial "others" and subscribe to anti-racist ideology.

CATHOLICISM AND LATINO IDENTITY

Because of the history of Spanish Catholic colonization, long have connections regarding Latino identity and Catholic identity been intertwined. Catholicism has long been the majority religion in Latin America.[11] This is particularly true for Latinos of Mexican origin; the largest Latino ethnic group in the United States.[12] Catholic iconography has historically been associated with Mexican identity, such as the Virgin of Guadalupe, who is seen as the patron saint of Mexico. Likewise, Catholicism was important in Latino civil rights movements in the United States. For example, Cesar Chavez used Catholic symbols, doctrine, and narratives to galvanize support for improving the work conditions of farm workers in the San Joaquin valley.[13]

Besides the long history of Catholicism in Latin American countries, Catholicism is an important mechanism for social and cultural participation among Latinos in the United States. Similar to Judaism, Catholicism has been described as a "quasi-ethnic"[14] religion, therefore leaving the Church to become Protestant indicates a significant shift in Latino identity. The movement may signal not only Latino assimilation into the American religious mainstream but also a loss of Latino identity. Indeed, as described in chapter 3, surveys have demonstrated that Latinos who are Protestant are more likely to exhibit characteristics of assimilation into U.S. society—including a greater likelihood of speaking English and privileging their religious identity over their ethnic identity.[15]

CONSTRUCTING A LATINO PROTESTANT IDENTITY

As we noted in our chapter 2 discussion of the history of Latino Protestantism in the United States, Latino Protestantism does not represent a new ethno-religious phenomenon in this country. Latino Protestant history in the Americas stretches back at least 150 years.[16] As a result, Latino theologians have been wrestling with the issue of Latino Protestant identity for quite some time. Well-known Latino Protestant theologians and historians, Odina González and Justo González, articulate in *Nuestra Fe (Our Faith)* the ways that a unique Christian history has been cultivated in Latin American for hundreds of years and the important role that Protestantism has played in that history.[17] Another notable example is found in a 1994 edited volume by Daniel Rodríguez-Díaz and David Cortés Fuentes written for the Hispanic Theological Education Association (Asociación para la Educacíon Teológica Hispana or AETH), an association founded by Justo González.[18] Many Latino Protestant theologians and historians offer essays in an effort to provide "an instrument to continue our discussions around the challenges facing the task of recovering and documenting Latino Protestantism."[19] Contemporary streams of Latino Protestant theological scholars have engaged with the racism, colonization, and status hierarchy of Latinos in the United States. These studies involve critical perspectives on how white Protestant theologians have ignored the experiences and roles of Latinos in Protestant history. According to Rodríguez-Díaz, "In Latino communities . . . the matter of identity burns in the heart of all. This is so because the history of exclusion is one of centuries of resistance. A history with characteristics of domination has produced tension and ambivalence."[20] These writers assert that a Latino identity can exist in the absence of Catholicism, yet their identity is not so easily captured in the survey data available.

A SPECTRUM OF LATINO PROTESTANT IDENTITIES

Latino Identity Engaged with Racism, White Supremacy, and Immigration

In our field research, we see that Latino Protestant churches vary in how they come to understand their identities as Latinos outside of Catholicism. In the following section, we show examples from our fieldwork where we see Latino identity articulated as (a) engaged with racism, white supremacy, and immigration; (b) replaced with "multicultural"; (c) all-encompassing; and (d) divisive. We suspect that Latino Protestant congregations articulate their identity in even more heterogeneous ways that will be revealed by our study in future years. Until then, we share early ethnographic glimpses of what we have found to this point.

Iglesia Mundial, a Latino Pentecostal congregation, sits a little more than two hours from the Mexican border in a large metropolitan city in Texas. Located in a mostly low-income area of the city, the church is primarily comprised of Latinos, including many recent immigrants from Mexico and Central America. It is a predominantly Spanish-speaking congregation, although in the last year, it has focused on trying to make Sunday services fully bilingual. The lead pastor of the church, Miguel Suárez, is Puerto Rican, differing in ethnic background from most of his congregants, while his wife is of Mexican descent. Pastor Suárez was born on the island, and his wife is also a first-generation immigrant. Both are bilingual and have high levels of education, with the pastor having studied at a prestigious seminary in the United States. They have been influenced by and actively participated in scholarly conferences on Latino Protestant theological thought and have close relationships with leaders in the field, such as historian and theologian Justo L. González.

When interviewing congregants and leaders about how they perceived Iglesia Mundial's racial/ethnic identity, they never hesitated in describing it as a "Latino Church." Like many of the congregations in our study, the members cited two obvious facts: First, the church is majority (and almost exclusively) Latino; and second, the services are bilingual with many of its programs conducted solely in Spanish. In addition to what members mentioned, we noted that the church held weekly classes related explicitly to Latino identity and Christian faith.

The church offered the classes twice on Wednesday night: one in Spanish, comprised of middle-age attenders and older, and the second in English, comprised of mostly high school and college students. These "Faith and Culture" Bible studies routinely engaged issues of racism, colorism, social inequality, and the marginalized status of Latinos in the United States. Designed like a college course, Pastor Miguel led the class, and indications of rigor included a detailed syllabus, assigned readings from theologians who have written on faith and Latino identity/history, and two written exams.

At Iglesias Mundial, immigration concerns are an important avenue in which Latino identity is discussed. During a regular Sunday church service, a well-known lay leader of the church, Antonio, offered testimony about being an unauthorized immigrant who was held in a federal immigrant detention center (discussed further in chapter 6). He was released with the church's and (according to him) God's help. While his message did not explicitly connect his experience to his identity as a Latino in the United States, Iglesia Mundial provided a platform for Antonio to share his story to a receptive audience. The church venue, then, offered Antonio an opportunity to humanize his experience as an unauthorized immigrant and bring attention in a public way to conditions of other Latinos. Overall, the leadership at Iglesia Mundial is not shy about addressing controversial and progressive issues of racial/ethnic heritage despite its conservative Pentecostal faith. We find that in this church a unique Protestant and Latino identity is being crafted devoid of Catholic ties.

Latino Identity Replaced with "Multicultural"

Word of Life, another Latino Protestant congregation in the Southwest, articulated its racial/ethnic identity differently than Iglesia Mundial. Word of Life described itself as a "multicultural" church rather than Latino. Founded by Pastor Steven Forest (who is a non-Latino white) and his son (Pastor Mark) and daughter (Pastor Libby), the church sits about twenty minutes from the Mexican border. All members of the family have college degrees, but whether any of the three received seminary training remains unclear.

While officially nondenominational, the church has deep connections to well-known leaders in the Charismatic "Word of Faith" movement.[21] Located in a predominantly Latino border city, the church reflects the region's racial composition in that its attenders are 80 to 90 percent Latino. This multigenerational church is mostly composed of Mexican Americans and immigrants, as well as Latinos of other national backgrounds (e.g., Salvadorian, Puerto Rican). Whites represent the second largest population at Word of Faith, followed by African Americans/African immigrants, and a few Middle Eastern and Asian Americans (less than 1 percent).

Almost all church services, classes, and events utilized English. Only one service was held in Spanish in a classroom. In contrast to the expansive audience in the main sanctuary, the Spanish service included one hundred to two hundred people led by Pastor Oscar Quintanilla, the associate pastor (often identified as "the Spanish pastor"), who is seminary trained and a first-generation Mexican immigrant. It was clear that the pastoral leadership cares deeply about the Spanish-speaking members of their church. Pastor Mark, who does not speak Spanish, would give short talks a few times a year at the Spanish service. He would convey his family's love for the members in the Spanish-speaking service and remind them that his family often prays for them. Even with such assurances, the Spanish ministry had a limited role and was not as integrated into the other aspects of the church's ministry and congregational life. Beyond this service, use of Spanish was minimal in the congregational life of the church—although it was available as a translation via radio transition during its night service on Saturday and three main English services on Sunday.

Several aspects of Word of Life are important with respect to its racial/ethnic identity. First, like many Latino Protestant congregations in the Southwest, elements of Latino culture (particularly Mexican culture) were present at times. This included mariachi music, traditional Mexican folk dance (*ballet folkórico*) during special events such as their annual Christmas show, and popular Mexican street food for sale during events. Members said that these cultural markers were "no big deal" and were simply expected due to the high percentage of Latinos in the area. Yet, the level of engagement with Latino identity did not go beyond customary and often obligatory cultural markers that operated in the background of church activities. Unlike Iglesia Mundial, Word of Life never intentionally or explicitly discussed racial/ethnic identity.

Most significantly, everyone interviewed (excluding the lead pastor) refrained from describing Word of Life as a Latino church. The only exception, Pastor Steven, indicated that he felt comfortable labelling Word of Faith a Latino church, but only to the extent he thought it made sense given the church's population. While the lead pastor may find it important to maintain the distinctiveness of being "Latino," all other leaders and members found that label to be too limiting. They preferred the label "multicultural"—even though the demographics of the congregation clearly indicate the membership being overwhelmingly Latino. Kyle, a young church member, captured this sentiment, saying: "No, it's multicultural . . . of course there's Mexican heritage here. They honor that sometimes." John, a white retiree at the Word of Life, agreed: "No, it is more of a Christian church than it is an ethnic church." For many members, the noticeable presence of non-Latino people at the church (although small) disqualified it from being a Latino church. One of the most visible parts of congregational life was the worship team, which, while majority Latino, also included prominent African American and Asian American singers. Others like Amie (age twenty-four), indicated that a high population of Latinos at Word of Faith did not necessarily translate into a Latino church identity. Instead, Christian identity trumped any ethno-racial identity: "It's not [a Latino Church]. I mean, yeah, a lot of Hispanics come here, but it's more than just a Hispanic church. Like, this is God's place because it's His house. We're just builders of His house, and there's all that it is." During a membership class orientation, the instructor plays a DVD of Pastor Steven to welcome new members of the church. In the recording, the minister looks directly at the camera and declares that Word of Life is "a *multicultural* church and we are proud of it."

Latino Identity as All-Encompassing

Just three minutes to the south of Word of Life, another nondenominational megachurch, Poderoso Amor, claims four thousand eight hundred weekly attendees.[22] Similar to Word of Life, Poderoso Amor is led by a white pastor, Jason Taylor. The minister grew up in Mexico in a missionary family, speaks Spanish fluently, and married a woman of Mexican descent. As described earlier in this chapter, Poderoso Amor was originally a church that was planted in the 1980s in Mexico in a large city on the U.S. border. Over time, many of the Mexican church members moved to the United States and continued to commute on Sundays to Mexico to attend church. Eventually, members living on the U.S. side of the border decided to open a campus in the United States. Since its founding in 2001, attendance at the U.S. campus surpassed that of the Mexican campus and the church has planted three other campuses in the same city. The church is majority Mexican immigrant, followed by those Latinos who are second generation and above. Other Latino national origin groups attend as well, such as Salvadorians, Puerto Ricans, and Chileans.

The church conducts almost all activities in Spanish. In fact, a large portion of leaders and volunteers at the church do not speak English at all. During Sunday sermons, the church provides English translation via radio transmission with a headset. Beyond that accommodation, though, English remains rarely used during worship services.[23] The church has a large number of attenders who live in Mexico, commute to the United States to attend church weekly, and express dedication to seeing the U.S. campus flourish. The international ties of Amor Poderoso run deep and most prominently through its music and youth ministries. Pastor Jason's family and Amor Poderoso México played an important role in establishing Mexico's first Protestant youth conference—highly influential among youth ministries throughout Latin America. Many high-profile Spanish-speaking Christian artists started their careers in the music ministry at Amor Poderoso. The quality of the showmanship of the musicians continues to be high. Currently, the youth band Amor Adolescentes has an international fan base in Latin America and has released several albums. The church band debuted its first album under a Latino Christian label for international sales online and in select Christian stores. In support of its outstanding music ministry, the church has a large recording studio and employs professional Christian music producers from other parts of Latin America.

Aside from the deep transnational ties both in its founding and through its music ministry, Pastor Jason demonstrates a particular sensitivity to church visitors who may be Latino Catholics or to church members who may have been formally Catholic. Often during services, the pastor uses Spanish words traditionally reserved for a Catholic service, such as calling services at the church *Misa* (Mass). During altar calls[24] at the end of his sermons, Pastor Jason would use the word *rezada* (traditional Catholic prayer) to ask the church to pray with him. The associate pastor at Poderoso Amor, Alfonso Leya, explains that this is done in order to "help people feel more comfortable," particularly since a large portion of visitors of the church are Latino Catholics. At the same time, Amor Poderoso would sometimes display iconography that played on stereotypes, such as fliers printed with images of men in dressed in *sarapes*, *sombreros*, and big mustaches. Pastor Jason regularly dressed this way in the church's videos and during sermons.

The church leadership and members regularly identified Amor Poderoso as a Latino church—perhaps not surprising given the history of the church's founding and transnational ties to Mexico. Pastor Alfonso, a Mexican immigrant and one of the original founding missionaries of the church, recognizes that the church's focus on the Latino population may limit who the church can attract as potential members. Pastor Alfonso recalled non-Latino visitors who never returned to the church due to the lack of English services. Some Latino members with primarily English-speaking children have also left the church. Pastor Alfonso did not seem alarmed by this these families or other members deciding to leave:

> Even though we have about two thousand [members] that profess their faith in Jesus, not everyone stays, and we understand because we don't think Amor Poderoso is the answer. Christ is the answer. So if you want to go to another church, I mean, go. What we want is for you to have an encounter [with Christ], and we want to be able to bring you to that encounter.

In contrast to other Latino Protestant congregations in our study who regularly dwell on their Latino racial/identity, Amor Poderoso never did. Leaders and members did not wrestle with the implications of Latino identity in regard to civic issues like racism and immigration in a manner similar to that of Iglesia Mundial. Pastor Alfonso and members at Amor Poderoso did not understand the church's identity as a Spanish-speaking, Mexican church plant as a barrier to the church's ministry. Instead, they believed that the church served a significant population in the city.

Latino Identity as Divisive

As mentioned earlier, Alabanza Hispanic Church is a Southern Baptist congregation in a large metropolitan city in the Southwest. The Sunday worship service includes attendance of about one hundred sixty, almost all of whom are Latino (about 98 percent). The church serves a largely middle-class Mexican American and Mexican immigrant population along with other Latino ethnic groups such as Puerto Rican, Cuban, Colombian, and Salvadorian. The church is largely second generation with some recent immigrants. Sunday rituals include two worship services and two Sunday school classes—each in both Spanish and English. Pastor Carlos is bilingual and teaches during the main services, while members of the pastoral team (and sometimes volunteer lay leaders) teach the Sunday school classes. Wednesday night Bible studies include both languages as well. Spanish use remains prominent in church activities and among the older congregants. Among the children and youth, however, English seems to be preferred.

As discussed earlier, during our observations the church had initiated a transition that included finding a new pastor and changing the congregational name. The modification included dropping the word "Hispanic" from the church title. The pastor and other church leadership felt the sign dissuaded some from coming to the church. Visitors had asked the pastor if they had to be Hispanic to come to the church and most did not return. These developments made Pastor Carlos worry that the church name gave an impression of exclusivity. He recalls the complaint of a Latina visitor to the church:

> She said, "The sign offends me." I think it offended her because we live in a world where . . . there is a lot of fighting and divisions over racial stuff. A lot of tension. People see that all over the news. . . . They are going to see that [the church sign] like, "Man, they are prejudiced. They are just trying to reach out to Hispanic people."

This visitor's complaint and those of a few others like her made a lasting impression on Pastor Carlos. The pastor and leaders in the church expressed concerns that that the sign would impede the church's ability to grow. The worship pastor, Alex, strongly articulated his dislike of the name of the church: "I hated the name of the church. I thought it was really ignorant and pretty stupid. We were putting ourselves in a box and also putting God in a box. I don't think God likes that. I know God doesn't favor people from one race over another." Pastor Carlos's vision was also to see the church's population change to be more racially/ethnically diverse, and the sign was a hindrance to that goal. For Pastor Carlos, the name not only made the church unappealing to non-Latinos but to non-Mexican Latinos as well. He observed, "My friend's parents were here; they are both from Nicaragua. . . . They heard the name Alabanza Hispanic Church, [and] they associated 'Hispanic' with just Mexican people. They didn't consider themselves Hispanic; they actually consider themselves Latinos."

It was clear in conversations with the leadership at Alabanza Hispanic Church that the sign appeared to present barriers for diversity on various fronts. Church leaders invoked "spiritual" reasons for changing the name. The pastor explained to the congregation that name changing occurs frequently in the Bible, noting that Jesus changed the name of Peter. He said that name change offered evidence of the Holy Spirit's work in revitalizing the church's vision. Another church leader, Kenny, indicated that no scripture could be used to justify having a church name with specific ethno-racial connections. He cited the apostle Paul, "There is neither Jew nor Greek, slave nor free, there is no male nor female, for you are all one in Christ Jesus,"[25] to demonstrate that Christianity should seek to erase divisions between people not create them.

Beyond the name change, the church adapted the musical style of the Spanish service. Historically, the church played hymns that were in the ranchera music style, a genre of traditional music in rural Mexico. Currently the transition has been to contemporary English and Spanish worship music. Alex's musical direction was the main reason for this transition, and he articulated that without a change in music, the church would get "too comfortable" and be unwilling to reach out to the new generation of young Christians. Alex strongly believed that the change in music was integral to growth of the church and that stretching the comfort zone of the older congregants musically was a necessary challenge. He said that he felt God tell him while praying that:

> Any church or generation that stays stuck where they are at is a dying generation. I started looking around, and in the Spanish chapel there was nothing but elderly people. There were no teenagers. There were not even people in their forties. I told the pastor team that I was changing songs because we needed to start training the people

after us, getting them involved and excited, but they're not even
here. We need to start drawing them [younger people] in somehow.

Alex explained that the oldest members of the congregation were the
most upset at this change and complained to him and Pastor Carlos
often; many left.

Alabanza Hispanic Church was clearly not in denial about the type
of population it served or ashamed of its Latino roots. Over and over in
interviews, congregants at the church were comfortable with the label
of "Latino church."[26] Spanish remains prominent in the church's formal
and informal activities. At the same time, church leaders felt the need
to emphasize that their identity as Christians superseded their Latino
identity, as Pastor Carlos notes:

> Definitely I think the church is more Hispanic. . . . You don't have to
> go into the church too far in to notice that obviously this is a Hispanic
> church, but I believe we don't have to promote it. Our promotion
> should be more about who we are as believers. I was born in Mexico;
> I'm not ashamed of that. I'm Hispanic and I'm okay with that, but at
> the same time, I don't want to limit [the] kind of people who can
> come to this church.

Alabanza Hispanic Church's decision to eliminate Hispanic from its
name was in tension with its forty-five-year history of serving a primarily
Latino community. The "Hispanic" title was seen as too divisive and too
political. Ironically, markers of a primary Latino congregation were not
entirely removed. The new proposed church sign included "*servicios en
Español*" (Spanish services), and the new name chosen was a biblical
Greek word easily pronounced in Spanish. Spanish language use continued to be prominent in sermons, worship, and in general congregational life.

THE DIVERSE PATHS OF LATINO PROTESTANT IDENTITY

The complexity of how Latino Protestant identity is articulated cannot
be fully captured by survey data alone. An observational study like the
Latino Protestant Congregation Project demonstrates paths forward for

scholars of race/ethnicity. Through those observations, we find that Latino Protestant congregations interpret racial/ethnic identity in a variety of ways, signalling that a monolithic definition of a Latino church offers an inadequate explanation. All the churches discussed in this chapter assert the significance of their Protestant Christian identities. For some, this translates into downplaying their Latino identity. For others, though, they saw no need for a reduction in their ethno-racial identity as Latinos. Latino Protestants appear to be able to preserve their cultural distinctiveness apart from their white Protestant counterparts. These Latinos redefine what it means to be Latino outside of the Catholic faith through the development of new cultural practices, new definitions, and newly modified yet Catholic-associated rituals (i.e., Protestant churches holding a service in celebration of a *quinceañera*). This is then filtered by the local contexts of the churches as well (e.g., Spanish predominance, location on the borderlands, immigrant population, etc.). Additionally, we see instances where Latino Protestants exercise influence within largely white-run Protestant denominations to which they belong by establishing annual Latino-centered conferences, nurturing Latino-authored theological discourse, and highlighting the challenges of Latino-inflected racism within their religious lives. Our research clearly demonstrates that despite the shadow cast by Roman Catholicism, Latino Protestants in the United States have forged paths where they have created and maintained their own unique ethno-religious identities. Latino Protestant congregations demonstrate no sweeping disavowal of Latino identity. Latino Protestant churches function as important institutional contexts in which Latino identity can be reified, reduced, or negotiated.

What Latino Protestant congregations provide is a platform in which the complexity of Latino identity is processed. In other words, the churches are microcosms of a larger, aggregate process of racialization in which Latino racial/ethnic identity is being ironed out. Latino identity in Latino Protestant congregations seems to mirror what Julie Dowling[27] argues about Latino racial identity in general—as an ideology existing in the form of a continuum (with some Latinos more likely to identify as "white," while others more readily identifying as racial "others"). We do see a continuum of identification in churches. In tandem, these churches appear to also be shaping the racial/ethnic discourses and racial ideologies Dowling describes as well.

In the end, Latino Protestant churches do not racialize in the same way—they push Latino identity down in prominence, keep it at bay, or magnify it. What churches do is provide tools for Latino Protestants to process their identities. It is important to emphasize that the categories of Latino identity formation showcased here are not necessarily mutually exclusive or static. And it is certainly possible that these churches could shift their orientation toward a more stable and consistent Latino identity in the future.

5

THE CENTRALITY OF "DOING CHURCH" AMONG LATINO PROTESTANTS

WHAT ARE THE PATTERNS OF LATINO PROTESTANT CONGREGATIONAL LIFE?

Latino Protestantism has no archetype of congregational life. Churches range widely in habits, beliefs, and expectations. More than that, Latino Protestant congregations do not remain static in their church practices. Scholars and writers have argued that *within* Latino Protestant congregations, the very practice of Christianity is being reshaped. What is certain is that church is central to Latino Protestantism. For example, in California, Pastor Rene Molina leads Restauracion Los Angeles—a congregation that had thirty members two decades ago and currently counts weekly attendance closer to three thousand. In a former movie theater in Crenshaw, Molina fosters an intimate experience for immigrants who have left family and friends behind. Juan Martínez, a vice provost down the road at Fuller Seminary, describes the emphasis of the worship at the church: "Society may have you in the shadows because of your immigration status or your economic status. But this is a church that says, in God's economy, you have total worth."[1] Bolstering that contention, attender Ricardo Romero describes his first visits to Restauracion: "It changed my life. There was a warmth, a spirit and ease that I had not encountered in a church before. And the pastor was urging us to love God and improve ourselves. . . . It was not about wealth or becoming rich. It was about becoming the best student, the best father, the best person and citizen we could be."[2] In this way, Latino Protestant congregation members themselves attest to the profound influence that their churches have within their lives.

With stories like Restauracion Los Angeles in mind, this chapter surveys the richness of Latino Protestant church and congregational life. As noted earlier, Latino Protestants, living in a religious country to begin with, demonstrate even more intensity than most Americans in both what they believe and how they practice those beliefs. Because of that commitment, churches function as a central feature of the social and spiritual lives of Latino Protestants. With that in mind, it is important to understand how congregational life shapes and outlines the practice of Latino Protestantism.

For our purposes, we see congregations as simply people gathering to worship in a particular location.[3] Moreover, congregations continue to be significant institutions in the United States: "More Americans are involved in a religious congregation than in any other type of association, group, or club."[4] Beyond that, we also note that these are complex and diverse organizations. With somewhere between three hundred thousand and four hundred thousand churches in existence in the United States, the places, rituals, narratives, and artifacts of congregational life are bound to vary. This is no less true within the congregations that comprise Latino Protestantism in this country.

The consistent trend of diversity among Latino Protestants continues to bear out when examining congregational behaviors and cultures. For instance, an aspect of Latino Protestant heterogeneity demonstrated in the Pew survey data is church attendance. Overall, attending church weekly is a much greater priority among Latino evangelicals than Latino Catholics. However, Latino mainline Protestants attend at even lower levels than Latino Catholics. We also see distinctiveness in the percentage of Latino Protestants who participate in weekly prayer or Bible study groups: 55 percent of evangelicals compared to 25 percent of mainline Protestants.[5] In this chapter we describe the variegated patterns of congregational involvement for Latino Protestants. Beyond that, we note the relative significance of congregations within the lives of Latino Protestants.

The diversity of religious orientation among Latino Protestants also leads to considerable heterogeneity in liturgical styles found within these churches. Many of these differences are due to varying theological priorities, denominational background, and alternate congregational practices. In this chapter we also pay careful attention to the Pentecostal and renewalist movements and their respective influence on Protestant Latinos as a whole. Latinos identify with the Pentecostal and renewalist movements at a much higher rate than the rest of the U.S. population, and that affiliation has had significant influence within many Latino churches that are not themselves Pentecostal in their orientations. Indeed, we find that Latino Pentecostalism threatens to overshadow other forms of Latino Protestantism.

Finally, in this chapter we also stress the significance of place, location, and context for Latino Protestant churches and their ministries. The demographic and built environments in which they find themselves have substantial implications for congregational practice and church constituency. In some cases, new churches sprout to accommodate the migration of Latinos. For instance, a study in Boston found that as the phenomenon of gentrification worked its way through the city, Latino Protestant families relocated from neighborhoods like the South End to more affordable places like Roxbury, and churches sprang up to follow these flowing and expanding Latino populations.[6] In other instances, Latinos have found membership in Anglo Protestant congregations to be conducive of community and economic acceptance. From the rural plains of the agricultural economy of Iowa to the density of core city neighborhoods in New England, we see all manner of Latino Protestants working, residing, recreating, and worshipping in all sorts of venues and circumstances. These myriad complexities of faith, habit, and practice can be difficult to discern, so we demonstrate how Latino churches affect and are influenced by modern demographic and socioeconomic issues using both existing studies and our own qualitative data.

ALWAYS A "FIESTA"? LATINO PROTESTANTS AND VARIETIES OF WORSHIP EXPRESSION

Worship Experience

When journalist Elizabeth Dias visited Calvary Foursquare Church in Silver Spring, Maryland, for her 2013 *Time* magazine cover story, she described an exuberant scene of five hundred worshippers. Instruments included guitars and trumpets. Children and adolescents dance and race down the aisles. An elderly woman delivers a prophecy in "screams" as the rest of the congregation falls silent. A man beats his fist against a pew while in prayer. As people kneel at the altar, the ministers anoint them with oil. A dozen girls in sequined sashes dance at the front of the sanctuary. While the service occasionally settles down into respites of quietude, the dominant mode of worship remains an ebullient celebration.

Dias notes that in her observations of Latino Protestants she witnessed adaptable worship that allowed for liberal doses of self-expression. Ten minutes away from Calvary, at Iglesia Roca de la Eternidad (an Assemblies of God church), the pastor delivers sermons that resist traditional three-point homilies. Instead, "the message at La Roca is theologically raw, unpolished, and aimed at the immigrant experience."[7] The pastor explains: "People are looking for a real experience with God. We do the best to preach with the Bible open. . . . They may have had religion, but they did not have an experience."[8] To nurture a sense of intimacy among the members, La Roca encourages small groups to meet weekly and keep account of members' prayer needs. Beyond that, every Sunday morning includes one dictate: before you listen to the sermon, every attender should greet ten other worshippers.

Both scholars and journalists describe much of Latino Protestant worship as charismatic. Dias explains "charismatic" as connoting "a belief in miracles, healing, divine intervention, speaking in tongues, and an active spirit world."[9] Such a statement echoes theologian Juan Martínez's assertion that Latino Protestant worship looks "like a fiesta."[10] In her journalistic observations, Dias witnessed a woman praying so hard that she vomited. Of course, it should also be noted that such an activity might not have been as spontaneous as assumed: Ushers stood by ready with plastic bags to contain any mess.

NOT ALWAYS A PARTY

While the vivid scenes and explanations of theology that Dias captures tell us something about worship and rituals, it should not be understood as the totality of Latino Protestant congregational life. Our own ethnographic research on Latino Protestants has offered the opportunity to glimpse congregational life in places that range from the Pacific Northwest to North Carolina. While Latino Pentecostals and evangelicals dominate most of the headlines and assumptions about the practices of Latino Protestants in general, it remains significant to remember that many Latinos in the United States worship in mainline congregations that engage in more formal rituals.

Beyond that, our time in these congregations has demonstrated quite clearly as well that not all Latino Protestant worship should be described as a "fiesta." A Latino Pentecostal—almost always assumed to be charismatic, spontaneous, and emotional in worship—congregation in Oregon, for instance, could be best described as orderly in its liturgy. In fact, when a member of our research team interviewed members of this church, she heard the phrase, "God is a god of order"[11] multiple times. Moreover, the concept of orderliness also governs the rituals of worship at the church. Services start punctually at the predetermined time. The movements of the liturgy (worship and praise, prayer, greetings, offering, sermon) follow a specified chronology and length of time. To ensure that these elements remain on schedule, a coordinator remains in the rear of the sanctuary and will indicate to worship leaders by raising his hands and pointing to his watch that they needed to transition to the next element of the worship service.

The rather staid, non-fiesta atmosphere also governs participants' activities during worship. While the service includes clamoring, crying out, and ecstatic utterances that would typically be associated with Pentecostal worship, extraneous bodily movement seems forbidden. No one dances. No running through the aisles. No shaking attacks of holy laughter. We witnessed no instances of parishioners being slain in the spirit. Instead, a church supervisor remains near the rear of the sanctuary vigilantly watching to protect the service from anyone "entering into emotionalism." Our researcher heard from two worship team leaders that they often will have the congregation be seated if they sense the worshippers are on the precipice of too much movement. There even seem to be gender-based protocols for acceptable movement: most women bend their arms at the elbows when they lift them while men tend to extend their arms up straight. The strict, ordered worship practiced at this Pentecostal church in Oregon seems oddly incongruent with any notion of fiesta.

Language, Sermons, and Sites

While levels of spontaneity may vary, overall, Latinos in the United States tend to be more uniform in the use of Spanish language for worship. Regardless of religious tradition, the majority of Latinos report attending a church where worship includes a Spanish language service. Catholics, though, report a higher percentage (86 percent) than either Latino evangelicals (81 percent) or mainline (72 percent). In addition, Latino churchgoers tend to largely be under the leadership of Latino clergy. Almost eight in ten Latino evangelicals (79 percent) and Latino Catholics (78 percent) worship in churches with Latino pastors. Interestingly, Latino mainline attenders report a significantly lower number (65 percent) worshiping under Latino clergy. In addition to more exposure to non-Latino clergy, less than half (48 percent) of Latino mainline Protestants attend churches that are mostly or all Latino. Both Latino Catholics (66 percent) and evangelicals (58 percent) have higher percentages of churchgoers who attend congregations where the majority of parishioners are Latino.[12]

So we know that Latino Protestants hear most sermons in Spanish, but what is the substance of the sermons they hear? Based on a Chicago study, their pastors have divergent views regarding the Bible. While roughly one in four (26 percent) Latino pastors believe the Bible stands as the literal word of God, about half (49 percent) understand the Bible to be divinely inspired but do not endorse a literal interpretation. While none of the Latino mainline pastors queried in Chicago believed the Bible to be literal, four in ten (41 percent) Latino Pentecostal pastors and one in three (33 percent) of Latino evangelical pastors promoted the Bible as the literal word of God.[13] By way of contrast, we would also note that evangelical Latinos hear different things from clergy than their Catholic counterparts. While almost half (48 percent) of Latino Catholics report hearing about immigration issues from clergy, only four in ten (38 percent) evangelical Latinos indicate the same. Interestingly, those numbers invert when the subject changes to laws regarding homosexuality: 47 percent of evangelicals and 36 percent of Catholics report hearing ministers speak on legislation related to homosexuality.[14] In short, the topics of sermons and homilies vary from religious tradition to religious tradition.

We note as well that Latino Protestants also, at times, worship in a variety of settings. New Life Covenant Church in Chicago includes four campuses that host seventeen thousand worshippers every Sunday. New Life holds eleven worship services every week—only two are Spanish language. The pastor, Wilfredo De Jesús, speaks English as his first language. He also earned a masters degree from North Park Theological Seminary and has published a book, *Amazing Faith*, that includes a foreword from fellow author and megachurch pastor Rick Warren. Worship services at New Life stream online and count viewers in states that range from Massachusetts to Arizona to Kentucky.[15] In sum, we see that Latino Protestant worship remains highly textured and resists un-nuanced categorization: some worship in small, intimate spaces, while others worship in large, anonymous arenas.

In the end, any conclusions regarding Latino Protestant worship should be held loosely: congregational life and worship practices can also be fluid and remain highly flexible. For instance, at the aforementioned Restauracion Los Angeles, the church maintained a long-standing tradition of seating during worship segregated by gender. In addition, there existed an expectation of formality and modesty in the dress of worshippers. Only men could preach. Eventually, though, "[Pastor Rene] Molina tossed it all out, starting with the dress code and gender separation. His wife, Hanelory, and other women began preaching. The band that once played Central American hymns moved to Christian rock. The sermons became less focused on castigating imperfection and more on the way God's love has sweeping power to change."[16] As Restauracion demonstrates, Latino Protestant worship continues to evolve and will continue to be influenced by religious tradition, context, and demographics.

Pentecostalism: A Prominent Faith within Latino Protantism

Though occasionally collapsed into one religious tradition category, sociologist Norman Ruano rightly insists that Latino Pentecostals and Latino evangelicals look and behave in different ways. Utilizing the Chicago Latino Congregations Study (CLCS), Ruano, for instance, finds dissimilarity among Latino Protestants in terms of gender and congregational involvement. Interestingly, Latino Pentecostals seem to be "most effective at attracting (or retaining) men to the pews."[17] While only one in four attenders at a mainline Latino Protestant church is a man, fully 38 percent of Latino Pentecostal congregants are men. In between, we see that a little more than three in ten (34 percent) Latino evangelicals are men. Congregational distinctions also arise when considering educational levels. The vast majority of Latino mainline (88 percent) and evangelical (78 percent) pastors have a Bachelor of Arts degree or more. However, fewer than half (46 percent) of Pentecostal pastors report the same level of education.[18]

Ruano also highlights variegated affiliations between Latino evangelicals and Latino Pentecostals. He finds, for instance, that Latino evangelicals tend to have some sort of association with established U.S. evangelicalism—either a denomination, an affiliation, or a network of some sort. Conversely, Latino Pentecostals either function as independents or find affiliation with Latin American or U.S. Latino denominations. Ruano claims that these distinctions have led Latino evangelicals down a road of political conservatism that looks similar to white evangelicalism, while Latino Pentecostals express more progressive views that translate into strong support for the Democratic Party.[19] Ruano concludes: "In the end, it is very important to separate Latino evangelicals and Latino Pentecostals for the sake of research. Although Latino evangelicals have some similarities with Pentecostals (moral issues, for instance) . . . they also have significant differences in social and political views and civic engagement behavior."[20] Again, we see that a finely filtered analysis of distinctiveness *within* Latino Protestantism yields intriguing texture and richness.

The Renewalist Movement: Charismatics within Latino Protestantism and Latino Catholicism

In discussing influences among Latino Pentecostals in particular, we would be remiss in not addressing the significance of the broader renewalist movement. Renewalist practices have profoundly impacted Latino Protestant congregational life in the United States—and not just Pentecostals. "Renewalist" Christians tend to include both Pentecostals and charismatics. Pew describes renewalist Christians as practicing "lively, highly personal faiths" that "emphasize the spiritually renewing 'gifts of the holy spirit.'"[21] Renewalist Christianity became a prominent movement throughout global Christianity during the twentieth century and continues to have significant sway among Latino Protestants (and Catholics[22]) in the United States. Fully two-thirds of U.S. Latino Protestants practice a Christianity that could be classified as renewalist.[23]

In terms of congregational life, renewalism manifests in worship practices that include speaking or praying in tongues, receiving direct revelations from God, divine healing, and witnessing evil spirits being driven out. For Latino Pentecostals, these rituals happen fairly frequently. Over half (59 percent) report observing an exorcism and a little less than half (49 percent) say that have spoken in tongues. The percentages, though, increase to almost two-thirds for Latino Pentecostals when they discuss receiving a divine healing (64 percent) or a direct revelation from God (64 percent again). However, for non-Pentecostal Latino charismatics, those reporting these types of renewalist experiences decline sharply. For instance, less than half indicate that they have received a divine healing (46 percent) and the exact same share (46 percent) report a direct revelation from God. Beyond that only one-third (33 percent) have witnessed the exorcism of evil spirits and a little more than one-fifth (22 percent) have spoken in tongues.[24] Thus we see even within the renewalist camp of Latinos significant distinctions between Pentecostals and charismatics.

For Latino Pentecostals who regular attend worship services, almost all (97 percent) indicate that they at least occasionally witness people engaging in "excited" and "enthusiastic" worship that could include raising hands, shouting, jumping, or clapping—compared to 86 percent of Latino charismatics. Similarly, the vast majority (96 percent) of churchgoing Latino Pentecostals also report that the worship services they attend at least occasionally include worshipers speaking in tongues, prophesying, or praying for miraculous healing while significantly fewer (70 percent) of Latino charismatics indicate the same type of worship elements. In stark divergence, though, about half of non-renewalist Latino Protestants told the Pew Research Center that they never observe these charismatic practices at their churches.[25]

In addition, there seems to be a relationship between renewalism and the prosperity gospel within Latino Pentecostalism. More specifically, about two-thirds (65 percent) of Latino Pentecostals believe that if they have enough faith that God will bless them with wealth and good health. That percentage drops to less than four in ten (39 percent) among non-renewalist Latino Protestants.[26]

As has been established, Latino Protestants overall demonstrate high levels of religious commitment. However, the renewalists within their midst report heightened religiosity in comparison. While 51 percent of non-renewalist Latino Protestants report attending worship services at least weekly, the percentages increase considerably for those within the renewalist camp of Latinos: 72 percent of Pentecostals and 64 percent of charismatics.[27] In the end, renewalism clearly wields a broad and deep influence throughout Latino Christianity: It transcends the religious tradition boundaries of Protestant and Catholic while encouraging more rigorous religious practice within its adherents.

THE CENTRAL ROLE OF CONGREGATIONS

The Wide Range of Church Subcultures

Latino Protestant congregations represent a growing wing of Christianity in the United States. In a larger context of significant disaffiliation with organized religion, how do we account for such an aberration among Latino Protestants?[28] Some scholars claim[29] that Latino Protestant congregational growth resides in the fact that many of the pastors of these churches "come from a Latino background, speak Spanish, share the daily hardships of the community, and have more of an egalitarian church service based on scripture."[30] In contrast, Latinos attending Catholic churches have less opportunity to have a priest who has Latino heritage. In this interpretation, Latino Protestant congregational life offers an ethnic familiarity and comfort that remains largely absent in many Catholic churches. Thus, in some cases, Latino Protestantism gains adherents by offering an ethno-religious refuge.

Of course, even though Latino Protestantism is growing, that does not mean that all Latino Protestants attend thriving, expanding churches. In fact, Latino Protestants gather in congregations that range from a handful of folks meeting in a living room to megachurches that contain upwards of twelve thousand attenders who worship in state-of-the-art sanctuaries. Despite the fact that we know there exists a range of Latino Protestant congregations, a nicely pixelated picture of these churches remains elusive. In some instances, that is simply because these congregations remain difficult to locate: Journalist Elizabeth Dias asserts in her 2013 *Time* magazine cover story ("Evangélicos!") that many Latino Protestant churches begin in basements and storefronts and may not have any signage to speak of.[31] The vast array of these churches also necessarily means that they have divergent ways of "doing church." So while the number of Latino Protestants is growing, the majority of them attend smaller congregations, often characterized by part-time pastors, relational intimacy, a high proportion of lay volunteers, and largely unobtrusive worship services and week-long ministries. Being small and largely independent, these churches are hard to find. Obscurity for researchers, though, should not be misinterpreted as insignificance. These small congregations hold influential places in the lives of millions of Latinos in America.

Expectations of Latino Protestant Church Membership

Different congregations will also cultivate different cultures and expectations of attenders' behavior and involvement. Based on the Pew Research Center's comprehensive study of Latino religious patterns in the United States, it remains difficult to make sweeping generalizations about Latino Protestants and their relationships to their churches. For instance, how often do Latino Protestants attend worship services? Even a seemingly straightforward question like this becomes muddled as different strands within Latino Protestantism are teased out. By way of example, we see that, overall, 62 percent of Latino Protestants attend worship on a weekly basis (compared to 40 percent of Latino Catholics). However, a closer examination reveals a significant contrast when Latino Protestants are sorted by evangelical (71 percent) and mainline (35 percent) categories. By filtering we see that evangelicals demonstrate the highest level of church attendance, while those of the mainline affiliation have percentages that slump below Latino Catholics.[32] Thus, a close examination *within* the category of Latino Protestantism reveals striking disparities in church attendance practices. In short, not all brands of Latino Protestants attend church with the same regularity.

Beyond worship attendance, Latino Protestants also demonstrate various levels of engagement in general congregational life (for example: Sunday school teacher, member of the council, small group leader, ministry coordinator, volunteer in the food pantry). Again, in terms of involvement in church leadership and volunteering, Latino mainline attenders look more like Latino Catholics than their fellow Protestants, Latino evangelicals. When asked if they have any involvement beyond worship, Latino Catholics and mainline Protestants responded at almost identical rates of 17 percent and 16 percent, respectively. In marked contrast, fully 42 percent of Latino evangelicals indicated some type of involvement in congregational life. In essence, then, Latino evangelicals have twice the involvement rate in congregational activities than any other churchgoing Latino religious category.[33] In all likelihood, those high levels of church participation function as residue from *conversion* to Protestantism—we know that converts have higher rates of congregational activities when compared to lifelong Protestant Latinos.

In addition to church volunteering, Latino Protestants also tend to have higher levels of participation in prayer or Bible study groups— associations that may or may not have formal affiliation with a congregation—than their Catholic counterparts. Overall, 48 percent of Latino Protestants report attending a prayer or Bible study group at least weekly. In contrast, only 17 percent of Latino Catholics indicated the same level of regularity with these types of meetings. Again, however, when examining closely, we note that Latino evangelicals have the most disparate habits: 48 percent report at least weekly attendance compared to only 25 percent of Latino mainline Protestants. It seems, though, that Latino evangelical Bible and prayer meetings in particular might be slipping as a priority. Whereas Latino Catholic and mainline weekly percentages largely held steady from 2006 to 2013, the rate of weekly participants among Latino evangelicals fell by 10 percentage points (from 65 percent to 55 percent).[34]

Another method for considering church commitment is amount of hours per week in which attenders engage in church-related activities. Latino Protestants also spend variable amounts of *time* each week involved in congregational events. When gauging congregational time commitments in his Chicago-based study, Ruano found Latino Pentecostals and evangelicals looking very different than Latino mainline Protestants and Latino Catholics. While the majority of both Latino Pentecostals (70 percent) and evangelicals (63 percent) spend at least three hours a week in church activities, only about three in ten mainline (36 percent) and Catholic (32 percent) Latinos demonstrate the same level of time commitment.[35] The same trends hold true when congregants reported whether they spent seven hours or more per week at church. Fully one in three Latino Pentecostals indicated that they spent more than seven hours per week engaged in church-related activities. Not far behind in church time commitment, almost two in ten (19 percent) of Latino evangelicals spend at least seven hours every week. Strikingly, only eight percent of Latino mainline Protestants reported that many hours of church activity.[36]

PUBLIC AND COMMUNITY INVOLVEMENT

Much as they have variable levels of time commitments to their congregations, Latinos also have a variety of opinions about how robustly the church should enter public debate and about whether it should register opinions regarding social and political issues. In general, almost as many Latinos say that the church should remain silent (44 percent) as say that religious institutions should (47 percent) enter public debates. Again, though, Latinos from different religious traditions tend to have distinctly divergent opinions on this matter. Latino mainline Protestants tend to favor silence from the church: only 37 percent indicated support for churches speaking out. On the other hand, six in ten (61 percent) evangelical Latinos indicated that they thought the church should express viewpoints on various social and political issues. Opinion regarding the role of the church in society, however, has not been static among Latinos in the United States. For instance, from 2006 to 2013 mainline Protestant Latinos became less enthusiastic about the church expressing views. The percentage approving church expression fell from 55 to 37 percent. Evangelical Latinos moved in the same direction but not nearly as dramatically: in 2006 64 percent noted approval compared to 61 percent in 2013.[37] In sum, then, Latino Protestants seem to have become more hesitant about the mingling of congregations and politics.

Of course, size of congregation and relative resources play a role in their ability to develop capacities for civic and social engagement. Based on the study from Chicago, very few Latino Protestant congregations generate budgets that would allow for robust levels of civic involvement. The vast majority (89 percent) of Latino mainline congregations in Chicago generate budgets of less than $101,000 annually.

Though fewer Pentecostal (71 percent) and evangelical (61 percent) churches have similarly small budgets, all three strands of Latino Protestantism still look quite sparse compared to Latino Catholic parishes in Chicago: 56 percent have budgets that exceed $201,999.[38] These types of revenue-generating discrepancies certainly play a role in determining the degree to which a congregation enters into social service delivery or civic engagement.

In Illinois, the CLCS noted that Latino Protestants also demonstrate different expectations for certain social behaviors. Compared as a composite group with their Catholic counterparts, Latino Protestants feel more pressure from larger congregational expectations to forgo the use of alcohol and tobacco. Only a small minority of Catholic churches expected attenders to abstain from alcohol or tobacco (23 percent and 8 percent, respectively). Thus, it could be concluded that there exists little stigma for Latino Catholics in the Chicago area to drink alcohol and use tobacco. In contrast, the aforementioned CLCS also found that almost nine in ten (89 percent) religious leaders from Latino evangelical congregations and almost eight in ten (77 percent) from Pentecostal congregations expected attenders to forgo tobacco use. On the same issue, only 27 percent of leaders from Latino mainline churches held the corresponding expectation. On the related topic of alcohol use, nine in ten (90 percent) Pentecostal leaders and a little more than eight in ten (83 percent) evangelical leaders expected abstention, while only half (55 percent) of mainline leaders held the same position. In sum, then, evangelical and Pentecostal congregations tend to have more profound restrictions regarding alcohol and tobacco use when compared to Latino mainline congregations. However, the evangelicals appear a bit more tolerant of alcohol while the Pentecostals exhibit higher levels of leniency for tobacco.[39] Thus, we see sometimes vast discrepancies in the social behavior expectations among Latino Protestants—sweeping assumptions undermine the complexities of the interplay between faith and behavior among members of this demographic group.

Social and Spiritual Support

Though many Latino Protestant congregations may be small, they tend to be potent forces within the lives of attenders. For instance, in her ethnographic study of the Lafayette, Indiana, area, Sujey Vega found that for Latino Protestants, "church engagement and active participation in a Spanish choir or Bible study provided a sense of spiritual agency that carried over to a sense of belonging."[40] Vega continues, "through ethnic solidarity and *ethno-spirituality*, these families defined what it meant to live and function in the area in ways familiar to them, making Lafayette work for them rather than abandoning themselves to the larger socioeconomic forces of Lafayette."[41] For immigrants in the "foreign land" of central Indiana, the Latino Protestant congregation acted as social-spiritual support. The rituals of attending worship services and "spending time with their faith-based social networks offered a much-needed break from the monotony of the workweek."[42] Many of the Latinos in central Indiana found themselves employed in strenuous work that taxed them both physically and emotionally. With that in mind, Latino church leaders frequently utilized Sunday afternoons as moments of familial socializing: "Indeed, the small but thriving Spanish-speaking Baptist community almost always held outdoor events. Christian music could be heard in the background of families eating; playing volleyball, soccer, or softball with one another; and enjoying the recreational moments with new-found friends."[43] Vega quotes Refugio, a recent Baptist convert from Catholicism: "In our church, one feels as if we're part of the same family."[44] When Refugio and his family first arrived in Lafayette, they attended the Spanish Mass at the local Catholic Church. However, they soon found themselves disenchanted with the anonymity of the church and what they perceived as the detached nature of Catholic polity and hierarchy. Refugio revealed that the appeal of the smaller Baptist church resided in its ability to provide a more intimate spiritual encounter.

With that in mind, Vega argues, "Faith-based community building among Latino Protestants also provided familiarity, social networks, and emotional strength for facing an environment that was not always welcoming to their presence." These Latino Protestants "created their own sacred places where their spiritual needs were met and ethnic familial bonds created. Sacralizing space and practicing one's faith publicly validated the right of Latinos to exist openly as ethnic beings in a predominantly White community."[45] One woman recounted how the church provided a space that validated her Latina identity as a girl when her Latina features attracted mostly negative attention at her mostly white school—from both students *and* administrators. Other women described their churches as offering networks where they had friends who spoke the same language as their parents and also had direct knowledge of "ethnic traditions specific to a U.S. Latino identity."[46] Moreover, 60 percent of the Latinas interviewed by Vega indicated that their religious experiences at church offered positive respites from the hostility they perceived in places like work and school.[47]

In another instance, the congregational life and the leadership opportunities afforded by Protestant church polity and practices (guiding Bible study groups and practicing public speaking through testimonies, for example) fostered confidence in attenders. Vega finds that pastors encouraged attenders to vocalize their marginalized status and confront personal and structural impediments. Affirming studies[48] that argue that the Protestant congregational structure leads to a possible "road to civic empowerment," Vega observes once-meek Latino Protestants emboldened by experiences in church leadership and now marching the streets of Indianapolis in protest. With the confidence earned at church, these Latino Protestants in Indiana developed a sense of autonomy among their ethnic peers.[49]

It seems that church acted as an integral support for those who consciously decided to remain in Lafayette and become Latino Hoosiers: it allowed for encounters with similar others who made the same decision to persevere in the area. For Vega, the distinctiveness of Latino Protestant churches resided in (1) the creation of sacred spaces, (2) the maintenance of spiritual needs and ethnic bonds, and (3) the provision of a venue for public faith within a predominantly white community. In these three ways, Latino Protestant congregational life serves as a buffer to the harshness of life in the rural United States.

Of course, it would be wrong to assume that all Latino Protestants are recent immigrants. Even for those whose ancestors have been in the United States for generations, though, the rituals and subculture of congregational life serve as a site of being known, belonging, and being comforted. For some, congregations serve as centers of ethnic identity maintenance. For others, though, the Protestant congregation offers an efficient route to assimilation into broader U.S. culture.

RELATIONSHIPS WITH NON-LATINOS AND NON-PROTESTANTS

Efforts to Accommodate Latino Protestants within Mainstream Christianity

While Latino Protestants reflect the patterns of broader Christianity, they also wield a significant influence of their own. The rapidly expanding number of Latino Protestants is transforming religious practices in the United States. Though many Latino congregations remain unaffiliated or nondenominational, established denominations such as the United Methodists and the Reformed Church in America have begun holding national meetings regarding how their churches might be more hospitable and attractive to Latinos. Another denomination, the Southern Baptist Convention (SBC) has set a goal of establishing seven thousand Latino Baptist congregations by 2020. Already in 2009 Richard Land, former president of the SBC's religious liberty commission, told his pastors to ignore Latino Protestants at their own risk. Dias quotes him, "Because if you left [Washington D.C.] and drove all the way to L.A., there wouldn't be one town that you'd pass that doesn't have a Baptist church with an *iglesia bautista* attached to it."[50] It should be noted that this has been building over the last number of decades: already since the 1970s, United Methodist, Presbyterian, and Baptist churches became mixed Anglo-Latino congregations as the formerly white surrounding neighborhoods became predominantly Latino.[51] In short, established, historically white/Anglo denominations have noted demographic trends and have started to respond to the growing presence of Latinos. Beyond the mainline denominations, the aforementioned Rick Warren of Saddleback Church in Southern California has played a role in launching thirty-five Spanish-speaking congregations in Orange County.[52] Established congregations and denominations find themselves scrambling to capture the growing Latino demographic in the United States. And, of course, in the context of Anglos leaving organized religion at a quickening rate, it becomes all the more pressing for these churches to garner new attenders and members.

Tension with Roman Catholics

Some of the attractiveness to Protestantism for Latinos rests in the congregational practices that differentiate these churches from Catholicism. For instance, in a 2015 article about the seeming lack of appeal of Pope Francis to Latino Protestants in the United States, a Latino covert to evangelicalism in New York City, Miriam Salam, noted that she appreciated the encouragement of her current pastor for her to read the Bible for herself. She said that as a Catholic, "the priest read to us, but we never read [the Bible]. Now we know." Priscilla Nieves, another convert from Catholicism, contrasted the worship practices: "At a Catholic Church, all you do is just hear hymns, Santa Maria, like a regular boring monotone. But with Pentecostal it's on fire, you feel the Holy Spirit, you sing the songs, and you dance and you use instruments to worship God." Relatedly, Gabriel Salguero, former senior pastor of the Lamb's Church on New York's Lower East Side, discussed the fact that many of his attenders were former Catholics.[53] The appeal for them in his congregation, he argued, rested on some of its distinctiveness from Catholicism: "our charismatic worship, our empowerment of indigenous leadership, our ordination of women."[54] In this way, Latino Protestantism sometimes revels in its contrasts with traditional Catholicism.

As already mentioned, Vega also recounts that for many of the Latino Protestants in central Indiana, the appeal of congregational life was also related to opportunities for lay leadership that did not exist within the protocols of Catholicism: "In addition to female-led prayer groups, the Protestant congregations also placed lay individuals in leadership roles with the youth ministry, adult Bible study groups, weekend retreats, and much more."[55] Furthermore, these leadership roles became vital experiences for Latinos to "locate their voice[s]" and confidently address issues of marginalization and adversity. Vega argues, "Asked to reflect on their interpretations of scripture and engage their faith actively, Latino Protestants developed a sense of autonomy and confidence among their ethnic peers."[56] Citing previous studies about Latino Protestant activism,[57] Vega also concludes that the Protestant tradition of "individual spiritual affirmation" within congregational life nurtures a skill set that translates easily into larger secular social and political participation that felt constrained within Catholicism: "Indeed, I observed this first-hand with individuals who initially struggled to lead their prayer groups but who months later project a much more assured presence in front of their congregation."[58] Vega contends that congregational opportunities nurtured capacities for civic engagement. Latino Catholics, on the other hand, had scant opportunity to lead their congregations and, subsequently, had fewer chances to cultivate autonomy and leadership skills. They would be hard pressed, compared to Latino Protestants, to find their political and social voices.

Latino Protestants in Non-Latino Protestant Congregations: Two Cases

It should also be noted that Latino Protestants do not solely worship within Latino Protestant congregations.[59] Instead, studies indicate that 16 percent of Latinos attend Protestant churches where fellow Latinos remain few or nonexistent. In other words, a significant portion of Latinos do not worship in "Latino congregations." How Latinos become affiliated with these churches also remains variegated and highly dependent on context and religious tradition. For instance, a study out of rural northwest Iowa by Jane Juffer documents Latino Protestants joining a Reformed congregation that started as a joint effort between two historically Dutch denominations: the Reformed Church in America (RCA) and the Christian Reformed Church in North America (CRC).[60] Halfway across the country, Laura López-Sanders studied a Protestant nondenominational church, Harvest, in an affluent suburb in South Carolina that had incorporated twenty Mexican families into their congregation.[61] In both instances, the hybrid congregations function as socializing institutions that mediate social and economic ties for Latino Protestants in Anglo-dominant communities. For these reasons, even non-Latino congregations have significance in the lives of Latino Protestants across the country.

A Case in Iowa

Juffer describes the Iowa church Amistad Cristiana as a hybrid site of Anglo and Latino worship that rearticulates the classic Reformed confessions, including the Heidelberg Catechism. Pastor Arturo Gomez, ordained in the CRC, leads the church along with three Latino deacons and two Anglo elders. While the congregation remains financially solvent because of support from both the RCA and CRC, they have moved toward financial independence to the point that they raise enough money to fund Pastor Gomez's salary.

At Amistad Cristiana, Juffer notes the influences of Reformed, Pentecostal, Southern Baptist, Church of Christ, Assembly of God, and Roman Catholic traditions in the beliefs of the members. While the church clearly maintains a Reformed identity, Pastor Gomez describes the theology as "trying to be Christ-centered, with a Reformed-flavor teaching. We understand the other perspectives, the other traditions, and we're trying to be open, not to impose."[62] In practice, then, Amistad adheres to the tenets of Reformed theology but also allows for contextual relevance. For instance, the congregation recently resolved a disagreement regarding infant baptism—a nonnegotiable in some Reformed church circles. However, for some Latinos at Amistad, the idea of infant baptism seemed contrary to their understanding of Christianity. In response, the council offered what Juffer describes as a hybrid solution. A communication from an Anglo leader noted: "Amistad . . . recognizes that there are members who come from other Christian denominations where infant baptism is not practiced and therefore do not have an understanding of infant baptism. In these circumstances, Amistad encourages these parents to study the doctrine of infant baptism in order that they may understand and then baptize their children."[63] In the end, it seemed that Anglo leaders, while deeply committed to infant baptism, decided against making it a litmus test. While the tone remains decidedly heavy-handed and paternalistic, Juffer notes that the church struggled to make the doctrine relevant to a new constituency—rather than just forcing it upon them.

Meanwhile, the Latinos of Amistad have transformed some of the traditional worship practices of the Dutch Reformed. Juffer describes the worship service as "more lively" and having a stronger sense of camaraderie. After initial hesitancy, many of the Anglos embraced the band and the more effusive music.

Juffer also asserts that Amistad plays a crucial role for Latinos in northwest Iowa. First, it provides a context for Latinos to worship, speak Spanish, and gain confidence about interactions with Anglos. Beyond that, the church serves as point of commonality for member Latinos with the Dutch Reformed throughout the community. Amistad attracts Latinos from a twenty-five-mile radius and includes not just

Sunday worship but also Tuesday evening Bible studies and Wednesday morning coffees for women and children. In the end, Juffer sees Amistad as becoming a site with countywide influence. Thus, we see that historically white ethnic congregations have found intentional inclusion of and hospitality for Latinos as a strategy that provides a form of service while also beneficially raising their local profile.

A Case in South Carolina

Although in a much different geographic context, Harvest Church provides similar social resources as Amistad. A largely Anglo congregation of about one hundred forty families, the pastor of Harvest described integrating Latinos into the congregation: "There was a core group of us, and we started with the idea and the prayer and the wish that we could engage the community and not just exist for ourselves. . . . We thought that the church should engage the community on all levels. And really from there we sort of almost in a way stumbled on the Hispanic community. In a sense, some of our people had a connection because they either work with the Latinos or . . . you know, they have employees that were Latinos, so of course in their minds a light went on when we prayed on how to engage the community."[64] The initial foray toward integration was limited to inviting Latino musicians to perform for worship services. Since then, the congregation has evolved to a point that services include bilingual interpretation with headphones and receivers. PowerPoint projections also include both English and Spanish text.

Though Harvest sees its role as simply integrating Latinos into its church and not as a social service provider, it has demonstrated a proclivity to offer assistance. For instance, when the owner of the trailer park where many of the Latino congregants resided threatened to close it without notice, the pastor of Harvest brokered a deal that allowed the families more time to find alternative housing. Beyond that, Latinos who attend Harvest express hope that their membership in the congregation offers a social cachet with certain employers.

In addition to these potential social and economic benefits, Latinos at Harvest indicate that they appreciate the "unconventional structure" of a congregation that has limited hierarchy. López-Sanders argues that the congregation makes "local decisions" that "respond to the need for flexibility in the Latino community."[65] The fact that Harvest refuses to ask Latino congregants to renounce their Catholicism provides a vivid example of this flexibility. With that permission in place, "some Latinos have reached a religious compromise, in which they attend services at Harvest but still maintain some Catholic traditions. Amelia, for example, baptized her baby at both Harvest and a Catholic church. Other Latinos at Harvest participate in Catholic celebrations every year."[66] Thus, Harvest's success at integrating is due both to its ability to adapt and the socioeconomic benefits that Latinos might garner from attending the church—including socialization and the nurturing of economic relationships.

Amistad and Harvest represent Anglo congregations attempting to incorporate Latinos. These hybrid churches, then, serve crucial roles in helping to negotiate and broker the inclusion of Latinos into certain geographic contexts within the United States. Thus, in some instances, non-Latino congregations play a crucial role in helping Latinos to integrate into communities and neighborhoods.

ETHNOGRAPHIC GLIMPSES OF LATINO PROTESTANTS AND CONGREGATIONAL LIFE

In just a year and a half of the LPC Project research team spending time in Latino Protestant congregations, we have already witnessed a tremendous amount of diversity in how church is done. Our reports from the field demonstrate that Latino Protestant congregations undermine attempts at sweeping statements that encapsulate the whole of the religious tradition. Rather than relying on vague assessments of Latino Protestant church life, our participant observation has yielded provocative nuance and distinctiveness among these congregations. Ethnographic evidence from Pentecostal, Episcopal, and Presbyterian Latino churches offers a strong sense of heterogeneity in Latino Protestant congregations.

For example, our research team has participated in liturgy in Latino Protestant congregations that included a statue of the Virgin of Guadalupe. In one instance, we learned of a family that felt they had been duped: They had been attending an Episcopal church thinking it was Catholic. While these Latino Protestant congregations use elements of

Catholicism to make worshippers more comfortable, others take the opposite tack and use Catholicism as a cudgel to insure in-group cohesiveness. And yet for others, the specter of Catholicism seems to not loom at all and has little influence on the individual church.

To demonstrate the diversity that exists in congregational life, we offer glimpses of congregations from Texas, North Carolina, and Indiana. In all these cases, our research team has spent months as participant observers and interviewed both attenders and leaders. These case studies provide a textured portrait of Latino Protestants that interrogates broad brush–style proclamations regarding "the typical" Latino Protestant congregational life. The churches considered here include Word of Faith, mainline, and Pentecostal.

The Word of Faith congregation in Texas has a worshipping body of well over two thousand attenders—over 80 percent Latino. Despite that vast majority, the church considers its identity to be "multicultural" rather than "Latino." A white pastor, his son, and his daughter lead the congregation as ministers. During the main worship service, English remains the only language spoken and Latino issues are not addressed. Worship service song lists contain plenty of Hillsong played by a rock band of six. The setting includes two jumbo screens and three narrower LCD screens about fifteen feet in height. Coordinated laser lights punctuate the sanctuary's typical darkness and seem reminiscent of a professional music concert. Worshippers raise hands, clap, and dance. Much of the discourse from the pulpit includes Word of Faith statements that encourage attenders to declare their own success and claim their own health and wealth. The phrase "God is on your side" functions as a congregational motto: It is displayed throughout the church, featured in local television commercials, and repeated in every worship service. The process of taking offering usually consumes around twenty minutes of the worship service as the ministers explicate the significance of tithing.

In an urban area of North Carolina, another congregation of Latino Protestants gathers and has a vastly different worship experience on Sunday afternoons. In a Presbyterian church (PCUSA), they gather at 1:30 in the afternoon—late enough to allow the earlier English service attenders to fully clear the facility. A typical Sunday includes about sixty attenders and the elements of the worship service are described in the bulletin: call to worship, confession, passing of the peace. A projection screen at the front of the sanctuary displays song lyrics and scriptural verses. A logo denoting the PCUSA affiliation of the congregation is included on every slide. During the songs, worshippers refrain from engaging their bodies through dancing, clapping, or raising of hands. Quietude is also the expectation during the sermon. Women in this church serve in roles of primary leadership. Relatedly, during prayer, the language of "mother" is utilized to address God. A member of our research team noted that during one prayer of confession, the minister began, "I confess to you, Dear God, Father and Mother." In addition, sermons did not avoid potentially divisive issues: One Sunday the minister directly addressed domestic abuse throughout his discourse. On another Sunday, the minister delivered a message that contrasted strikingly with what would be heard at the Word of Faith church in Texas: "If anyone told you that when you became a Christian, all of your problems would be solved, well, run away from them! Get your money back!" He went on to insist that having the peace of Christ did not necessarily mean that life would be absent of conflict.

In northern Indiana, a Latino Pentecostal (Church of God) congregation finds strong identity in being "*not* Roman Catholic." The congregation of about one hundred seventy attenders finds strong identity in maintaining a symbolic boundary that delineates distinctiveness over and against Catholicism. For this church, a perceived rivalry with Catholicism allows it to thrive. Leaders of the church equate Catholicism with a lack of knowledge, while they link conversion to Protestantism with a migration experience as a powerful metaphor.

In direct contrast, our research team has been in multiple Latino Protestant mainline congregations where the template for worship embraces some Catholic practices in an effort to make converts as comfortable as possible. These congregations include rituals such as crossing one's self, use of holy water, *las Posadas*, and the Stations of the Cross—one sanctuary even includes a statue of the Virgin of Guadalupe. One interviewee told a researcher that these Catholic-like practices give her comfort as she navigates her conversion to Protestantism while battling the "feeling of being a traitor" to her former Catholic faith. In short, Latino Protestants clearly have variegated relationships with and attitudes toward Catholicism.

As is clear in these case studies, the worship, liturgy, theology, identities, resources, and expectations of Latino Protestant congregational life vary widely. Congregational life occurs in both small, intimate store-fronts and in expansive arenas with state of the art technology—and in all sorts of venues in between. Worship ranges from rigidly formal to exuberantly informal. Theology includes the social gospel, the Prosper-ity Gospel, Calvinism, Methodism, and sometimes even pseudo-Cathol-icism (to name but a few). In short, Latino Protestant congregational life remains so varied that succinct descriptions fail to account for the diverse manifestations of worship, theology, and identity that occur within these churches. Moreover, these discrete versions of worship also lead to and foster variegated understandings of a congregation's proper role in broader public life. These modes of community and civic engagement will be the subject of our next chapter.

6

LATINO PROTESTANTS AND THEIR POLITICAL AND SOCIAL ENGAGEMENT

HOW ARE LATINO PROTESTANTS ENGAGED IN LOCAL COMMUNITIES AND THE BROADER SOCIETY?

On a rainy early spring morning in a modest brick Presbyterian church just outside the Fruitvale neighborhood of Oakland, California, sixty-four worshippers gather. The entire worship is in Spanish. During the sermon, the pastor makes a passing reference to how few of the attenders now live in Oakland proper, that many have to drive farther than ever for church services. The implicit message: the leadership of the church realizes that gentrification of San Francisco has spilled over the Bay Bridge and now threatens the availability of affordable housing throughout Oakland. In response, the congregation has started programs that offer legal advice for responding to rent-hiking landlords and identifying housing options around the city. Though resources and attenders tend to be somewhat scarce, the leadership has creatively organized in an effort to address the structural and policy concerns of housing. Beyond that, the pastor proudly notes that this church readily offers immigration status services, computer classes, and English classes.

Later that day, down the road forty-five miles in San Jose (still in the rain), over five hundred people gather in line outside the local Victory Outreach church for the second night of the theatrical production "Duke of Earl: Legacy." When the doors finally open, over one thousand attenders will overflow the sanctuary to the point that the foyer will be filled with folding chairs for viewing the drama on two flat-screen closed-circuit televisions. After warm-up acts that include a praise team, two separate Christian rap performances, and a free "Duke of Earl: Legacy" T-shirt being thrown to the loudest section of the audience by the head pastor, the drama begins. Impressive production values include fog, intricate lighting, stage prop cigarettes, a full band for musical performances, and copious gun battles with blanks that leave eardrums ringing. The entire event is in English. The plot of the play earnestly encourages the audience to leave behind drugs, gangs, and violence and to commit their lives to Christ and join a church. The evening ends with a well-received altar call that overwhelms the stage.

Both of the aforementioned churches reside in the San Francisco Bay Area. However, due to a host of reasons (including denominational background, neighborhood context, leadership, and resources), they engage their respective communities very differently. They have variegated blinders and telescopes—social issues on which they focus intensely, and those that they ignore or fail to notice. Moreover, while one congregation has an explicitly singular agenda, the other remains more multi-faceted. In multiple ways, then, these two congregations serve as a microcosm of the diversity with which Latino Protestants across the United States engage socially and politically.

POPULATION GROWTH AND GEOGRAPHIC DISPERSAL

Increasing Presence of Latinos

Latino Protestants continue to be a religious minority within an ethnic/racial minority[1] in the United States. However, both of these groups demonstrate robust growth in terms of percentage and raw population numbers. Moreover, as Latinos continue to expand in terms of numbers, they have also dispersed throughout the United States—arriving in rural, suburban, and urban places that heretofore had little to no Latino population. With that in mind, we know that Latino Protestants will likely have a bourgeoning influence on public life in new ways and new places in the United States. In this chapter we consider Latino Protestant attitudes and behaviors related to social and political issues. Consistent with the diversity seen in previous chapters, we see heterogeneity in how Latino Protestants and their churches approach social and political engagement. Moreover, any monolithic arguments about Latino religiosity and public policy preferences will be found wanting by the preponderance of social science evidence.

It remains difficult to overstate the critical role that Latinos have played in the shifting sands of the U.S. ethnic and geographic landscape in the last forty years. Owing to immigration and high fertility rates, the Latino population has surged to the point that they have surpassed African Americans as the largest minority in the nation. This population growth has been described as a "demographic revolution."[2] Studies indicate that nearly one million U.S.-born Latinos reach voting age every year.[3] Beyond that political power, they also have economic clout: U.S. Latinos have a purchasing power equivalent to the world's sixteenth-largest country.[4] The 2010 U.S. Census reported that 50.5 million people (16 percent of a total of 308.7 million) claimed Latino or Hispanic ancestry. Moreover, Latino population increases accounted for more than half of the overall growth in the total population in the United States from 2000 to 2010.[5]

In addition to population growth among Latinos, we have also seen population *dispersal*. These demographic shifts translate into new contexts for Latinos that likely demand adaptation of some sort—both on the part of the receiving communities and the freshly arriving Latinos themselves. The Census Bureau reports that the South and the Midwest experienced the most significant growth in Latino population between 2000 and 2010. Scholars have described these demographic movements as "unprecedented geographic scattering . . . where [Latinos] often revived dwindling nonmetropolitan communities" and "transformed" U.S. urban landscapes.[6] In short, while Latinos continue to cluster in traditional nodes in the Southwest and Northeast, they are also dispersing to unprecedented locales like the rural South and Midwest.[7]

With shifting demographics, we see that Latino residential patterns and geographic diffusion has not followed the pattern of African Americans. That is, the story of Latinos in the United States in no way serves as a replication of the African American narrative. In the early years of the twenty-first century, "Latino's geographic scattering is national in scope and involves a broad range of places, from global cities to rural boomtowns. Furthermore, it simultaneously involves concentration and re-segregation as well as dispersal and, presumably, social integration."[8] In contrast, the Latino population in the United States remains fluid and in flux. Part of the shift has included the Latinization of the U.S. South. Some have argued that Latinos settling in the South frequently receive the label of "undeserving outsiders" because of skin color and perceptions about citizenship.[9] Of course, the cold shoulder of the South has not been the uniform welcome for all Latinos in all corners of the country—as some communities recognize newly arriving Latinos as social and economic stimulators. These varying attitudes and contexts also play a role in how Latino Protestants position themselves within their local neighborhoods and the wider community.

Latinos and Residential Segregation

Even outside the South, Idelissa Malavé and Esti Giordani claim that the average Latino in the United States still "lives in a segregated, lower income neighborhood."[10] Moreover, while there has been a shift to more rural regions, 91 percent of Latinos continue to live in metropolitan areas.[11] That is, they tend to be in urban or suburban locales. However, they also note, "On average, between 1990 and 2009, affluent Latinos were more likely to live in neighborhoods with fewer resources than poor whites."[12] That dissonance between relative wealth and a lack of neighborhood resources festers because, similar to African Americans, Latinos in the United States have suffered from residential segregation: "The average or 'typical' Latino lives in a neighborhood that is 45 percent Latino, even though Latinos represent just 17 percent of the total population."[13] Of course, these patterns do not occur by chance: Latinos have experienced residential restrictions from real estate practices that include redlining, steering, and predatory lending. Beyond residential segregation, Latinos in the United States also suffer from lower earnings (even when held constant for similar types of work): "With a median annual household income at $39,000, Latinos earn $11,000 less than the median for the total U.S. population and have the lowest weekly earnings out of any other group."[14] The discrepancies grow starker when considering wealth: the median wealth of whites in the United States soars to almost twelve times the median wealth of Latinos.[15]

Marta Tienda and Norma Fuentes acknowledge that the diffusion of Latino populations has not always translated into socioeconomic mobility, saying, "Latinos residential dispersion evolved against a background of rising income inequality, industrial restructuring, population aging, increasing unauthorized immigration, and political polarization also has implications for their integration prospects" in the United States.[16] Beyond just exclusion, we would also note that Latino Protestants have been subject to what scholars have labeled a "double marginalization" that has consequences for their social and political beliefs and behaviors. In other words, Latino Protestants' racial minority status within a majority Anglo nation combines with a religious minority status as Protestants among a majority Catholic religious affiliation among their co-ethnics to situate them outside of the mainstream in two areas. As they wrestle with a doubly marginalized identity, Latino Protestants, in particular, demonstrate a fluidity in how they engage with larger communities both socially and politically.[17]

In the end, Latino populations in the United States are both growing and dispersing. Moreover, we see that in some instances Latinos have also been marginalized in major U.S. cities, including Los Angeles and New York, to the point that some scholars have described their residential situation as one of "hypersegregation."[18] Within this context, Latino Protestants must consider how they will engage their neighborhoods, communities, cities, and broader society.

CHURCHES BUILDING SKILLS AND PROVIDING SUPPORT

In the face of exclusion and discrimination, Latino Protestant congregations necessarily become both refuges and sites of public action and advocacy. That is, because religion remains so uniquely salient for Latino Protestants, it follows that their social and political engagement will, in most cases, bear residue and evidence of their faith. Moreover, those commitments will likely occur within the context of congregational life. With that in mind, it only follows that Latino Protestant churches serve as pivotal sites for social engagement.

Perhaps the most geographically focused and exhaustive study of Latino religious life occurred on the shores of Lake Michigan: The aforementioned Chicago Latino Congregations Study (CLCS). The authors describe CLCS as "a multi-level, comprehensive study of Latino churches in the Chicago area."[19] Though they suffer from double marginality (or possibly because of it), Latino Protestants, according to the authors of the CLCS, tend to be more politically active than their Catholic counterparts. The authors argue that, because of a more hierarchical church polity, Catholics learn comparatively fewer civic skills in their parishes.

A number of other scholars have also argued that Latino Protestants have more opportunities than their Catholic counterparts to enhance civic skills that translate into a form of social capital.[20] Proponents of this argument claim, again, that the hierarchical nature of Catholicism limits the ability of attenders to organize and practice relevant political tactics. Paul Djupe and Jacob Neiheisel find, indeed, that Latino Protestants receive more opportunities than Latino Catholics to "develop leadership skills and be recruited into politics through the church."[21] They argue that there exists more synthesis between congregation and community in Latino Protestant contexts: "In the broader, more Protestant society, the congregation is an independent community through which members make ties and acquire skills. In Latino communities, on the other hand, the congregation is better integrated into the community. Hence, attachment to a church in a Latino community helps the member to tap into community networks."[22] Thus, the synergy of church and community leads to a localized form of social capital.

Building on that notion of social capital, sociologist Norman Ruano finds that because of a lack of financial resources and histories of voluntarism, Latino Protestant congregations function as sites of civic and administrative skill development. The CLCS reported that well over half of all Latino Protestants indicated that they serve in some type of leadership role within their congregation. Latino Pentecostals led the way at 63 percent, followed closely, though, by Latino evangelicals and mainline at 59 and 58 percent, respectively.[23] Beyond that, it should also be noted that these Latino churches offer a locus for women to exercise leadership. In all of the Latino Protestant faith traditions a higher percentage of women than men reported holding positions of leadership. Of course, some of the gender-related leadership discrepancy relates to the fact that more women than men fill the pews of these congregations. Still, it seems quite clear that "Latino women . . . have power and influence at the church."[24]

In the end, Latino Protestant congregations, to varying degrees, have a tendency to nurture social capital for groups that have been historically marginalized. Beyond that, they provide both material and social services. As Elizabeth Dias (*Time* magazine journalist) notes, many Latino Protestant churches become "*de facto* healing centers for a population with limited health care benefits. They act as food banks for people with empty refrigerators. They house people avoiding street violence. There's a lot more going on there than just saving souls."[25] Latino Protestant churches, then, frequently serve as focal points of community engagement and social service delivery.

LATINO PROTESTANTS AND THEIR POLITICS

Political Party Affiliation

Overall, Latinos in the United States have shaded toward support of Democratic candidates.[26] The 2016 U.S. presidential election demonstrated that tendency in stark relief. In the months leading up to the election, 54 percent of registered Latino voters indicated that the Democratic Party demonstrated more concern than the Republican Party while only 11 percent said that the Republicans exhibited more—a 43 percent gap.[27] In the aftermath of the election, exit polls revealed that 66 percent of Latinos voted for Hillary Clinton—an overwhelming majority but a slip from the 71 percent received by Barack Obama in 2012. Moreover, despite his provocative comments regarding immigration and Mexicans, Donald Trump managed to garner 28 percent of the Latino vote—a decided minority, but one percentage point higher than Republican candidate Mitt Romney's 27 percent from 2012.[28] Latinos supported Trump in greater numbers than expected despite his strong anti-immigration news and comments about Mexicans as dangerous and undesirable. Also, although some pundits had described the Latino vote as the "sleeping giant" that could sway the election, Latinos failed to surge to the polls—even with the threat of mass deportation of undocumented Latinos and the stakes for the negative perception of legal residents where high.

Even the 2016 presidential primary elections revealed the complexities of Latino voting patterns. Two of the Republican candidates (Senator Ted Cruz of Texas and Senator Marco Rubio of Florida) highlighted their Latino roots and pollsters watched to see if either could rally a critical mass of Latino support. However, both senators' stances on policy issues like immigration caused many Latinos to withhold their backing. More than that, interviews with Mexican Americans who found little solidarity with Cruz and Rubio's Cuban background undermined any notion of a Latino voting bloc for a Latino candidate.[29]

Some scholars have noted, though, that Republican politicians in the United States have made particular efforts to embrace *evangelical* Latinos on the basis of shared conservative social values related to issues like abortion.[30] However, these invitations for alliance have found limited acceptance. In fact, in a May 2015 editorial in the *Wall Street Journal*, Russell Moore, president of the Ethics and Religious Liberty Commission of the Southern Baptist Convention (the largest Protestant denomination in the United States), warned Republican presidential candidates to be wary of offending both white and Latino evangelicals. He noted the growing political clout of evangelical Latinos and that all candidates would do well to respect them: "The most evangelistic, growing congregations in this country are filled with first- and second-generation immigrants. There is more salsa at our church potlucks lately, and we like it. . . . An immigrant brother in the next pew is a person, a creation of God, not a piñata for politicians. 'Born again' comes in Spanish as well as English versions—and so do voters." Moore noted that in the weeks before he wrote, Latino evangelicals by the thousands had gathered in Houston to discuss issues that included abortion, racial justice, and economic opportunity. His message was clear: Politicians who ignored evangelical Latinos did so at their own peril.[31]

Other studies have also confirmed the tendency of non-Catholic Latinos to be more likely to support Republican Party candidates than Catholic Latinos.[32] For Latino Protestants, frequent church attendance seems to have a relationship with social conservatism on some—but not all—issues. For instance, political scientist Ali Adam Valenzuela found that regular churchgoers were "significantly and substantively more likely than infrequent attenders to identify as Republican" and to oppose gay marriage and abortion.[33] However, when considering views regarding immigrant amnesty and economic welfare, Valenzuela found no differences between regular and infrequent churchgoers among Latino Protestants.

Committed, churchgoing Latino Protestants remain a tantalizing demographic for Republicans in the United States because when compared to Latino Catholics and the nonaffiliated they consistently report more conservative political preferences. Moreover, Valenzuela finds that Latino Protestants who consistently attend church demonstrate substantially more conservative philosophies than their less-committed fellow parishioners. [34] In fact, researchers at the Pew Research Center noted that in the 2012 U.S. presidential election, among the Latino electorate, religious identities played a crucial role in how individuals voted. While 80 percent of religiously unaffiliated Latinos and 75 percent of Latino Catholics claimed support for Barack Obama, only 50 percent of evangelical Latinos said the same. Similarly, on the eve of the 2016 election, the Pew Research Center reported a wide discrepancy in how Latinos planned to vote: While 59 percent of Latino Catholics indicated their support for Clinton, only 12 percent of Latino evangelicals said the same. [35] Perhaps not surprisingly, among Latinos in the United States, religious affiliation seems to have a degree of influence on voting patterns. [36]

Political Attitudes and Stances

More recently, in 2014, Pew found that, in general, Latinos in the United States tend to lean toward Democratic Party affiliations. Over half (56 percent) of Latinos indicated that they identified as Democrats while only one in five (21 percent) leaned toward the Republican Party. [37] Even when examining through the prism of religion, the Democratic tendencies remain: Latino evangelicals (48 percent), mainline Protestants (54 percent), and Catholics (58 percent) all lean more Democrat than Republican (evangelicals: 30 percent, mainline Protestants: 23 percent, and Catholics: 21 percent). [38] U.S. Latinos demonstrate a sharp break with their co-religionists on political party affiliation. A 2012 Pew study reported that 70 percent of white evangelicals leaned Republican—more than twice the percentage of Latino evangelicals. In a similar fashion, white mainline Protestants also leaned more Republican at a percentage (51 percent) more than twice that of mainline Protestant Latinos. [39]

From their exhaustive report related to Latino demographics, Idelisse Malavé and Esti Giordani also note that "Overall, religious affiliation does not have the same impact on party affiliation among Latinos as it does among white voters."[40] By way of example, they point to the stark contrast in preference for the Democratic Party between white and Latino evangelicals: while roughly half of Latino evangelicals affiliate with the Democratic Party, a scant 23 percent of white evangelicals do the same. Correspondingly, "almost three-quarters of white evangelicals (72 percent) identify or lean toward the Republican Party, while only 36 percent of Latino evangelicals do."[41]

Similar to African Americans, Latino Protestants with strong religious commitment appear to be "less motivated by the faith-based political conservatism observed in white Christian circles."[42] There also seems to be a common tendency for African American and Latino ministers to similarly focus more heavily on social justice issues than white religious assemblies. White congregations, as members of the dominant racial demographic in the United States, likely have less appetite for issues related to marginalized minority groups.[43]

The CLCS found that when examining contemporary issues that ranged from U.S. intervention in Iraq to the U.S. embargo against Cuba, mainline Protestant Latinos tended to express opposition to U.S. foreign policy almost as much as Latino Catholics, while a distinct minority of both Pentecostals and evangelicals expressed negative views regarding such foreign policy issues. It follows, then, that the same study revealed that more evangelical (53 percent) and Pentecostal (53 percent) leaders viewed themselves as politically conservative, while very few mainline (18 percent) labeled themselves the same way. Beyond political viewpoints, we also find differences among Latino Protestants in terms of political activities and engagement in Chicago. Interestingly, a full 93 percent of evangelicals claimed to never participate in political activities. Roughly 83 percent of mainline Latinos made the same claim. It should also be noted that the lack of citizenship status should be remembered as a variable that might inhibit some from participating in overt political action.[44]

While mainline Protestant Latinos show a slightly higher preference than their evangelical counterparts for the Democratic Party, no such discrepancy appears when considering the role and size of government. When queried about whether they would prefer a smaller government with fewer services or a larger government with more services, 62 percent of *both* evangelical and mainline Protestant Latinos indicated a preference for the latter. In short, both groups favor more government services. However, neither Protestant group favored larger government as much as Latino Catholics (72 percent). In addition, it should be noted that a similar percentage of the minority among Latino evangelicals and mainline Protestants indicated preference for smaller government (25 percent of evangelicals and 29 percent of mainline Protestants). In this regard, Latino Protestants are markedly divergent from the general public of the United States, where the majority (51 percent) prefers a smaller government and the minority (40 percent) prefers a larger government.[45]

In terms of attitudes toward international intervention by the United States, political scientist James L. Guth divides Latino Protestants into two categories: Traditionalists and Modernists.[46] He describes Traditionalists as those who would be included in fundamentalist, evangelical, charismatic, or Pentecostal camps. Modernists, then, include most of the mainline and any who identify themselves as liberal. Guth reports that more than six in ten (62.1 percent) Traditionalist Latino Protestants qualify as "Hardliners" (strong supporters of preemptive U.S. military intervention and "hawkish" foreign policy[47]) compared to less than three in ten (28.9 percent) Modernist Latino Protestants and about one in ten (10.4 percent) Latino Catholics.[48] Thus we also see that religious tradition predisposes Latino Protestant attitudes regarding international affairs.

Similarly, in their case study of Chicago, the CLCS noted that when examining political attitudes and behavior through the filter of religious tradition, a pattern emerges where Latino Catholics and mainline Protestants have more liberal inclinations than Latino evangelicals and Pentecostals. For instance, respondents within their study from "Catholic and mainline churches were more likely to vote for Democratic presidential candidates than respondents in evangelical and Pentecostal churches, and were more likely to disagree with the U.S. intervention in Iraq." The study's authors went on to "note that the divide is not between Catholics and Protestants more broadly, highlighting the importance of distinguishing between mainline Protestant and conservative Protestant groups."[49] Indeed, the heterogeneity of Latino Protestant sociopolitical beliefs manifest in myriad attitudes and behaviors.

Even in an issue like immigration, where uniformity of Latino opinions might be assumed, we see complexity. Not surprisingly, the majority of overall Latinos (53 percent) tend to identify immigration as a pressing issue for the United States. Somewhat counterintuitively, though, a comparable percentage of Latinos rank quality of public schools (55 percent), the federal deficit (54 percent), and the cost of college (53 percent) as critical issues for the country as well.[50] Corroborating these findings, the Pew Research Center also reports that while 73 percent of Latinos indicate that immigration reform is extremely important or very important to them, *more* say that issues of education (92 percent), jobs and the economy (91 percent), and health care (86 percent) are extremely or very important to them.[51] In short, Latinos in the United States do not monolithically focus on immigration as *the* political issue of significance. Moreover, Latino attitudes regarding the importance of immigration also diverge by religious tradition. The majority of both Catholic (59 percent) and mainline Protestant (57 percent) Latinos express the opinion that they understood immigration as a "critical" issue. Fewer evangelical (48 percent) Latinos see immigration as important.[52]

On the related issue of "path to citizenship," again, the majority (67 percent) of Latinos support the U.S. government "[allowing immigrants] a way to become citizens provided they meet certain requirements." Filtering by religious tradition, though, again also reveals a slight heterogeneity of opinions. While strong majorities of every Latino religious group support a path to citizenship for immigrants currently living in the country without documentation, Catholics (72 percent) and evangelicals (75 percent) report nearly identical rates and mainline Protestant Latinos dip to nearly two-thirds (67 percent). Interestingly enough, the religiously unaffiliated report the least amount of support (59 percent).[53] While half of Latino Catholics (49 percent) report hearing clergy speak about immigration, only about a third of Latino Protestants indicate the same (35 percent evangelicals and 37 percent of mainline Protestants). Moreover, when compared to Latino Catholics (26 percent), a very small percentage of Latino mainline Protestants (16 percent) and Latino evangelicals (12 percent) report their churches participating in immigration rights protests or boycotts.[54] Thus we continue to see that the contours of religion affect even issues that might be assumed to have consensus among Latinos.

PUBLIC ROLES OF LATINO PROTESTANT RELIGIOUS LEADERS

On an issue-by-issue basis, we see a complex picture of Latino religious leaders' political leanings. When asked directly about how they described themselves, about half of both evangelical (53 percent) and Pentecostal (also 53 percent) Latino leaders described themselves as conservative. In comparison, both mainline (18 percent) and Catholic (20 percent) leaders indicated significantly less inclination to do the same. However, these percentages should not be misinterpreted as meaning that substantial swaths of Latino Catholic and mainline Protestant leaders understood their political identity as liberal. Most, in fact, saw themselves as moderate (70 percent of Catholics and 64 percent of mainline). Among Chicago Latino religious leaders, very few defined their political leaning as liberal. Mainline and Catholics leaders had the highest percentages (19 percent and 10 percent, respectively). Interestingly, while 7 percent of Pentecostal leaders identified as liberal, *no* Latino evangelical leaders in Chicago indicated such a political identity. Thus, we see an admittedly narrow band of liberal political leanings within Latino Pentecostalism that does not manifest in that way within Latino evangelicalism. This unique conservatism among Latino evangelical leaders also bore itself out when the prompt asked about political party affiliation. Among all Chicago-area Latino religious leaders, only evangelicals identified with the Republican Party (33 percent) more than Democratic Party (24 percent). For Pentecostal leaders, the numbers were almost inverted: 32 percent Democrat and 22 percent Republican. Democrats saw even more support among Catholics and mainline Protestants. About half of both groups of Latino religious leaders identified as Democrats, and a very scant minority (2 percent of Catholics and 5 percent of mainline) labeled themselves as Republicans.[55]

Regardless of their religious leaders' political affiliations, the majority Latino Protestants want to hear political views from the pulpit. Latino evangelicals (65 percent), especially indicated appreciation for hearing clergy discuss political and social issues. Demonstrating the range of opinions within Latino Protestantism, a significantly lower percentage of Latino mainline Protestants (52 percent) agreed with that sentiment.[56]

Political Activities of Latino Protestant Attenders

Compared to Latino Catholics, Latino Protestants demonstrate as high (or higher) levels of political action.[57] However, a close look at the Latino churches within the Chicago study still reveals fairly low levels of political engagement. For instance, the CLCS also found that evangelical Latino attenders claimed very little political activity. When queried with whether they participated in a voter registration drive, volunteered for a political campaign, or donated money to a party, over nine in ten (93 percent) evangelical Latinos reported that they *never* participated in any of the mentioned activities—the highest of any of the religious traditions. Some of that seeming political apathy likely found resonance with issues of citizenship status among these evangelicals: U.S. citizens tended (16 percent) to be more likely to say that they had been involved in political action than noncitizens (9 percent). Overall, the vast majority of Latinos in the study, regardless of religious tradition, indicated high levels of political *inactivity*. Beyond evangelicals, the other three religious traditions all had rates of at least eight in ten congregants reporting having never participated in political activities.[58] Of course, it should be noted that the apparent lack of political activity might simply be a function of the survey question. When the same respondents reported whether they had contacted a religious official within the last year, the percentages of those reporting "never" dropped. Latino evangelicals still emerged as the most reticent with more than eight in ten (82 percent) indicating that they had never spoken with or contacted a public official within the last twelve months. Latino Pentecostals, mainline Protestants, and Catholics, though, should not be classified as activists: a high percentage of attenders from three religious traditions reported never contacting or speaking with a public official in the last year (Pentecostal: 76 percent, mainline: 70 percent, and Catholic: 67 percent).[59]

Limited congregational engagement, though, should not be interpreted as evidence of political withdrawal being preached from Latino pulpits. Instead, we see that almost half of the Latino religious leaders from Chicago had requested their members to call or write a public official. Beyond that, half of the religious leaders reported asking that their congregation sign a petition. Catholic (60 percent) and mainline (58 percent) leaders had a more pronounced tendency to ask that their congregants sign petitions than their counterparts in Pentecostal (40 percent) and evangelical (42 percent) traditions.[60]

Overall, we also see that Latino mainline Protestants and Latino Catholics tend to have similar views regarding the intersection of religious beliefs and politics. A little over one-third of each (38 percent of mainline Protestants and 36 percent of Catholics) agreed that religious beliefs played a "very important" role influencing their political thinking. In marked contrast, 62 percent of Latino evangelicals offered the same assessment of religion and politics.[61] Thus we see within Latino Protestantism a wide discrepancy in understanding how religion should interact with political issues.

LATINO PROTESTANTS AND SEXUAL AND FAMILY ISSUES

Attitudes Regarding Same Sex Marriage

Moving from politics to social issues, we also find multiple viewpoints among Latino Protestants. Overall, in terms of same-sex marriage attitudes, studies find that Latinos who have at least some ties to faith communities have demonstrated a resistance to progressive policies that allow for the establishment of same-sex marriage.[62] That is, Latinos of any religious background tend to articulate resistance to same-sex marriage. The assumption, though, that the cultural conservatism that exists among Latinos in the United States serves as evidence of cultural Roman Catholic residue has been proven erroneous. Instead, we see— similar to the general population—conservative *Protestant* Latino leaders and denominations have been at the forefront of those promoting traditional marriage while opposing any movement toward the legalization of same-sex marriage.

A 2012 study by Pew found that 66 percent of Latino evangelicals described themselves as strongly opposed to same-sex marriage. Similarly, a 2013 study by the Public Religion Research Institute reported that 8 in 10 (79 percent) Latino evangelicals opposed same-sex marriage. In short, Latino evangelicals, in particular, tend to be fairly uniform on the issue of same-sex marriage.[63] In the mid-2000s, for instance, the National Hispanic Christian Leadership Conference

(NHCLC), a consortium of Latino evangelical leaders, led an effort to mobilize against same-sex marriage. NHCLC materials couched their argument in a way that framed opposition as motivated by desire for the flourishing of the broader evangelical community. Their resistance, they claimed, was not about being "anti-gay or discriminating against anyone."[64] Rather, they argued that, along with faith in God, they simply saw families with both "a mother and a father" as "the primary deterrent in the Latino community to drug abuse, gang violence, teenage pregnancy, and other social ills." With that sentiment in mind, it should be noted that the NHCLC has sought to distance itself from "the media-exacerbated image of angry white evangelicals who oppose everything."[65] Thus in this narrative offered by the NHCLC, resistance to same-sex marriage should be understood as for the benefit of Latino communities, not as intolerance. Though the NHCLC lays claim to being largest Latino evangelical organization in the United States, they clearly do not represent all Latino Protestants. In fact, Christopher Ellison and colleagues noted that in 2008 Reverend Ignacio Castuera, a Methodist, argued in a televised debate that LGBT persons should have the right to marry: "The Bible has many different models of sexuality and many different models of family. . . . We cannot impose the Bible as the right belief onto a population with people who are multicultural and religiously diverse."[66]

Regina Branton and her colleagues found that Latino Catholics have a significantly higher probability of supporting civil unions for same-sex couples, when compared to Latino Protestants.[67] Christopher Ellison and his colleagues, though, note that evangelical Latinos, in particular, tend to be much more resistant to same-sex marriage than Latino Catholics. In fact, evangelical Latinos who attended church regularly had an 84 percent chance of being less likely to approve same-sex marriage than their Catholic counterparts. However, we begin to see disparity among Latino Protestants and their views regarding same-sex marriage when we widen the scope and consider mainline Protestant Latinos. It seems that within that subset, church attendance has salience: Ellison and his colleagues find that among mainline Latinos, regular attenders disapprove of same-sex marriage more than Catholics, while non-weekly attenders from the same religious tradition tend to be more supportive of same-sex marriage.[68] In sum, then, Latino Protestants have representatives on both poles of the same-sex marriage spectrum, while

Latino Catholics seem to embrace more relatively moderate views. Evangelicals and regular attenders among mainline Protestants tend to oppose same-sex marriage, while sporadic attenders among mainline Latinos tend to support same-sex marriage.[69]

In Chicago, when asked about same-sex marriage, Latino evangelicals and Pentecostals modify to the more traditional positions: nine in ten (92 percent) evangelicals and almost all (99 percent) of Pentecostals either "disagreed" or "strongly disagreed" with same-sex marriage. In contrast, only about half of mainline (45 percent) and Catholic (62 percent) leaders expressed the same reservations regarding same-sex marriage.[70]

Indeed, a 2012 Pew study found that among Latino Protestants while 46 percent of those who attended mainline churches favored same-sex marriage, only 25 percent of evangelicals felt the same way. Moreover, neither group of Latino Protestants registered as much support for same-sex marriage as Catholics (54 percent).[71] Beyond that, even among evangelical Latinos, views regarding same-sex marriage remain diverse: 71 percent of those who attend church at least weekly oppose same-sex marriage, while those who attend less often expressed less resistance (58 percent).[72]

Attitudes Regarding Divorce, Cohabitation, and Casual Sex

As already noted, for Latino Protestants, church attendance has salience for other social issues as well. In assessing Latino Protestant views regarding marriage, divorce, cohabitation, and casual sex, Ellison, Wolfinger, and Ramos-Wada found that those who attended church more regularly also tended to report more traditional views. Beyond that, evangelical Latinos also reported more traditional views than their Catholic counterparts. Again, Ellison and his colleagues note that such a finding undermines the long-held assumption that Latino cultural conservatism results as a simple by-product of Catholicism. In fact, in only one of the four issues under discussion, sanctity of marriage, do Latino Catholics and evangelicals maintain the same level of conservatism. In terms of opposition to divorce, cohabitation, and casual sex, evangelical Latinos "are substantially more conservative than Catholics."[73] Ellison and his colleagues claim that these views can be directly traced to the evangelical tendency to believe "that the Bible is the Word of God and that it is without error and contains necessary and sufficient information to guide most human affairs, especially those involving faith and family."[74] That is, a strict interpretation of biblical injunctions leads to social traditionalism among Latino evangelicals.

Attitudes Regarding Abortion

Religious tradition matters significantly when exploring how Latinos in the United States feel about the issue of abortion. Likely due to their overall higher levels of religiosity, Latinos generally express more opposition to abortion than Anglos. However, when we analyze differences among religious traditions, we see that evangelical Latinos are especially hostile to abortion—more so than their Catholic counterparts. Regina Branton and her colleagues report that Latino Catholics have a higher probability of also supporting legal abortion in all circumstances than Latino Protestants.[75] On this score, Latino Catholics represent the middle ground: About half indicate that abortion should be illegal in all or most circumstances. Among Latino Protestants, though, there exists a wide range of opinion. While seven in ten (70 percent) evangelical Latinos say abortion should be mostly or entirely illegal, only 46 percent of mainline Protestants agree with that sentiment.[76]

In interpreting their opposition to abortion, John Bartkowski and his colleagues argue that these conservative Protestant Latinos have transposed religious schemas from broader evangelicalism in the United States.[77] That is, while both white and Latino Catholics seem more prone to selectively embracing Vatican judgments regarding social issues like abortion, both white and Latino evangelicals demonstrate strong opposition to abortion. Beyond that, it may be the case that Latino evangelicals embrace the antiabortion positioning of white evangelicals in order to negotiate their double marginality: "Strong opposition to abortion situates evangelical Latinos squarely within the broader universe of conservative Protestantism. At the same time, these convictions distinguish them from the 'lukewarm' commitment to Christian principles exhibited by their Catholic peers."[78] Of course, such a stance by Latino evangelicals should not simply be interpreted as cynical political maneuvering. However, it should be noted that such attitudes regarding abortion might have the latent function of creating alliances with white evangelicals.

Attitudes Regarding Gender Roles

Compared to the overall U.S. population, Latinos in the United States resist embracing traditional gender roles related to marriage and the family. In fact, the vast majority (79 percent) express a preference for having both wife and husband working and sharing child care and house management as opposed to a more traditional arrangement where the husband functions as sole provider (supported by only 18 percent). In that way, Latinos articulate a predilection for traditional gender and family life at a rate less than the general population of the United States (given that 62 percent indicated support for traditional family structures).[79]

Among Latinos, though, a discrepancy in attitudes regarding family and marriage patterns emerges when examined through the filter of religion. Whereas 26 percent of Latino Protestants expressed support for more traditional roles, only 15 percent of Latino Catholics agreed. Among Latino Protestants, evangelicals emerged as more traditional in this regard than mainline Protestants (29 percent versus 19 percent). In teasing out this idea further, Pew asked "whether a husband should have the final say in family matters."[80] Overall, about six in ten (63 percent) of Latinos rejected the statement. A religious breakdown, however, proved insightful. Unaffiliated Latinos led the way in disagreeing with the statement at a rate of 74 percent, followed by Catholics at 67 percent. Among Protestant Latinos, 55 percent of those in the mainline rejected while only 43 percent of evangelicals did the same. In other words, evangelicals were the only religious tradition among Latinos in the United States to have a majority (53 percent) completely or mostly agree with the statement, "a husband should have the final say in family matters."[81] The theme of gender dynamics within Latino communities also emerged in other studies. Instead of examining gender roles in marriage, a 2009 Pew study queried about gender based *religious* roles within families. When asked whether "men have a duty to serve as religious leaders in the marriage and family," the majority of Protestant Latinos (70 percent) agreed with that sentiment while Catholic Latinos remained split (50 percent). However, evangelical Latinos expressed a higher level of enthusiasm (75 percent supported) than did mainline Latinos (55 percent).[82]

VIEWS ON ECONOMICS AND POVERTY

Beyond family and gender issues, studies on Latino Protestants yield interesting insights on their views regarding economic issues. Based on their more conservative leanings demonstrated thus far, perhaps it should not be surprising to learn that Latino Protestants, when compared to their Catholic counterparts, are less likely to indicate that the poor face hardship because of a dearth of government interventions. Although there is danger in oversimplifying the nuances of how individuals think about the sources of poverty, it remains instructive to note that the dialogue traditionally has two dominant camps: (1) those who argue that poverty results largely from structural causes and (2) those who claim that the attitudes, behaviors, skills, and talents of individuals delineate who will be poor in the opportunity-filled United States.[83] With that dichotomy in mind, studies indicate that devout (frequent attenders of worship services) evangelical Latinos are 55 percent less likely than devout Latino Catholics to articulate a sense that the poor face difficulty because of a lack of government recourses. In other words, evangelical Latinos express less sympathy toward the poor than Catholic Latinos.

These divergent attitudes toward the poor are consistent with trends seen among other racial demographics in the United States and the manner in which religious identity influences attitudes toward the poor. It seems that the idiosyncratic nature of Catholic and Protestant ethics remain robust in spite of a racial or ethnic distinction: the "Catholic ethic emphasizing sharing and material generosity" and the "conservative Protestant ethic being much more individualistic and moralistic with regard to material wealth."[84]

The fact that evangelical Latinos look similar to white evangelicals when explaining the sources of poverty, though, fails to translate into a wholesale endorsement of identical social and political attitudes within the religious tradition. For instance, Latino evangelicals and white evangelicals look very different when pulling the ballot box lever. The Pew Research Center found that white evangelicals supported Mitt Romney's 2012 presidential bid at a rate of almost three out of four (74 percent) while only four out of ten (39 percent) of evangelical Latinos did the same.[85]

Of course, in the United States economic issues tend to be entwined with issues of race. In their landmark tome about race and religion in the United States, *Divided by Faith: Evangelical Religion and the Problem of Race in America*, sociologists Michael Emerson and Christian Smith noted that many white evangelicals embraced a "miracle motif" regarding racial reconciliation in the United States. That is, white evangelicals tended to assume that as more and more individuals converted to the Christian faith, racial alienation would decrease. In a seeming test of the miracle motif regarding all social ills, Pew asked Latinos if they agreed with the statement, "If enough people were brought to Christ, social ills would take care of themselves."[86] Perhaps not surprisingly—since Emerson and Smith identified the miracle motif as a uniquely evangelical manifestation—we see a discrepancy in whether Protestant Latinos would endorse such a statement. While about two-thirds (65 percent) of evangelical Latinos agreed with the statement, only about half (51 percent) of mainline Protestants concurred.[87] Thus we see that the evangelical "cultural tool kit" identified by Emerson and Smith transcends some racial boundaries.

PROVISION OF SOCIAL SERVICES BY LATINO PROTESTANT CONGREGATIONS

Amount and Types of Social Service Delivery

Social engagement, of course, means more than social positions and politics. Congregations of all religious orientations and racial backgrounds have entered into social service delivery, and Latino Protestants are no different in that regard. In fact, Gastón Espinosa has argued that "Latino Protestant churches are more likely to provide social services than their Catholic counterparts" in many measures of social action.[88] Individually, about one-third (32 percent) of Latino Protestants volunteer with a neighborhood organization, a business, or a youth agency. Evangelical Latinos (34 percent) do so just slightly more than mainline Protestant Latinos (29 percent). For both sets of Protestants, though, the amount of volunteering declines when the engagement changes focus to tutoring or school programs (23 percent for evangelicals and 25 percent for mainline Protestants).[89]

Of course, churches engage in social service delivery in multiple ways. A Hudson Institute national survey of 452 Latino Protestant congregations found that 72 percent offered social service programs.[90] Beyond that, the CLCS found that *every* one of the Latino religious leaders they interviewed indicated that their congregations provided some sort of health care–related service delivery to their respective communities in Chicago. However, Latino Protestants tend to offer interventions like health services less frequently than their Catholic counterparts—an interesting phenomenon because a higher percentage of Latino Catholics (61 percent) agree that guaranteeing health care for all citizen's should be the government's responsibility compared to Latino mainline Protestants (53 percent) and evangelicals (50 percent).[91] While Catholic churches average over five different types of health service, Latino mainline Protestants (3.38), evangelicals (3.56), and Pentecostals (2.61) all offer less. The authors attribute the stark contrast between Catholics and Pentecostals especially as explained by the fact that Catholic churches tend to be much larger than their Pentecostal counterparts and, thus, have more resources and capacities for health-related services.[92]

The percentage of health services programming among Latino Protestant churches also varies among the mainline, evangelicals, and Pentecostals depending on the health service being delivered. The report considers five areas of health services: Alcoholics Anonymous, sex education, diabetes screening, nutrition information, and blood pressure screenings. Except for the area of sex education, a higher percentage of Catholic congregations offered health services when compared to the Latino Protestant congregations in the study. Beyond Catholic-Protestant distinctions, however, it should be noted that discrepancies exist among evangelical, mainline, and Pentecostal congregations as well. For instance, evangelicals (35 percent) are more likely to offer sex education than mainline (24 percent) or Pentecostal (27 percent) congregations. Evangelical congregations also lead the way (31 percent) on offering nutrition information (mainline: 19 percent and Pentecostal: 13 percent). On the other hand, mainline churches offer more (33 percent) opportunities for blood pressure screenings than those of the evangelical (31 percent) or Pentecostal (24 percent) traditions.

Of course, in all these instance of health services rendered by Latino Protestant congregations it should be noted that the vast majority of these programs are largely informal structures that lack robust organization.[93] At the same, though, it could be argued that these congregations possess invaluable knowledge of networks and neighborhoods that might allow for more incisive health care delivery that targets the needs of the population. In the end, the strand of religious tradition within Protestantism has significant influence on how these Latinos engage the larger community in terms of health services programming.

Latino Pentecostalism and Community Engagement

With all this evidence, it does seem clear that different strains of Latino Protestantism have different concerns, priorities, and behaviors when it comes to social and civic engagement. How do we account for this heterogeneity? Some have argued that Pentecostalism, especially, stands out among other faith traditions within Latino Protestantism. Gastón Espinosa, in his comprehensive tome, *Latino Pentecostals in America: Faith and Politics in Action*, claims that Latino Pentecostals, in particular, avoid the traditional evangelical and mainline tendency to decouple evangelism and social justice.[94] In other words, Latino Pentecostals meld an evangelistic social work that assumes an outreach that demonstrates "the love and saving grace of Jesus Christ to a broken and suffering world."[95] It seems that Latino Pentecostals reject notions of the Social Gospel and Liberation Theology as they see both movements as "not Christ-centered enough."[96] Indeed, among some Latino Protestant congregations there seems to be a strong sense that social engagement is not necessarily a political act. In our ethnographic research of a Latino Protestant church in the Bay Area of California, we heard attenders/leaders tell us, "Feeding the poor is not a political act." In other words, that particular congregation simply understood social engagement as the church being the church—they did not see it as a political statement.

Ruano argues that a significant number of Latino Pentecostal congregations find themselves located in neighborhoods plagued by poverty and other attendant social problems. Because of that context, it becomes "imperative to understand the types of civic skills and civic engagement opportunities afforded to the congregants and whether they translate into engagement outside of the church, and if so, under what circumstances."[97] While Pentecostalism has long been assumed to be a faith that fosters closed, inward-facing communities, congregations like Pastor Rene Molina's Restauracion Los Angeles hear messages that encourage attenders to become active in political and social issues. Molina states that anyone who has citizenship has a responsibility to vote, and if they cannot do that, they should be in marches that seek to change restrictive immigration laws. Molina does not counsel his congregation to turn inward—in fact, he actively engages the broader community of Los Angeles by organizing with local African American pastors on issues of racial reconciliation.[98]

While those congregations organize around racial reconciliation, other congregations coalesce around other issues. For example, Victory Outreach (highlighted earlier in the chapter), a coalition of six hundred churches worldwide, finds focus in building "a tightly knit community among recovering gang members."[99] Sociologist Edward Flores describes Victory Outreach as an "evangelical-Pentecostal" network that emphasizes a hard rupture with old communities and intensive involvement with the church—including evenings, weekends, and holidays—as a method of "un-becoming a homie and joining the non-gang society."[100] Other scholars have described Victory Outreach as an "emotional rescue ministry."[101] Church leaders encourage members to forgo relationships, hobbies, and jobs that might interfere with participation in congregational worship and events. Moreover, Victory Church mimics the Pentecostal church's decentralized hierarchies and rigid religious boundaries to promote what Flores describes as a "segregated redemption" for former gang members.[102] Though Victory Outreach churches might stand as an outlier with their singular and aggressive focus on gang rehabilitation, it does represent the energy that Latino Pentecostal congregations have developed for certain issues.

In the end, numerous studies have indicated that most congregations tend to provide some type of social service program—if not multiple programs. Latino Protestant churches are no different. However, it is also clear that among Latino Protestants the rationales for and modes of community engagement differ markedly based on religious tradition and context.

LATINO PROTESTANTS AND LOCAL PARACHURCH COMMUNITY ORGANIZATIONS

Of course, not all of Latino Protestant social and political life occurs under the auspices of church. Instead, we see that they have crafted other institutions and organizations "whose very purpose is to provide some type of social service for the community they serve."[103] These faith-based organizations (FBOs) maintain religious foundations, but because of Internal Revenue Service regulations, they are required to eschew proselytizing while providing a social service. Catherine Wilson closely examined two of the largest Latino Protestant FBOs. The first, the Latino Pastoral Action Center (LPAC), is located in the South Bronx in New York and is led by a Pentecostal minister, Reverend Raymond Rivera. The second, Nueva Esperanza, is located in North Philadelphia and is led by an evangelical pastor, Reverend Luis Cortés Jr. Consideration of these FBOs proves instructive because they allude to the scope and diversity of Latino Protestant social and political engagement—they help to extrapolate the values, culture, and beliefs of these faith communities. As Wilson contends, "along with congregations, FBOs help the Latino community to mediate its religious sensibilities and, in doing so, prepare this community for social and political involvement."[104] In other words, along with congregations, FBOs have become integral organizing institutions for focusing Latino Protestant social engagement in the United States.

Wilson, in her study of Latino FBOs, claims that these organizations tend to emphasize "the incarnation of Jesus Christ, the kingdom of God on earth, and personal salvation at the end of one's earthly journey."[105] Despite the doctrinal differences that have divided the Latino communities over the years, Wilson argues that especially in cities, "social, political, and economic injustices" have caused various strands of Protestants and Catholics to ally. Wilson goes on to note that Justo González, a United Methodist and prolific theological author, has argued that the best path forward for urban Latinos in the United States includes Protestants and Catholics aligning to "[walk] the same path."[106]

The aforementioned LPAC includes a local network of over three hundred clergy and a mailing list that boasts over two thousand clergy addresses. The FBO focuses on intentionally grooming indigenous leaders.Wilson claims that the theological underpinnings of LPAC can be found in "the Pentecostal worldview."[107] That is, the flexibility and spontaneity associated with Pentecostalism leads directly to the informal and adaptive responses of LPAC to the old and new social issues of the South Bronx. While Pentecostalism has often been described as "otherworldly," LPAC directly addresses current socioeconomic issues. Wilson notes that Rivera, the founder and director, has stated that his job is not confined to saving sinners but also "to do something about the problems in the neighborhood."[108] LPAC's programming includes job readiness workshops, gang prevention, English-as-a-second-language classes, alternative late-night entertainment for youth, recreational opportunities, and collaborating with local agencies on the issues of at-risk youth. LPAC's collaborators in these initiatives have ranged from the New York City Department of Probation to Quaker Friends to Buddhist temples. In other words, LPAC has demonstrated a robust emphasis on community partnership formation that undermines assumptions about a more insular Pentecostal community. These partnerships, though, all have to align with LPAC's focus on the "whole person" and to help them transform their lives. In the end, Wilson describes LPAC as a "ministry of personal outreach."[109]

In somewhat of a contrast, Wilson portrays Nueva Esperanza as a ministry of institutional development. In fact, Nueva's mission rests on a "commitment to the creation of Hispanic-owned and operating institutions that serve the economic and spiritual well-being of the community."[110] Yet both FBOs find similarity in a deeply rooted belief in the transformative power of the Christian message. Nueva has grown from a $60,000 one-year grant in 1987 to cohosting President George W. Bush at the first National Hispanic Prayer Breakfast in 2002. Indeed, there remains little doubt that Nueva stands as a high-profile example of Latino Protestant social and political engagement. As further evidence, Wilson also notes that a January 2005 issue of *Time* magazine declared Cortés held a position among the "25 Most Influential Evangelicals" in the United States.

At least a portion of their fledgling influence should be traced to the FBOs' strategic political maneuvering. Indeed, Nueva has been decidedly nonpartisan in its governmental alliances. Cortés has described his political affiliations: "I'm not red, and I'm not blue. I'm brown."[111] In essence, Cortés, in making such a proclamation declares himself a supporter of those who would advance the cause of Latinos in the United States. To that end, Nueva has hosted high-profile politicians ranging from Hillary Clinton to John McCain. Nueva refuses to limit itself with any type of partisan affiliations.[112]

The organization ultimately wants to spend political and social capital in ways that holistically benefit Latino communities and individuals. Nueva understands that "the Latino community struggles simultaneously with both material and spiritual needs."[113] With that in mind, the institutional development catalyzed by the FBO assumes that material conditions of extreme want must be addressed before there can be a resolution of spiritual issues.[114] Wilson contends that since it views its ministry as a business, "Nueva is a model of faith-based entrepreneurship."[115]

To that end, Nueva engages in educational, health, and social issues. Tangible examples of these efforts include Laundromats, housing units (including one project that consisted of fourteen units and cost $1.6 million that reflected a Spanish Revival-style architecture desired by the inhabitants), and the establishment of the Career Link Center (for job training and work readiness).[116] In all these multifaceted efforts, Nueva sees itself as a ministry primarily of institutional development.

At a national level, Nueva has been a vocal advocate for comprehensive immigration reform. Cortés himself, in fact, testified in July of 2006 before the Senate Judiciary Committee against a bill that included uncompromising language regarding any individual who "assists, encourages, or induces a[n] [undocumented] person to reside in or remain in the United States."[117] Wilson notes that Cortés asserted that "such a provision amounted to the criminalization of all Hispanic clergy and non-Hispanic clergy aiding the undocumented."[118] In multiple ways, then, Nueva exceeds what some might assume an evangelical FBO would focus on.

Nueva and LPAC offer a glimpse of the breadth and range of Latino Protestant social engagement. Though outsiders might discern negligible differences in the theological foundations of the two FBOs, they actually manifest in starkly different orientations to community social service provision. While LPAC operates, as we might expect, from an evangelical orientation—a focus on the individual and relationships—we see that Nueva operates somewhat counterintuitively: still an evangelical organization, but with a strong emphasis on institutions and structures.

NATIONAL PROFILE LATINO PROTESTANT ORGANIZATIONS

Local FBOs, though, are not the only forms of parachurch organizations that Latino Protestants have formed. The nonpartisan posture assumed by Nueva has also been adopted by the aforementioned National Hispanic Christian Leadership Conference (NHCLC) and the National Latino Evangelical Coalition (NaLEC). As evidence, the NHCLC makes frequent use of a metaphor that they follow not the "donkey" (the Democratic Party) or the "elephant" (the Republican Party), but the lamb (a symbol of Jesus Christ). Led by the charismatic Reverend Samuel Rodriguez, the NHCLC claims to be "America's largest Hispanic Christian Evangelical organization, representing more than 100 million evangelical Latinos who worship in more than 40,000 congregations throughout the United States."[119] In addition, the NHCLC reports that it represents seventy-five denominations and faith-based organizations.[120] The organization's website declares the intention "to reconcile Evangelist Billy Graham's message of salvation through Christ with Dr. Martin Luther King's march of prophetic activism."[121] In other words, NHCLC positions itself as similar to traditional evangelicalism in the United States—but with a social edge that pushes harder for issues of reconciliation. Indeed, language from the organization's promotional documents demonstrates a desire to exceed the traditional evangelical emphasis on gaining conversions to Christianity. The vision statement asserts that NHCLC seeks to "engage and reform the culture by engaging, empowering and equipping Hispanic Christ following born again men and women to emerge as key influencers in all spheres of society and the marketplace." And in the event that outsiders disregard the organization as another predictably conservative organization, the NHCLC distances itself by noting their efforts to "enrich the narrative of American Evangelicalism by replacing the media exacerbated image of angry white evangelicals who oppose everything to a convicted yet compassionate multi-ethnic kingdom culture community committed to sharing truth with love." Yet NHCLC remains a decidedly evangelical organization when they refer to their emphases on rejecting "moral relativism," "spiritual apathy," and "cultural decadence" while "elevating biblical marriage" and striving to "champion life."[122] Such terms likely function as codes that nod to the more typical white evangelical social concerns.

As a burgeoning player in national politics, news organizations will frequently seek NHCLC's opinion on issues and politicians as representative of evangelical Latinos. In fact, during the prologue to the 2016 U.S. presidential election, Rodriguez served as a prominent voice, representing evangelical Latinos and how they might respond to the candidates. A Reuters article quoted Rodriguez discussing Ted Cruz's seeming lack of appeal for Latino voters: "At times, Senator Cruz finds it difficult to identify or engage with his Latino heritage."[123] The article also described NHCLC as a "key conservative group" in the United States. As further evidence of the political clout of the NHCLC, it should be noted that President Barack Obama's administration "regularly contacted" its leaders "about their Latino, Evangelical, and faith-friendly policies."[124] Moreover, as the Obama administration regularly sought the counsel of Rodriguez, they have broadened the scope of the relationship to the point that they have also discussed religious liberty, marriage, immigration, and health care.[125]

Though not as large as the NHCLC, the NaLEC, led by Gabriel Salguero, has also attained a rather high profile as well. The NaLEC has similarly positioned itself as a "nonpartisan voice" for evangelical Latinos and Latinas "committed to the common good and justice in the public sphere." In fact, when Tony Campolo and Shane Claiborne (two progressive white evangelical leaders) offered their assessment of the 2016 presidential election in the pages of the *New York Times*, they insisted that the future of evangelical Christianity no longer resided with whites. Instead, they identified Salguero and the NaLEC by name and asserted that such leaders and organizations represented the future of evangelicalism in the United States.[126] Salguero has also served in an advisory role to President Obama and is regularly sought by journalists for quotes on policy issues. The NaLEC displayed some of the breadth of their policy concerns in early 2015 when Salguero announced the coalition's plan to organize around issues of childhood poverty, to support body cameras as "a necessity" for all police, and to announce their opposition to the death penalty.[127] In the end, both the NaLEC and the

NHCLC stand as only two examples of the nascent civic and social engagement of Latino Protestants.

A STORY OF IMMIGRATION IN A LATINO PROTESTANT CHURCH

At a Latino Protestant church in Texas, we heard a testimonial from a prominent lay pastor, Antonio—a sixty-two-year-old of Salvadoran descent. He related how he had been riding in a car with a friend driving when police stopped the vehicle for tailgating. During the procedure, the officer eventually asked for documentation. Neither man having any, the officer arrested both Antonio and his friend and they would be transferred and detained at a large immigration center in Pearson, Texas, for a month. As Antonio related his story to the rest of the congregation, he described his stay at the detention center as "marvelous." Through the filter of his religious tool kit, Antonio reframed an experience that sounded less than marvelous as miraculous and abounding with signs of God's provision.

Antonio explained in detail being forced to take off all his clothes and remain undressed except for his undergarments for at least an hour in a cold cell. He recalled being able to hear men crying out loud in cells next to him. Once he received his uniform, he described to the congregation that his minimalist meals included one packet of crackers and a small juice—once a day. Ultimately, Antonio tells the congregation not to feel sorry for him: through his suffering he garnered the strength to comfort others and preach the gospel to them. More than that, Antonio expresses his gratitude that the church held enchilada sales to hire lawyers who crafted the paperwork that allowed him to be released. At multiple points, Antonio mentions that his lawyers indicated that his past criminal history made it likely that he would be deported. However, because of the character references and testimonials of the church leadership and pastors, Antonio received an atypical release. With a dramatic conclusion, Antonio announced that God had the last word on his detainment and decided to release him. Claps and shouts of "Hallelujah" and "Amen" fill the sanctuary as Antonio returns to his seat.

The church provided Antonio a platform to share his story and a receptive audience by which he could humanize his experience as an unauthorized migrant. Additionally, the religious framing allowed him to highlight the conditions of others at this center in a public way. While Antonio likely would not describe it as political, the message indeed carried policy implications. Indeed, in his role as a pastor of the church, he remained in communication with the families of other detainees. Moreover, he continues to do religiously motivated activist work with the detention center.

Antonio's case demonstrates how some Latino Protestant congregations function as sites of civic activism. Many of these churches do not have the luxury of choosing their "mission" or how they might consider socially engaging their community. Instead, as larger social issues like immigration embroil congregational attenders, the church has no choice but to become to some degree social activists. In these moments, though, church leaders and attenders use their faith to frame the situation and offer hope for future resolution.

In other instances, Latino Protestant churches have started to offer proactive programs related to immigration. A congregation our research team observed in Fresno, California, has initiated a number of programs to allow members to remain in the United States. The church understands serving the spiritual and economic needs of undocumented Latino immigrants as one of its primary ministries. On a personal level, the pastor writes letters of recommendation to be used for "deferred action programs" or to apply for local jobs. Collectively, the congregation raises money for farm laborers and undocumented families who struggle financially. In implementing these efforts, the church intentionally stays within the framework of U.S. laws. When our research team asked the pastor what boundaries he might push, for instance, to reunite a family, he resolutely responded, "I don't work against the laws of the U.S. This is my country, and I respect the law." We found in this and other congregations that though the church empathized with undocumented Latinos, they established limits to intervention.

In effect, for undocumented church members who experience the daily threat of deportation in Fresno, the leaders of the church affirm the law by telling members to "stay put" and not attempt to reenter the country illegally. In addition, the church encourages undocumented members to obtain Individual Taxpayer Identification Numbers (ITIN) from the Internal Revenue Service so that they may declare their tax liability. The leadership describes the practice as a method for establishing a "good record" that will be rewarded when immigration policy reform eventually grants them legal status or citizenship.

THE MANY CONCERNS OF LATINO PROTESTANT CONGREGATIONS

The many attitudes, behaviors, and organizations of Latino Protestants undermine sweeping assessments.[128] The population growth and dispersal of Latino Protestants has contextually influenced how they choose to engage. For instance, while immigration policy may be at the forefront for many Latino Protestants, it certainly does not stand as the *only* issue for which they demonstrate concern. Context matters. And even within the same region, one church may feel pressed by gang issues among their youth while another attempts to cope with gentrification. Moreover, theology matters. Religious traditions *within* Latino Protestant populations have also led to various political attitudes and social activities. Scale matters as well: Latino Protestant engagement includes everything from highly localized congregations to national organizations that make news with press releases and have the ear of the president of the United States. In the end, the bulk of social science evidence clearly demonstrates a complexity in how Latino Protestants engage in community and public life that remains to be fully disentangled.

7

LATINO PROTESTANTS AND THE FUTURE OF AMERICAN CHRISTIANITY

WHAT DOES THE RISE OF LATINO PROTESTANTISM MEAN FOR THE DEVELOPMENT OF CHRISTIANITY IN THE UNITED STATES?

Due to immigration and high birth rates, Latinos are rapidly growing as a proportion of American society—faster than any other racial-ethnic group—and are widely dispersed throughout the United States.[1] Moreover, a growing number of U.S. Latinos are not *Catholic* but *Protestant*.[2] Pew Research reported a 12 percent drop of Latino adults identifying as Catholic from 67 percent to 55 percent between 2010 and 2013,[3] and an even greater drop—19 percent—among those foreign-born, and patterns of religious "switching" reveal that the majority of these former-Catholic Latinos are now Protestant.[4] Not only are the numbers of U.S. Latinos growing, they are also becoming more "Protestant."

Latino Protestants represent a diverse and thriving segment of American Christianity, yet a few commonalities highlight their significance for religion in the United States: Latino Protestants tend to emphasize their *religious identity over their ethnic identity*,[5] have *much higher* church attendance compared to whites, and are *significantly higher* in their church attendance compared to Latino Catholics.[6] Robert Putnam and David Campbell reported that 85 percent of Latino evangelicals indicate religion is very important in daily life, *significantly higher* compared to 75 percent of white evangelicals and 72 percent of Latino Catholics.[7] Other data from both Pew and Gallup indicate that Latino Protestants (again, whether evangelical, Pentecostal, or mainline) are simply *more religiously active* than their Catholic counterparts—as well as both white Protestants and black Protestants.[8] In short, compared to Latino Catholics, white Protestants, and black Protestants, Latino Protestants are *more actively committed* to their congregations, their churches are *more central and more integral* to their religiosity, and their churches are *more central* to their lives. Latino Protestant churches capture and channel Latino Protestant religiosity. Latino Protestant churches are among the most strategic arenas for grasping a growing but neglected religious group that will become a more visible and prevalent force in American life.

In this chapter we conclude by once again highlighting the complexity and richness of Latino Protestants and their churches. The chapter synthesizes important findings, considers significant issues yet to be addressed, and speculates about potentially rich and generative avenues of inquiry related to Latino Protestant churches. In fact, the compelling heterogeneity and complexity of Latino Protestants demands disciplined, systematic, and rigorous research and analysis. This chapter provides a proposal for framing questions toward understanding the future of Latino Protestantism, raises issues to be pursued (like legalization and citizenship), and considers personal, organizational, and cultural issues that will be most pressing for Latino Protestants in the coming decades. Even more, many Latino church leaders claim generalizable knowledge based on personal experience or anecdotal data. While they may certainly be familiar with individual churches or even multiple congregations over a long period of time, utter speculation on Latino Protestants and their churches is rampant, and their knowledge has yet to be studied in a methodic, empirical manner. What is claimed as "fact" are empirical patterns that require investigation and sociological dynamics that need to be analytically unpacked. Because we intend for this volume to be a *social scientific* introduction to Latino Protestants and their churches, we also use this final chapter to suggest an agenda for further research.

HIGHLIGHTS AND SIGNIFICANT ISSUES
YET TO BE ADDRESSED

This rise in Latino Protestants will be significant not only for their own churches but also for denominational leaders who strive to reach and minister to a diversifying population, for political leaders who confront issues and craft alliances, for educational leaders—of religious and non-religious institutions—assessing needs for curriculum and training, for business leaders providing training and expanding services, and for average citizens in understanding and accepting this diffuse and growing portion of their everyday lives. While there are many stereotypes that surround Latino religion, our work represented in this book provides an accessible introduction to the variety and nuance of Protestantism and the various implications of differing religious orientations, national origins, and streams of American acculturation.

While we strive to honor the ethnic and racial distinctions found among Latinos throughout this book, careful work at further distinguishing at what point race and ethnicity really matter for individual and corporate faith remains a fruitful arena for research. There is not room enough in these pages to consider all the variations of history, migration, and generational succession for Latino groups; we acknowledge that such distinctions of context, origins, and age matter. We hope our work here contributes to finding new and better ways for considering such variances.

While much of our writing stresses what is "new" or "largely unknown" about Latino Protestants, our narrative emphasizes that Latino Protestants are not new to the United States. We have traced the fascinating and differing migrations of Latinos in the United States, yet many forget that the United States abruptly annexed a large number of Latinos at the end of the Mexican American War. The success of missionary efforts resulted in a distinctive "borderland Protestantism," whose cultural vestiges remain today. At the same time, the condescending and racially superior attitudes found among many of those missionaries further contributed to stigmatization and prejudice. Thus, the cultural residue of racism and white privilege also remain today. Finally, yet another remnant is anti-Catholicism, a religious divide that still poses a barrier among American Latinos.

Regardless of race or ethnic heritage, Latino Protestants routinely encounter difficulty among friends and family who adhere to the Catholic faith. We found many Protestants have experienced tensions, anger, alienation, and being "cut off" from their families as a result of their conversions. We also discovered unexpected situations where Latinos became active members of congregations they believed to be Catholic—attending sometimes for years—only to be shocked when they realized it was actually a Protestant church. These unintended and conflicted Protestants are not ignorant; instead, their situations result from church leaders deliberately obscuring denominational identities in an attempt to create culturally relevant churches that attract Latinos. In some cases, Anglo church leaders embrace stereotypical notions of Latino religion (such as having a prominent statue of the Virgin Mary in the front of their sanctuary) and thereby create a form of Latino Protestantism that is due less to the inherent faith of their members than to the cultivation of a type of Protestant *Latinidad* that curiously defines how Protestantism is practiced in the United States. Attention to the tensions and conflicts not only among Latinos of differing religious orientations but also *within* Latinos who "switch" from Catholicism to Protestantism is likely to be an increasingly pressing issue.

Another constant is how much congregations matter to Latino Protestants. Latino Protestants express their spirituality through their church involvements. We expect that these communal structures should factor more prominently into our understandings, decisions, and solutions that concern them. Moreover, any explanations and productive interventions will be strategic to the extent they consider the centrality of congregations to Latino Protestants—rather than merely focusing on their individual beliefs and attitudes. As Latino Protestants mobilize more members and gain economic means to construct larger structures, we should not be surprised at the emergence of larger, more prominent, and more public churches who take on roles of spokesmanship and representation among Latino Protestants. Should these bigger congregations follow the pattern seen among American megachurches, their voices will be significant for the visibility of Latino Protestants, and the power of their vision for their people will become more pervasive. Moreover, Latino pastors are creating affinity groups within denominational bodies, and Latino seminary leaders are creating programs and networks to resource and support expanding ministries.

As Latino Protestant congregations attain greater independence, they try to balance distinctively religious concerns with the material needs of their congregation. Higher income, good health, and greater education remain challenges among Latino Protestants today, their religiosity sometimes helping and sometimes hurting their efforts—especially when concerns of personal morality seem to outweigh less tangible and more abstract political issues. Latino mainline Protestants appear to achieve the highest socioeconomic status; however, differences in research methods and sampling obscure the clarity of the overall results. Moreover, geographic and cultural differences muddy the findings (e.g., Latino mainline Protestants tend to live in the North rather than the South). How Latino religious orientation affects resilience and well-being is one of the most vital arenas of research today.

The need to attend to resilience and well-being among Latino Protestants stimulates innovative efforts. To address such significant and complicated matters, the more recent consolidation of Latino Protestant parachurch organizations (like the Asociación para La Educación Teológica Hispana, the National Hispanic Christian Leadership Conference, the Hispanic Mega Church Association, and the National Latino Evangelical Coalition) is especially significant. The mission of these groups encompasses community needs and political issues, providing perspectives and mobilizing people to address pressing concerns on their behalf. Latino Protestants tend to connect their religiosity to supernatural experiences rather than to social and material needs. Therefore, it is significant (and perhaps inevitable) that Latino parachurch organizations feel compelled to attend to broader civic concerns on their behalf. Representatives of these parachurch organizations are given a seat at the table more so than local pastors in local, state, and national organizations, essentially parachurch representatives becoming delegates for the "Latino Protestant Church" on matters vital to their communities. While such representation is not always *public*, it is increasingly *pervasive*. Indeed, the more frequent interactions of Latino parachurch organizations with civic and business structures means that policies affecting Latino Protestants are more likely to come from these boundary-crossing delegates.

How does language use fit into Latino churches and parachurch alliances? Part of the challenge of studying Latino Protestants is to cope with the complexities of language adoption and use. History, migration, and the founding of independent Latino Protestant churches all bear on the languages routinely spoken among Latino Protestants and the various sites in which one language may be preferred over another. Surely, the ministries of churches and parachurch organizations are dependent on the strategic use of language for mobilizing members and alliances, yet our research on language cautions against easy assumptions. Specifically, Latino religion is not necessarily oriented around Spanish.

While the majority of Latino Catholics indicate Spanish is their primary language, only one-third of Latino Protestants report the same. Moreover, Latino Protestant converts are twice as likely to be English dominant. Language use may be tied to the deeper connections fostered among Latino Catholics to their ancestral culture compared to Protestants, although this is understudied. Latino Protestant churches are readily found that use Spanish, English, and even K'iche' (among the Mayan of Guatemala). In fact, while the majority of Latino Protestants are English dominant, the majority of their church services are conducted in Spanish. So, while most Latino Protestants use English as their primary language, the primary language of their churches appear to be Spanish. Even so, we find churches may be characterized by use of only one language; others accommodate bilingualism. A Latino megachurch in Texas conducts their main services in English, segregating a small group of members into a "Spanish Service" in another part of the building. Parachurch organizations implicitly demand fluency in Spanish and English, Spanish to be inclusive of all potential constituents, and English to be inclusive of all potential partners and providers across the United States. Therefore, the demands of bilingual fluency in the work of Latino Protestant parachurch organizations means their leaders are more likely to be more highly educated, politically savvy, and culturally fluent with social institutions characterized by white privilege compared to their Latino constituents. Overall, the examination of language use becomes significant for investigating the connections between culture and religion as well as indicating the possibilities for diverse congregations that incorporate non-Latinos. In the end, language use is both fascinating and understudied, with profound issues of immigration, acculturation, and identity being intertwined.

Thinking about the complexities of language use draws us into an appreciation of the complexities of Latino ethnic identity. While we assert no singular, monolithic understanding of Latino Protestant identity, there appear to be some more generalizable characteristics. First, Latino Protestants are inherently multicultural, representing a wide-ranging spectrum of language, culture, and religious conviction. In other words, Protestantism encompasses several religious orientations, which we often collapse into mainline, evangelical, and Pentecostal. Second, Latino Protestants regularly contend with racism and white privilege, although their struggles and oppression may not be expressed with specificity within their own churches. Essentially, Latino Protestants are not uniformly equipped by their leaders or their theology for addressing ever-present difficulties and needs stemming from work, school, or civic engagements. Third, Latino Protestants express their religious lives in ways that may be *Latino* but are not necessarily *native to their ancestral cultures*. Latino Protestant churches in America bear the marks of missionary efforts; transnational groups hybridize practices that can emphasize continuity with home cultures but often do not; well-meaning efforts by Anglo church leaders often establish liturgical and ministry practices based on stereotypes that assert a *Latinidad* that may not be native to the members who eventually participate; and some Latino churches assert they are not "Latino" but simply "American." Thus, amid the variety and heterogeneity of Latino Protestants in America, they coalesce around particular congregational forms that all have their distinctive origin in the United States—the American congregationalization of their religion[9] —and that come to define for the group assembled in those places what it means to be properly devoted, pious, and religious. Finally, we should not neglect the presence of Latino Protestants in non-Latino churches. How do their identities, relationships, and religious experiences differ from those immersed in Latino (or multi-Latino) churches?

ARENAS FOR FURTHER INQUIRY ON LATINO PROTESTANTS IN AMERICA

By far, the greatest challenge in establishing an agenda for further exploration regarding Latino Protestants and their churches is the pervasiveness of *ethnoracial essentialization*.[10] In our narrative, we discussed the vague assessments that confidently assert Latino Protestants have "worship services with a Latino flavor"[11] or characterized by "the

spirit of fiesta."[12] Such tautological and racialized stereotypical statements have no analytic value. They fail to describe—less explain—any
concrete dynamics or mechanisms operating in these churches.[13]

Journalists, scholars, and church leaders should all avoid such front-
loaded, racialized assumptions and use careful sampling, listening, and
observation to pursue dynamics and nuance among Latino Protestants
and their churches. Rather than reduce complex dynamics to vague
generalities, interested observers must preserve variety and texture in
observing and describing Latino Protestants and their churches to then
follow up on substantive structures that both define and affect Latino
Protestants and their congregations. How will we consciously give attention to differences in nation of origin? What distinctions even matter? Also, it is not immediately clear whether this term signals a church
of immigrants or whether they are some type of acculturated Americans
(maybe neither? both?).

Moreover, an important question to answer is whether there is anything truly "indigenous" to Latino Protestantism in the United States.
Despite claims of "Latino culture" attached to various aspects of Latino
Protestant religious practice, we know congregations that originate
from "seeker church" models, orient around the prosperity gospel, or
infuse themselves with other distinctly American religious developments. Appreciating and apprehending the breadth of difference that
exists among Latino Protestants would contribute to revealing the type
of nuances we believe an agenda for future inquiry would want to
explore.

The considerable growth and diversity of Latino Protestants makes
full apprehension of this ethno/racial/religious subgroup tremendously
elusive. With that in mind, we suggest a coalescing around a common
set of interests. Such commonalities are not meant to be tightly framed
or narrowly defined but generally agreed arenas of focus for the sake of
building a body of shared understanding. To that end, we suggest the
following:

Worship and Liturgy

Religious and congregational life continues to revolve around worship.
Future observations and reports on Latino Protestants should seek to
capture the variety and complexity of liturgical patterns (order of wor-

ship, style, artifacts) and religious practices (singing, preaching, Bible readings, and evangelizing) of Latino Protestants and their congregations in relation to dynamics of leadership, power, and decision making at the local and denominational level.[14] Systematic, empirical exploration should consider individual and corporate worship practices in light of theological and liturgical traditions as well as national background and regional location of the Latino Protestants.[15] Investigations would also include the individual religious experiences of participants (both adults and children) as framed within the life of the congregation as a whole.

Musical worship, of course, remains an area of considerable interest and debate. For example, some Latino Protestant leaders confidently say that *salsa* is acceptable as worship music, but others react to *salsa* by pronouncing that such music comes "from the devil." An important question emerges: What is the scope of agreement on the sanctity of different forms of music? Also, what styles of music are actually present in Latino Protestant congregations? Is the music of Marcos Witt the standard music of the Latino Protestant churches (as some claim)? Or is some form of indigenous music the norm? We have observed churches that feature distinctive rhythms of *mariachi*, *cumbia*, and *merengue*, as well as Spanish-translated contemporary Christian music. Even more radically, our research has taken us from Latin-rhythm-inspired worship to nightclub, seeker church atmospheres to scenes of staid, rigidly controlled Pentecostals—all of which were Latino Protestant. But we do not know which are prominent or what accounts for the variation in choices of sacred music. Beyond style of music, how are praises and adoration actually practiced?

Also, the issue of gender is surely significant. How do the practices and experiences of women vary among Latino Protestants? What are the leadership roles of women who participate in Latino Protestant congregations? Are there limitations, and if so, what are they? What is the role of power in gender relationships among Latino Protestants? Even with formally defined sanctions prohibiting women's religious actions, we may find that women among Latino Protestants have considerably more power then men. Also, is *machismo* (another word that essentializes Latinos) a key dynamic of importance? Even more, how are specific types of masculinities and femininities shaped, leveraged, or reinforced among different Latino Protestants?

More generally, what are the meaningful structural differences among evangelical, Pentecostal, and mainline Latino Protestants? How are symbolic boundaries marked as individual Latino Protestants relate to one other and "compete" for religious legitimacy? Looking beyond what happens in their churches, how do Latino Protestants practice their religious devotion in their homes, schools, and workplaces?

Ethnic and Racial Identity

The Latino community in the United States is astonishingly diverse in terms of race, ethnicity, age dynamics, social class, level of acculturation, citizenship or legal status, and country of origin. For this reason, any observers aiming to shed light on the multifaceted nature of Latino Protestants should pay attention to the intersection of individual religious practice, involvements in religious spaces, and ethnoracial identity. How do Latino Protestants sustain their ethnic and identity?[16] Will we find that Latino Protestants "de-ethnicize" as found among other groups, or will they reconnect to their "Latino roots"?[17] How should we analytically consider Spanish-language use?[18] What is revealed when we focus on the intersection of race, ethnicity, and gender dynamics within particularistic Latino groups?[19]

Ethnicity and racial identity can be productively examined through the category of "age."[20] Looking at age dynamics, what of the place of children as well as the elderly? There is a label applied to young adults among Latinos: *jóvenes*. At what age are young adults still *jóvenes* (loosely translated "young people")? In our observation, people can be quite "mature" and yet be labeled *jóven*, which suggests that being labeled *jóven* has less to do with *age* and more to do with *power*, specifically, the ability of people to express opinions and exercise binding decision making at both the interpersonal level (conversations) and the organizational level (organizational policies). *Jóvenes* may have less power because they have not yet "proven" themselves in handling mature responsibilities attributed to marriage, stable jobs, and children. Given that *jóven* also signifies *unmarried*, how are Latino Protestants promoting expectations about marriage and the reproduction of particular family structures? How are various age groups organized and formed in their faith, for example, in regulating sexuality (birth control, family planning, same-sex relationships, cohabitation) or maintaining ethnic identity markers (music, food, types of occupations, and leisure activities)?

Scholarship on race and ethnicity (often buttressed by U.S. Census data) also indicate meaningful differences between "race" and "ethnicity" in the designation of a person who is Latino. Therefore, when a person in the United States says she is Latino, she could be white, she could be black, or she could even have her ancestral origin in Asia. What difference do the sociological dynamics of race and ethnicity make for Latino Protestants? How does the observation that Latinos—regardless of being first, second, or third generation—are perceived as *perpetual foreigners* affect their experience and practice of worship?[21] Do Latino Protestant congregations' worshiping practices have a bearing on the development of transnational cultural networks between Latino Protestants and Latin American countries? Furthermore, given the observed frequency of religious switching from Catholicism to Protestantism, how does conversion to a Latino Protestant congregation from Catholicism affect ethnic identity in relation to families and other groups that would otherwise form solidarities?

Community Involvement and Civic Engagement

Latino Protestants are embedded within their surrounding communities—although the depth of their "embeddedness" may be uneven.[22] For example, Rubén Armedariz asserts that Latino Protestants "do not deal efficiently with the communities in which they are located. One particular survey. . . indicated, overwhelmingly, that its own members recognized their lack of involvement in the issues affecting the community. Part of the reason is that most members of these congregations do not actually live in the community [but are] commuters to church activities."[23] Yet we know that some Latino Protestants consider engagement with and advocacy on behalf of socioeconomic disadvantaged Latinos a vital part of their mission. Consequently, an agenda for sociological research will contribute to understanding Latino Protestants that confront the challenges of wage inequality, undocumented immigration, criminalization/incarceration, and the general lack of health services and educational opportunities among Latinos—as individuals, through congregations, as well as through parachurch organizations.[24]

First, the role of religion, citizenship, and document status is a rich and largely untapped arena of exploration. More than simply looking at the personal experience of undocumented Latino immigrants in relation to Protestantism, what are the workings and impact of social structures affecting citizenship and document status? For example, what determines the attitudes and services provided to undocumented immigrants in Latino Protestant churches? All of our observed churches offer some form of support. While informal care and coping is always evident, many congregations have gone on to create formal ministries featuring distributed pamphlets, detailed processes, and dedicated volunteers. Such assistance appears to be in service to the state such that Latino Protestants reinforce through such ministry programs normative political ideologies, yet sometimes the programmatic approach to undocumented status takes on greater advocacy and political contention with the state. One way to theoretically frame themes regarding citizenship focuses on the opportunities and constraints stemming from broader civic structures. More specifically: how do state structures of legality/illegality shape the experiences of Latino Protestants? Do congregations merely enforce mainstream ideas of making "desirable" American citizens who are law-abiding, crime-avoiding, and hard-working students and laborers? Where do we find Latino Protestants inhabiting countervailing structures that question the pervasive racialized sorting found throughout American educational and occupational structures?[25] More generally, how should we conceptualize the workings of religion in relation to questions of citizenship and document status?

Next, what is the role of geography and the built environment (whether rural, suburban, or urban)? Are there regional distinctives among Latino Protestants? It is likely that where Latino Protestants are located is significant, both in terms of the background and circumstances of the Latinos found there and their tenure in the region. Long established Latino enclaves and "gateway" destinations are likely to have significantly different histories, networks, and coalitions of support in comparison with new destinations and more rural areas Latinos have been spreading into as they follow economic opportunities. The dynamics of geographic location and migration of Latinos connect with the more general question of the relationship between social class and citizenship for Latino Protestants. How do structures of legality and illegality shape the dynamics of the place of religion in their lives? Acknowledging the importance of undocumented Latinos, what are the individual practices, corporate theologies, and shared rites that characterize unauthorized/undocumented Latinos?[26] In what ways do Latino Protestants channel resources (e.g., time, money, people) and practices (e.g., prayer, rallying, voting) at the local, regional, national, and global level in order to advance the social conditions of their local communities?

Finally, how do Latino Protestants perpetuate and challenge broader issues of gender inequality, class inequality, and racism among Latinos? We know that Latino Protestants are more conservative than their Catholic counterparts on issues related to abortion,[27] same-sex marriage,[28] and attitudes toward marriage in general,[29] but we are not clear on the role of Latino Protestants in relation to these issues. Do Latino Protestant churches consider civic engagement to be a worship practice? What is the impact of broader political discourse on the ways Latino Protestants engage with society? What about Latino Protestants who remain apolitical and not otherwise civically engaged? Generally speaking, how do leaders and members of Latino Protestants define and engage "the world?"

STIMULATING INTEREST IN LATINO PROTESTANTS AND THEIR CHURCHES

The three arenas for further exploration suggested above for Latino Protestants and their churches are quite general, and the questions proposed are far from exhaustive. In short, there remains much for church leaders, editors, scholars, and journalists to absorb. Rather than seeking to discover what the current "research on Latino Protestants and their churches" is and try to fit new analysis within that, it is more important at this point to stimulate *multiple* lines of exploration with *intersecting* questions and issues from *various* sub-areas with an active *integration* of heuristic conceptual tools to search out potentially fruitful avenues of investigation.[30] Moreover, by suggesting that we give attention to congregations we do not mean a narrow focus on membership or attendance, nor do we mean to imply that Latino Protestant religiosity is solely "explained" by a focus on congregational structures. Our suggestions here urge interested observers to move beyond individual-based survey responses and examine congregations and parachurch organizations as strategic sites for beginning to build a more complex understanding of Latino Protestants. Productive investigations would focus not only on what happens "inside" organizations, but also on what happens outside and around them, what affects their constituents, how Latino Protestant structures are shaped and affected, and the manner in which Latino Protestants have an effect (if any) not only on their Latino members but also the community, the market, and the state—even on broader Christian developments in America.

The goal of *Latino Protestants in America* is to offer a map of a route that leads to a deeper understanding of Latino Protestants. Certainly much remains to be learned. As Latino Protestants continue to grow as a percentage of the U.S. population, their influence will be undeniable. Astute observers, scholars, and religious leaders will do well to invest significant resources into assessing the breadth and depth of Latino Protestant diversity because—even if we choose to ignore it—Latino Protestantism will be a significant phenomenon for the future of America.

APPENDIX

Qualitative Sources and Research Methodology

THE LATINO PROTESTANT CONGREGATIONS (LPC) PROJECT

The basis our observations and illustrations used throughout the narrative of *Latino Protestants in America* were drawn from the work of the Latino Protestant Congregations (LPC) Project. The LPC Project is a research grant awarded to Davidson College in September 2013 funded by Lilly Endowment. With this generous funding, an interdisciplinary team of social scientific researchers have been conducting "ground level" observations and interviews across the United States to capture the diversity of liturgy and worship, ethnic and racial identity, and community and civic engagement in Latino churches. The LPC Project is directed by Dr. Gerardo Martí (Davidson College) and Dr. Mark Mulder (Calvin College).

As a joint endeavor consisting of the LPC Project Directors and a team of LPC Research Fellows, we have been conducting a team-based examination of Latino Protestants in the United States. Our research design of multiple ethnographies by multiple researchers in multiple regions across the nation aims to illuminate the variety and complexity of Latino Protestants and their churches using a qualitative approach. Our motivation for a larger project on Latino Protestant churches comes not only from a realization of how distressingly little we know but also from a conviction that direct observation and careful interviewing is effective for challenging commonsense assumptions when needed and for teasing out what researchers, denominational leaders, and local church pastors should be paying attention to. Our research draws data from all strands of Protestantism (evangelical, Pentecostal, and mainline); is attentive to gender dynamics (among pastors, lay leaders, and members), to age dynamics (children, *jóvenes,* and adults), to generational dynamics (new immigrants to well-established Hispanics)—both documented and undocumented—while giving notice to alternative liturgical structures (language dominance, places of worship, styles of music and preaching) and being sensitive to the levels and degrees of transnational and various religious influences and potential resistances.

In recruiting LPC Research Fellows, we invited advanced graduate students, post-doctoral researchers, and junior faculty to participate in a three-year research fellowship starting in June 2014. A team of ten researchers was selected to conduct qualitative observations and interviews in Latino Protestant churches across the United States. All LPC fellows are fluent in Spanish. LPC Fellows were expected to gain entrée to local congregations in their geographic region and complete profiles for each, including field notes and audio interviews. Audio interviews were transcribed for each LPC fellow; more specifically, if interviews were conducted in Spanish, they were translated and transcribed into English for analysis. Throughout our collaboration, LPC fellows and the LPC project directors gathered annually at Calvin College to plan, collaborate, and debrief during the funding period. Our meetings over readings and observations focused on shared insights, cumulative learning, and strategic planning and discussions of our ongoing experiences and interpretations.

Most importantly, our research resists homogenizing "Latinos" to be a singular ethnic or racial group but explicitly acknowledges that Latinos in the United States are made of groups that are both recent arrivals and longtime residents with different countries of origin and different linguistic characteristics. In capturing the variety of Latino Protestantism, we wish to bring knowledge-driven attention to how important these churches are to the present and future of American religion.

PARTICIPANT OBSERVATION

The backbone of our collaborative research was participant observation. We attempted to immerse ourselves in various Latino Protestant churches in America. There is a long tradition of participant observation in the social sciences, which appreciates that "hanging out" with purpose can be the source of rich data.[1] Participant observation requires listening skills and attention to detail, including the ability to focus one's attention on what people say and how they say it, and to note what people do and how they do it.[2]

Though a small literature on Latino Protestants exists (especially the excellent quantitative survey work from the Pew Hispanic Center), our work is distinctive in its ethnographic focus. Participant observation is especially well suited to allowing researchers to discover how people themselves interpret their own worlds, including their subjective inner experiences.[3] Watching and listening, participant observers identify how people give meaning to their daily, mundane tasks, as well as to the institutions of work and leisure in which they participate. We were interested in micro-level processes including how people's religious orientations had developed, how they structured the communal life of their congregations, and how they lived in the "real world" outside the walls of their congregations. We strived to cultivate thick, narrative descriptions of Latino Protestant congregational life guided by those who experience and live in it. Our inductive approach acknowledges the leaders and attenders of these congregations as the experts. This is not to say that they fully understand either themselves or their congregations but that attention to their lifeworlds is critical to uncovering the more subtle dynamics we seek.

We believe research at the intersection of Latino Protestants as an ethno-racial group and their congregations as sites of worship is strikingly relevant to the academy as well as the broader American church. Therefore, this research involves understanding the timing and circumstances of the founding of Latino-focused churches and services, changes in these congregations over time, the character and functions of decision making, the dynamics of formal and informal power relationships, what it means to be a member of such congregations, and even what it means to be properly religious. While their social lives may seem unremarkable and self-evident to participants themselves, social scientists seek to order people's patterns of behavior and then relate them to wider sociological concepts—or develop new concepts based on their observations. This necessitates drawing insights from participants themselves as much as possible, rather than relying on secondary data sources that confirms researchers' prejudices or preconceived notions.

Of course, participant observers are aware that their very presence *as researchers* changes the social interactions of the people they are observing. Participants' awareness of the researcher may subtly (or not so subtly) change what they say or do. This makes it especially important for researchers to gain the trust of research participants so that their interactions are as natural as possible. As such, the relative success of participant observation can depend on researchers' relationships with the observed.

Although our data collection will continue at least through 2018, at the time of writing we drew on fieldnotes and interviews collected by the LPC Project Research Fellows from twenty Latino Protestant congregations. More specifically, data were collected from 2014 through 2016 from congregations in diverse regions across the United States, specifically from California's Bay Area, San Joaquin Valley, and Orange County; northern Indiana; eastern Massachusetts; the Research Triangle area of North Carolina; central and west Texas; northern Oregon; and Rhode Island. (Supplements to data collected by the fellows include additional information solicited by LPC Project Directors during the same period from a variety of sources, including: meetings with Latino Protestant church and seminary leaders, participating in denominational gatherings, consultations with church and parachurch leaders, as well as attendance at conferences and seminars dedicated to history and contemporary developments in Latino Protestantism.) In structuring our attention to Latino Protestant congregational life, we began our research by framing the understanding around the activities, artifacts, and accounts of Latino Protestant leaders and church members. Analytical tools used in qualitative congregational studies (e.g., observations of people, processes, and properties; congregational histories; membership patterns) are used to create thick, narrative descriptions of Latino Protestant congregational life guided by those who experience and live in it. As is heuristically productive, we freely draw on preestablished "hypotheses" while preferring to engage a methodology that allows salient patterns and structures to emerge. The end result is the cultivation of a series of compellingly rich narratives used to fuel analysis to illuminate this growing wing of Protestantism in the United States.

In order to properly research anything regarding "Latino Protestant congregations," a geographically broad sample is crucial. We worked to include places like Southern California and South Florida, border states like Texas and New Mexico, and destinations with surges in Latino populations like Charlotte and Chicago. In short, the study is national in scope in an effort to tease out regional distinctiveness while uncovering significant commonalities. In addition, we attempted to capture the locational discrepancies that arise in urban, suburban, and rural contexts.

Each researcher sought out Latino Protestant congregations in a broad geographic region (usually within an hour's driving distance from the researcher's home), and strategically selected sites that appeared to be particularly rich and appropriately diverse in size, ethnic composition, date of founding, and religious oreintation within Protestantism (i.e., evangelical, mainline, Pentecostal). The entrée to particular church sites often began with a conversation with the lead pastor, who granted explicit permission to conduct research. Main worship services were a priority (usually on Sundays), but observations of other church gatherings—formal and informal—also contributed to the data from each congregation. In addition to noticing what was happening, who was there (e.g., number of people, age, gender, ethnicity, languages spoken, class, clothing, etc.), and what people say and do, each researcher also took time to note other critical dynamics: body language, moods, or attitudes; the general environment; interactions among participants; and other information that could be relevant. Jotting down quick notes was used to help remember observations or, if notes could not be taken at the time, written down soon after leaving. These field notes were collated into a central filing system. In addition, researchers crafted research "memos" reporting on each congregation's history, information supplying important context for each church, and highlights of what appeared to be socially signifcant dynamics in the congregation.

Our national collaboration, our mix of social scientific methodologies, and our broad range of data comprise an attempt to overcome bias and blind spots. Pictures are constructed to create a synthetic whole out of the various pieces presented from our observations and the reported experiences of our respondents. When information does not match or is seemingly contradictory, we consider the source and weigh the evidence to obtain the best interpretive sense of what is happening sociologically. Concepts are provided throughout the text in the hope of their utility to future researchers.

IN-DEPTH INTERVIEWS

In-depth interviews built on the insights we gained from our participant observation. Interviews, both formal and informal, as well as the structured conversational interactions of focus groups, allow researchers like us to access information that may not be available through observation alone.[4] Participant observation and background reading may help researchers formulate questions, but it is in the interaction of the interview where participants can make sense and put order on their everyday thoughts and actions. Researchers listen closely and ask follow-up questions that might not have otherwise occurred to them. In-depth interviews allow researchers to solicit detailed life stories and life histories that cannot be gained by observing or hanging out.[5]

Each congregation studied included interviews with pastors, lay leaders, and members. Interviews were semistructured, which means we prepared an interview guide but allowed conversations to move into other areas through follow-up questions if these areas were relevant. Each question of the interview schedule was designed to open different lines of conversation along the three primary focal points of our work together: "liturgy and worship," "ethnic and racial identity," and "community and civic engagement." People were recruited from within the congregation, sometimes with help from the pastoral staff but more often based on the network of new acquaintances established by each researcher as a consequence of their involvement in the congregation. After a few warm-up and introductory questions ("How did you get to [*this church*]?"), interviewees were asked a series of questions they were able to answer based on their own participation in the congregation. Many details regarding their experiences and observations were solicited, with additional questions designed for the lead pastor and for those involved in the planning and conducting of worship. Throughout the interview, not only were there follow-up questions to secure more

instances and examples but also unexpected, ironic, or otherwise surprising avenues were pursued.

TEXTUAL SOURCES

Finally, we consulted secondary sources with relevant observations
from other scholars on Latino Protestants as they were available. These
texts included published books from Christian publishers. When texts
were largely theological, apologetic, or polemical in nature, they were
not considered data sources, although they provided some help in
understanding aspects of Latino Protestantism.

NOTES

PREFACE

1. For more on the LPC Project, see Appendix.

2. Gerardo Martí, "Latino Protestants and Their Churches: Establishing an Agenda for Sociological Research," *Sociology of Religion: A Quarterly Review* 76 (2015): 145–54.

1. LATINO PROTESTANTS ARE MORE THAN "NOT CATHOLIC"

1. Pew Research Center, "America's Changing Religious Landscape," Washington, DC, May 12, 2015, accessed March 22, 2016, http://www.pewforum.org/2015/05/12/americas-changing-religious-landscape/.

2. Pew Research Center, "Hispanic Population Reaches 55 Million, But Growth Has Cooled," Washington, DC, June 25, 2015, accessed March 22, 2016, http://www.pewresearch.org/fact-tank/2015/06/25/u-s-hispanic-population-growth-surge-cools/.

3. Pew Research Center, "The Shifting Religious Identity of Latinos in the United States," Washington, DC, May 7, 2014, accessed May, 15, 2014, http://www.pewforum.org/2014/05/07/the-shifting-religious-identity-of-latinos-in-the-united-states/ and Pew Research Center, "Changing Faiths: Latinos and the Transformation of American Religion," Washington, DC, April 25, 2007, 7, accessed March 28, 2014, http://www.pewforum.org/files/2007/04/hispanics-religion-07-final-mar08.pdf.

4. Pew Research Center, "The Shifting Religious Identity."

5. Wes Granberg-Michaelson, "Think Christianity Is Dying? No, Christianity Is Shifting Dramatically," *Washington Post*, May 20, 2015, accessed June 14, 2016. https://www.washingtonpost.com/news/acts-of-faith/wp/2015/05/20/think-christianity-is-dying-no-christianity-is-shifting-dramatically/. As another point of comparison, it should be noted that Latino evangelicals alone now outnumber Jewish Americans. See David Rennie, "America's Hispanics: From Minor to Major," *Economist*, March 14, 2015, 8, accessed February 22, 2016. http://www.economist.com/sites/default/files/20150314_sr_hispanics.pdf.

6. Elizabeth Dias, "Evangélicos!" *Time*, April 15, 2013, 20–26.

7. Pew Research Center, "The Unique Challenges of Surveying U.S. Latinos," Washington, DC, November 12, 2015, accessed, February 12, 2016, http://www.pewresearch.org/2015/11/12/the-unique-challenges-of-surveying-u-s-latinos/. We also acknowledge that a low response rate has been a criticism of the Pew data. However, we argue that the data remains highly useful for establishing a landscape of what we currently know regarding Latino Protestants.

8. For instance, see Robert P. Jones, Daniel Cox, and Juhem Navarro-Rivera, "How Shifting Religious Identities and Experiences Are Influencing Hispanic Approaches to Politics," Public Religion Research Institute," September 2013, accessed March 29, 2016, http://publicreligion.org/site/wp-content/uploads/2013/09/2013_HVS_FINAL.pdf.; and Juhem Navarro-Rivera, Barry A. Kosmin and Ariela Keysar, "U.S. Latino Religious Identification, 1990–2008: Growth, Diversity, & Transformation," American Religious Identification Survey 2008, accessed March 29, 2016, http://commons.trincoll.edu/aris/files/2011/08/latinos2008.pdf.

9. For more on the LPC Project, including methodology and scope, please see appendix.

10. Pew Research Center, "A Milestone En Route to a Majority Minority Nation," Washington, DC, November 7, 2012, accessed April 1, 2016, http://www.pewsocialtrends.org/2012/11/07/a-milestone-en-route-to-a-majority-minority-nation/. Recent studies indicated that, at the very least, Latino population in the United States will double to 108 million by 2050. See Pew Research Center, "With Fewer New Arrivals, Census Lowers Hispanic Population Projections," Washington, DC, December 16, 2015, accessed April 2, 2016, http://www.pewresearch.org/fact-tank/2014/12/16/with-fewer-new-arrivals-census-lowers-hispanic-population-projections-2/.

11. And we know that religion has deep salience for Latino youth as well. See Tomas V. Sanabria, "Personal and Religious Beliefs and Experiences," in *Pathways of Hope and Faith among Hispanic Teens: Pastoral Reflections and Strategies Inspired by the National Study of Youth and Religion*, ed. Ken Johnson-Mondragón (Stockton, CA: Instituto Fe y Vida, 2007), 71.

12. See Robert Putnam and David Campbell, *American Grace: How Religion Divides and Unites Us* (New York: Simon & Schuster, 2010), 285–87.

13. Pew Research Center, "The Shifting Religious Identity," 46–49.

14. For example, see Juan Martínez, *Los Protestantes: An Introduction to Latino Protestantism in the United States* (Westport, CT: Praeger, 2011) and Daniel Rodriguez, *A Future for the Latino Church: Models for Multilingual, Multigenerational Hispanic Congregations* (Downers Grove, IL: IVP Academic, 2011).

15. Rodriguez, *A Future for the Latino Church*, 26.

16. Ibid.,158.

17. Martinez, *Los Protestantes*, 105.

18. Ibid., 100.

19. Juan Martinez, *Walk with the People: Latino Ministry in the United States* (Nashville, TN: Abingdon Press, 2008), 57.

20. Rodriguez, *A Future for the Latino Church*, 57.

21. Martinez, *Los Protestantes*, 100; Rodriguez, *A Future for the Latino Church*, 57.

22. Rodriguez, 2011, 158.

23. Martinez, *Los Protestantes*, 105.

24. For an analysis of how racialized stereotypes affect worship and liturgy, see Gerardo Martí, *Worship across the Racial Divide: Religious Music and the Multiracial Congregation* (New York: Oxford University Press, 2012).

25. Pew Research Center, "The Shifting Religious Identity," 5.

26. Pew Research Center, "Changing Faiths," 50

27. Ibid., 12.

28. Manuel A. Vasquez, "Pentecostalism, Collective Identity, and Transnationalism among Salvadorans and Peruvians in the U.S." *Journal of the American Academy of Religion* 67, no. 3 (1999): 617–36.

29. Gerardo Martí, *A Mosaic of Believers: Diversity and Innovation in a Multiethnic Church* (Bloomington: Indiana University Press, 2005). See also Gerardo Martí, "The Diversity Affirming Latino: Ethnic Options and the Ethnic Transcendent Expression of American Latino Religious Identity," in *Sustaining Faith Traditions: Race, Ethnicity, and Religion among the Latino and Asian American Second Generation*, ed. C. E. Chen and R. Jeung (New York: New York University Press, 2012).

30. Jane Juffer, "Hybrid Faiths: Latino Protestants Find a Home among the Dutch Reformed in Iowa," *Latino Studies*, 6, no. 3 (2008): 290–312.

31. Laura López-Sanders, "Bible Belt Immigrants: Latino Religious Incorporation in New Immigrant Destinations," *Latino Studies* 10, nos. 1–2 (2012): 128–54.

32. For more on Juffer's and López-Sanders's respective studies, see chapter 5.

33. See Pew Research Center, "The Shifting Religious Identity" and Charles F. Westoff and Emily A. Marshall, "Hispanic Fertility, Religion, and Religiousness in the U.S.," *Population Policy Research Review* 29 (2010): 441–52.

34. Gastón Espinosa, "'Today We Act, Tomorrow We Vote': Latino Religions, Politics, and Activism in Contemporary U.S. Civil Society," *The Annals of the Academy of Political and Social Science* 612 (2007): 152–71.

35. Gastón Espinosa, "Separated Brothers: Latinos Are Changing the Nature of American Religion," *Economist* (July 16, 2009), accessed February 19, 2016, http://www.economist.com/node/14034841.

36. For more on the increasing academic interest in Latinos and religion, see Rogelio Sáenz and Maria Cristina Morales, *Latinos in the United States: Diversity and Change* (Cambridge, MA: Polity Press, 2015), 142–143.

37. See James Fitzpatrick, *Puerto Rican Americans: The Migration to the Mainland* (Englewood Cliffs, NJ: Prentice-Hall, 1971); Sidney Mintz, *Worker in the Cane: A Puerto Rican Life Story* (New York: W.W. Norton, 1974); and Renato Poblete and Thomas O'Dea, "Anomie and the Quest for Community: The Formation of Sects among Puerto Ricans in New York," *American Catholic Sociological Review* 27 (1960): 18–36.

38. Andrew Greeley, "Defection among Hispanics," *America*, July 30, 1988, 61–62. For yet another perspective on the Pentecostal attraction in particular, see Luís León, "Born Again in East LA: The Congregation as Border Space," in *Gatherings in Diaspora: Religious Communities and the New Immigration,* ed. R. Stephen Warner and Judith G. Wittner (Philadelphia: Temple University Press, 1998), 163–96. See also Vasquez's 1999 article where he argues that, when discussing the Pentecostal appeal, "local inflections" should be taken into account—rather than just assuming that "Pentecostalism does *x* for Latinos" (631). That is, in his ethnographic sites, Vasquez finds variegated rationales for the attraction of Pentecostalism. In one instance, the Pentecostal church serves as "a petri dish where pan-Latino identity is fashioned." Yet, in another case, the church acts as a place where national origin identity is bolstered, as the congregation acts as an inward-focused, buffering enclave (632). Thus, the Pentecostal draw remains complex and context-specific.

39. Marie Friedmann Marquardt, "From Shame to Confidence: Gender, Religious Conversation and Civic Engagement of Mexicans in the U.S. South," *Latin American Perspectives* 32 (2005): 27–56.

40. Espinosa, "Separated Brothers."

41. For example, theologian Timothy Matovina contends that Protestant churches have won Latino converts from Catholicism due to the attraction of

more intimate religious communities and active congregational engagement in *Latino Catholicism: Transformation in America's Largest Church* (Princeton, NJ: Princeton University Press, 2012).

42. Luis Guillermo Pineda, "Parishes Fail to Market Catholicism to Hispanics," *National Catholic Reporter* 43 (2007), accessed February 22, 2016, http://www.thefreelibrary.com/Parishes+fail+to+market+Catholicism+to+Hispanics.-a0158524887.

43. Pew Research Center, "Changing Faiths."

44. Aida I. Ramos, "Understanding Reasons for Latino/a Catholic to Protestant Conversion," unpublished manuscript, George Fox University.

45. For more on ethno-racial identity, see Tomás R. Jiménez, Corey D. Fields, and Ariela Schachter, "How Ethnoraciality Matters: Looking Inside Ethnoracial 'Groups,'" *Social Currents* 2 (2015): 107–15. Also, see an insightful discussion of Latino identity in Idelissa Malavé and Esti Giordani, *Latino Stats: American Hispanics by the Numbers* (New York: The New Press, 2015), 122–32. For a discussion that teases out issues of identity specifically regarding Mexican Americans, see chapters 8 and 9 in Edward E. Telles and Vilma Ortiz, *Generations of Exclusion: Mexican Americans, Assimilation, and Race* (New York: Russell Sage Foundation, 2008).

46. See, for instance, the Pew Research Center and their analysis of "Hispanic Trends." All of their reports within the "Hispanic Trends" research portfolio include "a note on terminology" that indicates the interchangeable usage of "Hispanic" and "Latino."

47. Gilbert Guerra and Gilbert Orbea, "The Argument against the Use of the Term 'Latinx,'" *Phoenix*, November 19, 2015, accessed August 25, 2016, http://swarthmorephoenix.com/2015/11/19/the-argument-against-the-use-of-the-term-latinx/. For more discussion on the use of "Latino," see Sáenz and Morales, 2015, 3–4. In addition, Sáenz and Morales offer a complex theoretical overview to interpret the multifaceted lives of Latinos in the United States.

48. Pew Research Center, "Is Speaking in Spanish Necessary to Be Hispanic? Most Hispanics Say No," Washington, DC, February 19, 2016, accessed February 22, 2016, http://www.pewresearch.org/fact-tank/2016/02/19/is-speaking-spanish-necessary-to-be-hispanic-most-hispanics-say-no/.

49. Pew Research Center, "English Proficiency on the Rise among Latinos: U.S. Born Are Driving Language Changes," Washington, DC, May 12, 2015, accessed March 20, 2016, http://www.pewhispanic.org/ 2015/05/12/english-proficiency-on-the-rise-among-latinos/. See also Pew Research Center, "A Majority of English-speaking Hispanics in the U.S. are Bilingual," Washington, DC, March 24, 2015, accessed March 20, 2016, http://www.pewresearch.org/fact-tank/2015/03/24/a-majority-of-english-speaking-hispanics-in-the-u-s-are-bilingual/.

50. Jiménez, et al., "How Ethnoraciality Matters," 111.

51. Larry Ortiz, "Latino Migration to Protestantism: A Historical, Socio-cultural, Ecclesiastical Analysis," *Journal of Sociology and Social Welfare* 41 (2014): 35.

52. Marquardt, "From Shame to Confidence," 38.

53. Ibid., 37–39. Marquardt here discusses outreach to Latinos among historic Protestant denominations.

54. Pineda, "Parishes Fail to Market Catholicism to Hispanics,".

55. Ortiz, "Latino Migration to Protestantism," 24.

56. Espinosa, "Separated Brothers."

57. Lucila D. Elk, "Language and Literacy in the Pentecostal Church Public High School: A Case Study of a Mexican ESL Student," *The High School Journal* 92 (2008): 1–13.

58. Edward Flores, "'I am Somebody': Barrio Pentecostalism and Gendered Acculturation among Chicano Ex-Gang Members," *Ethnic and Racial Studies* 32 (2009): 96–116.

59. Fermin Leal, "Templo Calvario Debuts New $11 Million Sanctuary," *Orange County Register*, July, 5, 2009, accessed June 22, 2016, http://www.ocregister.com/articles/new-168362-church-sanctuary.html.

60. Timothy Morgan, "Death Penalty Repeal Gains Support from Latino Evangelical Coalition," *Christianity Today*, March 31, 2015, accessed February 20, 2016, http://www.christianitytoday.com/gleanings/2015/march/death-penalty-ban-gains-support-from-latino-evangelical-coa.html.

61. Carlos Campo, "What the New Majority-Minority Public Schools Mean for Christians," *Christianity Today*, August 22, 2014, accessed February 20, 2016, http://www.christianitytoday.com/ct/2014/august-web-only/what-new-majority-minority-public-schools-mean-for-christia.html.

62. Abe Levy, "God Wants You to Graduate," *Christianity Today*, April 17, 2013, accessed February 20, 2016, http://www.christianitytoday.com/ct/2013/april-web-only/god-wants-you-to-graduate.html.

63. Pew Research Center, "Mapping the Latino Population, by State, County, and City," Washington, DC, August 29, 2013, accessed June 22, 2016, http://www.pewhispanic.org/2013/08/29/mapping-the-latino-population-by-state-county-and-city/.

64. Pew Research Center, "The Impact of Slowing Immigration: Foreign-Born Share Falls among 14 Largest U.S. Hispanic Origin Groups," Washington, DC, September 15, 2015, accessed June 22, 2016, http://www.pewhispanic.org/2015/09/15/the-impact-of-slowing-immigration-foreign-born-share-falls-among-14-largest-us-hispanic-origin-groups/.

65. Dias, "Evangélicos!"

66. Aida I. Ramos, Robert Woodberry, and Christopher G. Ellison, "The Contexts of Conversion among U.S. Latinos," unpublished manuscript, George Fox University.

67. Pew Research Center, "The Shifting Religious Identity, 44–49.

68. Ibid., 120–31.

69. Jessica Hamar Martínez, Edwin I. Hernández, Rebecca Burwell, Milagros Peña, and David Sikkink, *The Politics of the Latino Church: Understanding the Political Views and Behaviors of Latino Congregations in Chicago* (South Bend, IN: Center for the Study of Religion and Society, University of Notre Dame, September 2012), accessed June 14, 2015, https://latinostudies.nd.edu/assets/95361/original/thepoliticsofthelatinochurch_final.pdf.

70. Ibid. and Edwin I. Hernández, Jeffrey Smith, Rebecca Burwell, Milagros Peña, and David Sikkink, *Healing Hands: The Health of Latino/a Churchgoers and Health Outreach among Latino Congregations in Chicago* (South Bend, IN: Institute for Latino Studies and Center for the Study of Latino Religion, University of Notre Dame, 2010), accessed May 20, 2016, https://latinostudies.nd.edu/assets/95269/original/congregations_final_pages.pdf.

2. THE EARLY HISTORY OF INDIGENOUS AND IMMIGRANT LATINO PROTESTANTS

1. See Chapter 4, "The Demography of Latinos" in Rogelio Sáenz and Maria Cristina Morales, *Latinos in the United States: Diversity and Change* (Cambridge, MA: Polity Press, 2015).

2. Marta Tienda and Norma Fuentes, "Hispanics in Metropolitan America: New Realities and Old Debates," *Annual Review of Sociology* 40 (2014): 500.

3. Marta Tienda and Norma Fuentes, "Hispanics in Metropolitan America: New Realities and Old Debates," *Annual Review of Sociology* 40 (2014): 500.

4. For more on the historical linkages between Latin American countries, immigration, and the United States, see Sáenz and Morales (2015), chapters 2 and 3.

5. Pew Research Center, "Hispanic Nativity Shift," Washington, DC, April 24, 2014, accessed, February 22, 2016, http://www.pewhispanic.org/2014/04/29/hispanic-nativity-shift/

6. Daniel R. Rodríguez-Díaz and David Cortés-Fuentes, *Hidden Stories: Unveiling the History of the Latino Church* (Decatur, GA: AETH, Asociación para la Educación Teológica, 1994), xi.

7. Manuel G. Gonzales, *Mexicanos: A History of Mexicans in the United States* (Bloomington: Indiana University Press, 2009.)

8. Martha Menchaca, *Recovering History, Constructing Race: The Indian, Black, and White Roots of Mexican Americans* (Austin: University of Texas Press, 2001), 181–206.

9. Laurie F. Maffly-Kipp, *Religion and Society in Frontier California* (New Haven, CT: Yale University Press, 1994).

10. Armando Alonzo, *Tejano Legacy: Rancheros and Settlers in South Texas, 1734–1900* (Albuquerque: University of New Mexico Press, 1998), chap 1; See also Gonzales, *Mexicanos*, chap 4.

11. Edward M. Telles and Vilma Ortiz, *Generations of Exclusion: Mexican-Americans, Assimilation, and Race* (New York: Russell Sage Foundation, 2008), 75.

12. Arnoldo De León, *They Called Them Greasers: Anglo Attitudes toward Mexicans in Texas, 1821–1900* (Austin: University of Texas, 2010), 17. See also Telles and Ortiz, *Generations of Exclusion*, 78.

13. Gonzalez, *Mexicanos*, 84; Telles and Ortiz, *Generations of Exclusion*, 75.

14. Gonzalez, *Mexicanos*, 83.

15. Richard Griswold Del Castillo, *The Treaty of Guadalupe Hidalgo: A Legacy of Conflict* (Norman: University of Oklahoma Press, 2002), 48.

16. Ibid., 49.

17. Alonzo, *Tejano Legacy*, 147.

18. David Montejano, *Anglos and Mexicans in the Making of Texas, 1836–1986* (Austin: University of Texas Press, 2010), 123.

19. De León, *They Called Them Greasers*, 20.

20. John L. Kessell, *Spain in the Southwest: A Narrative History of Colonial New Mexico, Arizona, Texas, and California* (Norman: University of Oklahoma Press, 2002), xiv.

21. Robert H. Jackson, *From Savages to Subjects: Missions in the History of the American Southwest* (New York: M.E. Sharpe, 2000), xii, 59.

22. Juan Francisco Martínez, *Sea la Luz: The Making of Mexican Protestantism in the American Southwest, 1829–1900* (Denton, University of North Texas Press, 2006), 28.

23. Ibid., 29.

24. Paul Barton, *Hispanic Methodists, Presbyterians, and Baptists in Texas* (Austin: University of Texas, 2006), 2.

25. Martínez, *Sea la Luz*, 110.

26. Susan Mitchell Yohn, *A Contest of Faiths: Missionary Women and Pluralism in the American Southwest* (Ithaca, NY: Cornell University Press, 1995), 17.

27. Michéle Butts, "'I Could Realize What Sodom and Gomorrah Might Have Been': Image vs. Reality for Presbyterian Missionaries in New Mexico, 1872." *Journal of Presbyterian History* 774 (1997): 225.

28. Ibid., 223.

29. Butts, "'I Could Realize,'" 223. See also Martínez, *Sea la Luz*, 31.

30. Daisy L. Machado, *Of Borders and Margins: Hispanic Disciples in Texas, 1888–1945* (New York: Oxford University Press, 2003).

31. Martínez, *Sea la Luz*, 91. See also Butts, "'I Could Realize,'" 224, and Randi Jones Walker, *Protestantism in the Sangre de Cristos, 1850–1920* (Albuquerque: University of New Mexico Press, 1991).

32. Walker, *Protestantism in the Sangre de Cristos*, 20.

33. Butts, "'I Could Realize,'" 224.

34. Ibid., 224

35. Ibid., 1997, 223. See also Martínez, *Sea la Luz*, 20.

36. Walker, *Protestantism in the Sangre de Cristos*. See also Butts, "'I Could Realize,'" 227.

37. Butts, "'I Could Realize,'" 227.

38. Walker, *Protestantism in the Sangre de Cristos*.

39. Martínez, *Sea la Luz*, 133.

40. Butts, "'I Could Realize,'" 229.

41. Walker, *Protestantism in the Sangre de Cristos* and Martínez, *Sea la Luz*, 169.

42. Walker, *Protestantism in the Sangre de Cristos*.

43. Ibid., 1991.

44. Butts, "'I Could Realize,'" 230.

45. Martínez, *Sea la Luz*, 98; Butts, "'I Could Realize,'" 229.

46. Martínez, *Sea la Luz*, 15.

47. Robert Woodberry, "The Missionary Roots of Liberal Democracy," *American Political Science Review* 106 (2012): 244.

48. Butts, "'I Could Realize,'" 223.

49. Walker, *Protestantism in the Sangre de Cristos*.

50. Butts, "'I Could Realize.'"

51. Ibid., 228.

52. Martínez, *Sea la Luz*, 80.

53. Yohn, *A Contest of Faiths*.

54. Martínez, *Sea la Luz*, 151.

55. Ibid., 77.

56. Ibid., 109.

57. Ibid., 79.

58. Walker, *Protestantism in the Sangre de Cristos*, 30

59. Ibid., 29,.

60. Ibid., 30.

61. Martínez, *Sea la Luz*, 108.

62. Maffly-Kipp, *Religion and Society in Frontier California*, 2.

63. Martínez, *Sea la Luz*, 3.

64. Ibid., 112.

65. Martínez, *Sea la Luz*, 136.

66. Ibid., 146.

67. Barton, *Hispanic Methodists*, 136.

68. Butts, "'I Could Realize,'" 229.

69. Joe Creech, "Visions of Glory: The Place of the Azusa Street Revival in Pentecostal History." *Church History* 65 (1996): 405. Also see Daniel Ramirez, *Migrating Faith: Pentecostalism in the United States and Mexico in the Twentieth Century* (Chapel Hill: University of North Carolina Press, 2015), 35.

70. Gastón Espinosa, *Latino Pentecostals in America* (Cambridge, MA: Harvard University Press, 2014): 22.

71. Ibid., 24.

72. Ibid., 47.

73. Cecil M. Robeck, *The Azusa Street Mission and Revival* (Nashville, TN: Thomas Nelson Press, 2006), 56.

74. Espinosa, *Latino Pentecostals in America*, 35.

75. Espinoza, *Latino Pentecostals in America*, 51.

76. Jonathan E. Calvillo, "The Living Borderlands: The Persistent Borderland Presence in Southern California Latino Protestant Congregations," in *Religion in Los Angeles*, ed. Richard Flory (Berkeley: University of California, forthcoming).

77. Pew Research Center, "Hispanics of Puerto Rican Origin in the United States," Washington, DC, June 19, 2013, accessed May 6, 2016. http://www.pewhispanic.org/2013/06/19/hispanics-of-puerto-rican-origin-in-the-united-states-2011/.

78. Samuel Cruz, *Masked Africanisms: Puerto Rican Pentecostalism* (Dubuque, IA, Kendall/Hunt Publishing Company, 2005), chap 2.

79. Ibid., chap 2.

80. Lorrin Thomas, *Puerto Rican Citizen: History and Political Identity in Twentieth-Century New York City* (Chicago, IL: University of Chicago Press, 2010), 35.

81. Martha Menchaca, *Naturalizing Mexican Immigrants: A Texas History* (Austin: University of Texas Press, 2011), chap 4.

82. Rogelio and Morales also discuss the complexities of the Bracero Program, 32–34.

83. Virginia Sanchez Korrol, *From Colonia to Community: The History of Puerto Ricans in New York City* (Berkeley: University of California Press, 1994), 17.

84. Thomas, *Puerto Rican Citizen*, 256.

85. Korrol, *From Colonia to Community*, chap 2.

86. María Cristina García, "Exiles, Immigrants, and Transnationals" in *The Columbia History of Latinos in the United States since 1960*, ed. David Gutiérrez (New York: Columbia University Press, 2004), 81.

87. Ruth E. Wasem, "Cuban Migration to the United States: Policy and Trends." Library of Congress Congressional Research Service, Washington, DC, June 2, 2009 accessed May 1, 2016, http://fpc.state.gov/documents/organization/125936.pdf. See also David G. Gutiérrez, "An Historic Overview of Latino Immigration and the Demographic Transformation of the United States," National Park Service U.S. Department of the Interior, 2013, accessed April 10, 2016, https://www.nps.gov/heritageinitiatives/latino/latinothemestudy/immigration.htm.

88. Sarah J. Mahler and Katrin Hansing, "Toward a Transnationalism of the Middle: How Transnational Religious Practices Help Bridge the Divides between Cuba and Miami," *Latin American Perspectives* 32, no. 1 (2005): 121–46.

89. Migration Policy Institute, "Central American Immigrants in the United States," Washington DC, September 2, 2015, accessed June 1, 2016, http://www.migrationpolicy.org/article/central-american-immigrants-united-states.

90. Norma Stoltz Chinchilla and Nora Hamilton, "Central American Immigrants: Diverse Populations, Changing Communities," in *The Columbia History of Latinos in the United States since 1960*, ed. David Gutiérrez (New York: Columbia University Press, 2004), 146.

91. Gutiérrez, "An Historic Overview of Latino Immigration."

92. Chinchilla and Hamilton, "Central American Immigrants," 146; Migration Policy Institute, "Central American Immigrants in the United States."

93. Pew Research Center, "With Help from Mexico, Number of Child Migrants Crossing U.S. Border Falls." Washington, DC, April 28, 2015, accessed, April 12, 2016, http://www.pewresearch.org/fact-tank/2015/04/28/child-migrants-border/.

94. Peggy Levitt, *God Needs No Passport. Immigrants and the Changing Religious Landscape* (New York: The New Press, 2007).

95. Pew Research Center, "Unauthorized Immigrant Population: National and State Trends," Washington, DC, February 1, 2011, accessed, April 6, 2016, http://www.pewhispanic.org/2011/02/01/unauthorized-immigrant-population-brnational-and-state-trends-2010/. See also Pew Research Center, "Modern Immigration Wave Brings 59 Million to U.S., Driving Population Growth and Change Through 2065," Washington, DC, September 28, 2015, accessed, March 26, 2016, http://www.pewhispanic.org/2015/09/28/modern-immigration-wave-brings-59-million-to-u-s-driving-population-growth-and-change-through-2065/.

96. See Peggy Levitt, "God Needs No Passport: Trying to Define the New Boundaries of Belonging," in the *Harvard Divinity Bulletin*, Autumn 2006, accessed April 2, 2016, http://bulletin.hds.harvard.edu/articles/autumn2006/god-needs-no-passport.

97. Vegard Skirbekk, Eric Kaufmann, and Anne Goujon, "Secularism, Fundamentalism, or Catholicism? The Religious Composition of the United States to 2043," *Journal for the Scientific Study of Religion* 49 (2010): 293–310.

98. Larry L. Hunt, "Hispanic Protestantism in the United States: Trends by Decade and Generation," *Social Forces* 77 (1999): 1623.

99. Pew Research Center, "'Nones' on the Rise." Washington, DC, August 23, 2016, http://www.pewforum.org/2012/10/09/nones-on-the-rise/. For more on Latino secularization, see Rogelio Sáenz and Maria Cristina Morales, *Latinos in the United States: Diversity and Change* (Cambridge, MA: Polity Press, 2015), 155–156.

100. In 2013, 18 percent of Latinos in the Pew Research Survey of Latino Adults identified as being religious unaffiliated.

101. Pew Research Center, "The Shifting Religious Identity of Latinos in the United States," Washington, DC, May 7, 2014, accessed April 4, 2016, http://www.pewforum.org/2014/05/07/the-shifting-religious-identity-of-latinos-in-the-united-states/.

102. Ibid.

103. Virginia Garrard-Burnett, *Protestantism in Guatemala: Living in the New Jerusalem* (Austin: University of Texas Press, 1998) and David B. Barrett, George T. Kurian, and Todd M. Johnson, *World Christian Encyclopaedia* (New York: Oxford University Press, 1998).

104. Skirbekk et al., "Secularism, Fundamentalism, or Catholicism?," 293–310.

105. Andrés Villarreal, "Explaining the Decline in Mexico-US Migration: The Effect of the Great Recession," *Demography* 51 (2014): 2203–28, and Douglas S. Massey, "Immigration and the Great Recession," Stanford Center on Poverty, October, 1, 2012, accessed May 31, 2016, https://web.stanford.edu/group/recessiontrends/cgi-bin/web/sites/all/themes/barron/pdf/Immigration_fact_sheet.pdf.

106. Pew Research Center, "5 Facts about Mexico and Immigration to the U.S.," Washington, DC, June 11, 2016, accessed March 28, 2016, http://www.pewresearch.org/fact-tank/2016/02/11/mexico-and-immigration-to-us/.

107. Pew Research Center, "More Mexicans Leaving Than Coming to the U.S.," Washington, DC, November 19, 2015, accessed March 28, 2016, http://www.pewresearch.org/fact-tank/2016/02/11/mexico-and-immigration-to-us/.

108. Pew Research Center, "US Population Projections: 2005–2050," Washington, DC, February 11, 2008, accessed March 28, 2016, http://www.pewhispanic.org/2008/02/11/us-population-projections-2005-2050/.

109. Pew Research Center, "10 Demographic Trends That Are Shaping the U.S. and World," Washington, DC, March 31, 2016, accessed June 3, 2016, http://www.pewresearch.org/fact-tank/2016/03/31/10-demographic-trends-that-are-shaping-the-u-s-and-the-world/.

110. Pew Research Center, "The Shifting Religious Identity of Latinos in the United States."

111. Idelissa Malave and Esti Giordani, *Latino Stats: American Hispanics by the Numbers* (New York: The New Press, 2015), 63.

112. Matthew 28: 16–20 NIV.

113. "Azusa Now LiveStream 04.09.2016," on YouTube last modified April 9, 2016, https://www.youtube.com/watch?v=ZK2DkDKejcs.

114. Aida I. Ramos. "What Makes a Latino Church?" (paper presented at the annual meeting for the Society of the Scientific Study of Religion, Newport, California, October 23–25, 2015).

3. THE LATINO REFORMATION TODAY

1. Chesnut, R Andrew, *Born Again in Brazil: The Pentecostal Boom and the Pathogens of Poverty* (New Brunswick, NJ: Rutgers University Press, 1997), chap 1; and Timothy J. Steigenga and Edward L. Cleary, *Conversion of a Continent: Contemporary Religious Change in Latin America* (New Brunswick, NJ: Rutgers University Press, 2007), 7.

2. Ana Maria Diaz-Stevens and Anthony M Stevens-Arroyo, *Recognizing the Latino Resurgence in U.S. Religion: The Emmaus Paradig* (Boulder, CO: Westview Press, 1997),; and Larry L. Hunt, "Hispanic Protestantism in the United States: Trends by Decade and Generation," *Social Forces* 77 (1999): 1623.

3. Gastón Espinosa, Virgilio P Elizondo, and Jesse Miranda, *Latino Religions and Civic Activism in the United States* (New York: Oxford University Press, 2005), 6.

4. Pew Research Center, "The Shifting Religious Identity of Latinos in the United States," Washington, DC, May 7, 2014, accessed April 4, 2016, http://www.pewforum.org/2014/05/07/the-shifting-religious-identity-of-latinos-in-the-united-states/.

5. Juhem Navarro-Rivera, Barry A Kosmin, and Ariela Keysar, "U.S. Latino Religious Identification, 1990–2008: Growth, Diversity, & Transformation," (Hartford, CT: Trinity College, 2008), accessed March 29, 2016, http://

commons.trincoll.edu/aris/files/2011/08/latinos2008.pdf. Note that in the Trinity report the greatest proportion of growth was in the category of Latino "nones," those who claimed no religious affiliation.

6. For more on the LPC Project, see the appendix.

7. While Catholics are, of course, also Christians, this is a colloquial term sometimes used among Latinos Protestants to describe themselves.

8. Elizabeth Dias, "Evangélicos!" *Time*, April 15, 2013, 20–26.

9. Pope Pius XII, "Divino Afflante Spiritu," Encyclical of Pope Pius XII on Promoting Biblical Studies, Commemorating the Fiftieth Anniversary of Providentissimus Deus, 1943.

10. Christian Smith and Robert Faris, "Socioeconomic Inequality in the American Religious System: An Update and Assessment," *Journal for the Scientific Study of Religion* 44(1) (2005): 95–104; and Lisa A. Keister, "Religion and Wealth: The Role of Religious Affiliation and Participation in Early Adult Asset Accumulation," *Social Forces* 82 (2013): 175–207.

11. Lisa A. Keister, *Faith and Money: How Religion Contributes to Wealth and Poverty* (Cambridge, UK: Cambridge University Press, 2011), 70.

12. Scott Fitzgerald and Jennifer Glass, "Conservative Religion, Early Transitions to Adulthood and the Intergenerational Transmission of Class," *Research in the Sociology of Work* 23 (2012): 49–72; Conrad Hackett and D. Michael Lindsay, "Measuring Evangelicalism: Consequences of Different Operationalization Strategies," *Journal for the Scientific Study of Religion* 47 (2008): 499–514.

13. Alfred Darnell and Darren E. Sherkat, "The Impact of Protestant Fundamentalism on Educational Attainment," *American Sociological Review* (1997): 306–15; Lisa A. Keister and Darren E. Sherkat, *Religion and Inequality in America: Research and Theory on Religion's Role in Stratification* (Cambridge, UK: Cambridge University Press, 2014), 107.

14. Fitzgerald and Glass, "Conservative Religion, Early Transitions."

15. "Facts for Features: Hispanic Heritage Month 2014: Sept. 15–Oct. 15," last modified September 8, 2014, http://www.census.gov/newsroom/facts-for-features/2014/cb14-ff22.html.

16. Larry L. Hunt, "Hispanic Protestantism in the United States: Trends by Decade and Generation," *Social Forces* 77, no. 4 (1999):1601–24.

17. Pew Research Center, "Changing Faiths: Latinos and the Transformation of American Religion," Washington, DC, April 25, 2007, accessed April 4, 2016, http://www.pewhispanic.org/2007/04/25/changing-faiths-latinos-and-the-transformation-of-american-religion/.

18. Juhem Navarro-Rivera, Barry A. Kosmin, and Ariela Keysar, "U.S. Latino Religious Identification, 1990–2008: Growth, Diversity, & Transformation,"

Hartford, CT: Trinity College, 2008, accessed March 29, 2016, http://commons.trincoll.edu/aris/files/2011/08/latinos2008.pdf.

19. Ibid., 11.

20. Lisa A. Keister and E. Paige Borelli, "Religion and Wealth Mobility: The Case of American Latinos," in *Religion and Inequality in America: Research and Theory on Religion's Role in Stratification*, edited by Lisa A. Keister and Darren E. Sherkat (New York: Cambridge University Press, 2014), 119–45.

21. Ibid., 108.

22. Esmeralda Sánchez, "Latina, Pentecostal, and College-Bound," *Christianity Today*, last modified December 2014, acessed June 10, 2016, http://www.christianitytoday.com/women/2014/december/latina-pentecostal-and-college-bound.html.

23. Juhem Navarro-Rivera, Barry A. Kosmin, and Ariela Keysar, "U.S. Latino Religious Identification, 1990–2008: Growth, Diversity, & Transformation," Hartford, CT: Trinity College, 2008, accessed March 29, 2016,http://commons.trincoll.edu/aris/files/2011/08/latinos2008.pdf.

24. Edward E. Telles and Vilma Ortiz, *Generations of Exclusion: Mexican Americans, Assimilation, and Race* (New York: Russell Sage Foundation, 2008), 187.

25. Navarro-Rivera et al., "U.S. Latino Religious Identification," 17.

26. "Changing Faiths: Latinos and the Transformation of American Religion," 9.

27. Aida I. Ramos, Robert Woodberry, and Christopher Ellison, "The Contexts of Conversions among Latinos," under review, George Fox University, 2016.

28. Navarro-Rivera, Kosmin, and Keysar, "U. S. Latino Religious Identification", 15.

29. Jonathan E. Calvillo and Stanley R. Bailey, "Latino Religious Affiliation and Ethnic Identity," *Journal for the Scientific Study of Religion* 54, no. 1 (2015): 57–78.

30. Ramos, Woodberry, and Ellison, "The Contexts of Conversion among U.S. Latinos, 17."

31. David B. Barrett, George Thomas Kurian, and Todd M. Johnson. *World Christian Encyclopedia: Religionists, Churches, Ministries: A Comparative Survey of Churches and Religions in the Modern World* (New York: Oxford University Press, 2001).

32. Ibid, 6.

33. Pew Research Center, "Changing Faiths," 1–151.

34. Laurence R. Iannaccone, "Voodoo Economics? Reviewing the Rational Choice Approach to Religion," *Journal for the Scientific Study of Religion* 34,

no. 1 (1995): 76–88; Rodney Stark and William Sims Bainbridge, *A Theory of Religion* (New York: Peter Lang, 1987).

35. Iannaccone, "Voodoo Economics," 76–88.

36. Darren Sherkat, "Embedding Religious Choices: Preferences and Social Constraints into Rational Choice Theories of Religious Behavior," in *Rational Choice Theory and Religion*, edited by Lawrence A. Young (New York: Routledge, 1997), 65–68.

37. Christopher G. Ellison and Darren E. Sherkat, "The 'Semi-involuntary Institution' Revisited: Regional Variations in Church Participation Among Black Americans," *Social Forces* 73, no. 4 (1995): 1415–37.

38. Ramos, Woodberry, and Ellison, "The Contexts of Conversions among Latinos."

39. Norma Williams, *The Mexican American Family: Tradition and Change* (Lanham, MD: AltaMira Press, 1990).

40. Virginia Garrard-Burnett, *Protestantism in Guatemala: Living in the New Jerusalem* (Austin: University of Texas Press, 1998), 67.

41. David Martin, *Tongues of Fire: The Explosion of Protestantism in Latin America* (Cambridge, MA: Blackwell Publishers, 1990). See also Luís León, "Born Again in East LA: The Congregation as Border Space," in *Gatherings in Diaspora: Religious Communities and the New Immigration*, edited by R. Stephen Warner and Judith G. Wittner (Philadelphia, PA: Temple University Press, 1998), 163–96.

42. Elizabeth E. Brusco, *The Reformation of Machismo: Evangelical Conversion and Gender in Colombia* (Austin: University of Texas Press, 2011).

43. León, "Born Again," 165.

44. David Smilde, *Reason to Believe: Cultural Agency in Latin American Evangelicalism* (Berkeley: University of California Press, 2007), 98.

45. León, "Born Again," 188.

46. Marie Friedmann Marquardt, "From Shame to Confidence: Gender, Religious Conversation and Civic Engagement of Mexicans in the U.S. South," *Latin American Perspectives* 32, no. 1 (2005): 27–56.

47. Aida I. Ramos, "Understanding Reasons for Latino/a Catholic to Protestant Conversion," unpublished manuscript, George Fox University.

48. Stuart A. Wright, "Reconceptualizing Cult Coercion and Withdrawal: A Comparative Analysis of Divorce and Apostasy," *Social Forces* 70, no. 1 (1991): 125–45.

49. Debbie Berho, "Not Segregated: Mutual Collaboration and Shared Worship among Spanish- and English-Speaking Congregations of Oregon," (paper presented at the annual meeting of the Society for the Scientific Study of Religion, Newport Beach, CA, October 23–25, 2016).

4. ETHNIC IDENTITY AND VARIETIES OF LATINO PROTESTANT CHURCHES

1. In order to ensure confidentiality and privacy of research participants, all names of churches names and people are pseudonyms.

2. Richard Schaefer, *Encyclopedia of Race, Ethnicity, and Society* (Thousand Oaks, CA: Sage, 2008), xlvii.

3. Ibid., xlvii.

4. Edward E. Telles and Vilma Ortiz, *Generations of Exclusion: Mexican Americans, Assimilation, and Race* (New York: Russell Sage Foundation, 2008), 236.

5. Craig A. Kaplowitz, *LULAC, Mexican Americans, and National Policy* (College Station: Texas A&M University Press, 2005), 30.

6. G. Cristina Mora, *Making Hispanics: How Activists, Bureaucrats, and Media Constructed a New American* (Chicago: University of Chicago Press, 2014), 38; Dina Okamoto and G. Cristina Mora, "Panethnicity," *Annual Review of Sociology* 40 (2014): 219–39.

7. Mora, "Panethnicity," 40; Pew Research Center, "Census History: Counting Hispanics," Washington, DC, March 3, 2010, accessed February 5, 2016, http://www.pewsocialtrends.org/2010/03/03/census-history-counting-hispanics-2/.

8. Linda Martín Alcoff, "Latino vs. Hispanic: The Politics of Ethnic Names," *Philosophy & Social Criticism* 31, no. 4 (2005): 395–407.

9. G. Cristina Mora, "Cross-Field Effects and Ethnic Classification: The Institutionalization of Hispanic Panethnicity, 1965 to 1990," *American Sociological Review* 79 (2014): 183–210.

10. Julie A. Dowling, *Mexican Americans and the Question of Race* (Austin: University of Texas Press, 2014), 6.

11. Pew Research Center, "Religion in Latin America: Widespread Change in a Historically Catholic Region," Washington, DC, November 13, 2014, accessed December 23, 2015, http://www.pewforum.org/2014/11/13/religion-in-latin-america/.

12. Sharon Sandomirsky and John Wilson, "Processes of Disaffiliation: Religious Mobility among Men and Women," *Social Forces* 68 (1990): 1213.

13. Luis D. León, *The Political Spirituality of Cesar Chavez: Crossing Religious Borders* (Berkeley: University of California Press, 2014), 2.

14. Sandomirsky and Wilson, "Processes of Disaffiliation," 1211–29.

15. Jonathan E. Calvillo and Stanley R. Bailey, "Latino Religious Affiliation and Ethnic Identity," *Journal for the Scientific Study of Religion* 54 (2015): 57–78; Aida I. Ramos, Robert Woodberry, and Christopher Ellison, "The Con-

texts of Conversions Among Latinos," Unpublished manuscript, University of Texas at San Antonio, 2016.

16. Daniel R. Rodríguez-Díaz and David Cortés-Fuentes, *Hidden Stories: Unveiling the History of the Latino Church* (Decatur, GA: AETH, Asociación para la Educación Teológica, 1994), xi.

17. Justo González and Odina González, *Nuestra Fe: A Latin American Church History Sourcebook* (Nashville, TN: Abingdon Press, 2014).

18. Daniel R. Rodríguez-Díaz and David Cortés-Fuentes, *Hidden Stories: Unveiling the History of the Latino Church* (Orlando, FL: AETH, Asociación para la Educación Teológica Hispana), 1994.

19. Ibid., xiii.

20. Ibid., 3.

21. Milmon F. Harrison, *Righteous Riches: The Word of Faith Movement in Contemporary African American Religion* (New York: Oxford University Press, 2005); Gerardo Martí, *Hollywood Faith: Holiness, Prosperity, and Ambition in a Los Angeles Church* (New Brunswick, NJ: Rutgers University Press, 2008); Kate Bowler, *Blessed: A History of the American Prosperity Gospel* (New York: Oxford University Press, 2013).

22. This includes adults and children.

23. The exception would be the youth who use it at times for certain words.

24. The part of the sermon in which people are asked to publicly commit their lives to Christianity by "accepting Jesus Christ" though a prayer commonly known as "The Sinner's Prayer" or "Prayer for Salvation."

25. Galations 3:28 NIV

26. Only one informant emphasized that they hoped that that term could be inapplicable one day and that there would be people of many race/ethnic labels at the church.

27. Dowling, *Mexican Americans and the Question of Race*, 20.

5. THE CENTRALITY OF "DOING CHURCH" AMONG LATINO PROTESTANTS

1. Kurt Streeter, "Spreading the Pentecostal Spirit," *Los Angeles Times*, February 2, 2014, accessed July 22, 2015, http://www.latimes.com/local/la-me-latino-pentecostal-20140202-story.html#page=1.

2. Ibid.

3. See James P. Wind and James W. Lewis, ed., *American Congregations, Volume 1: Portraits of Twelve Religious Communities* (Chicago: University of Chicago Press, 1994), 1.

4. Robert Putnam and David Campbell, *American Grace: How Religion Divides and Unites Us* (New York: Simon & Schuster, 2010).

5. Pew Research Center, "The Shifting Religious Identity of Latinos in the United States," Washington, DC, May 7, 2014, 52, accessed May 15, 2014, http://www.pewforum.org/2014/05/07/the-shifting-religious-identity-of-latinos-in-the-united-states/.

6. Marilynn Johnson, "'The Quiet Revival:' New Immigrants and the Transformation of Christianity in Greater Boston," *Religion and American Culture: A Journal of Interpretation* 24 (2014): 231–58.

7. Elizabeth Dias, "Evangélicos!" *Time*, April 15, 2013, 25.

8. Ibid.

9. Ibid., 26.

10. Juan Francisco Martínez, *Los Protestantes: An Introduction to Latino Protestantism in the United States* (Westport, CT: Praeger, 2011).

11. Likely a paraphrasing of 1 Corinthians 14:33: "For God is not a God of disorder but of peace." New International Version.

12. Pew Research Center, "The Shifting Religious Identity," 76–83.

13. Norman Eli Ruano. "The Holy Ghost Beyond the Church Walls: Latino Pentecostalism(s), Congregations, and Civic Engagement," (PhD diss., Loyola University-Chicago, 2011), 255.http://ecommons.luc.edu/luc_diss/267.

14. Pew Research Center, "Latinos, Religion and Campaign 2012: Catholics Favor Obama, Evangelicals Divided," Washington, DC, October 18, 2012, 9, accessed June 13, 2015, http://www.pewforum.org/2012/10/18/latinos-religion-and-campaign-2012/.

15. Dias, "Evangélicos!," 28.

16. Streeter, "Spreading the Pentecostal Spirit."

17. Ruano, "The Holy Ghost Beyond the Church Walls," 241.

18. Ibid., 249.

19. Ibid., 282.

20. Ibid., 283.

21. Pew Research Center, "The Shifting Religious Identity," 93

22. Ibid., 93–109. The study reports that over half (52 percent) of Latino Catholics can be classified as renewalists.

23. Ibid., 94.

24. Ibid., 95.

25. Ibid., 95–96.

26. Ibid., 103.

27. Ibid., 98.

28. For more on religious disaffiliation, see Pew Research Center, "America's Changing Religious Landscape," Washington, DC, May 12, 2015, 4, accessed March 22, 2016, http://www.pewforum.org/2015/05/12/americas-

changing-religious-landscape/. Pew notes a drop in percentage of Christians in the United States from 78.4 percent in 2007 to 70.6 percent in 2014.

29. For instance, see David T. Abalos, *Latinos in the United States: The Sacred and the Political* (South Bend, IN: University of Notre Dame Press, 2007).

30. Ibid., 139.

31. Dias, "Evangélicos!," 23–24.

32. Pew Research Center, May 7, 2014, 46.

33. Ibid., 49.

34. Ibid., 52.

35. Ruano, "The Holy Ghost Beyond the Church Walls," 266.

36. Ibid., 269.

37. Pew Research Center, "The Shifting Religious Identity," 124.

38. Ruano, "The Holy Ghost Beyond the Church Walls," 251.

39. Edwin I. Hernández, Jeffrey Smith, Rebecca Burwell, Milagros Peña, and David Sikkink, "Healing Hands: The Health of Latino/a Churchgoers and Health Outreach among Latino Congregations in Chicago" (South Bend, IN: Institute for Latino Studies and Center for the Study of Latino Religion, University of Notre Dame, 2010), 4, accessed May 20, 2016, https://latinostudies.nd.edu/assets/95269/original/congregations_final_pages.pdf.

40. Sujey Vega, *Latino Heartland: Of Borders and Belonging in the Midwest* (New York: New York University Press, 2015), 79.

41. Ibid.

42. Ibid., 87–88.

43. Ibid., 88.

44. Ibid.

45. Ibid., 97.

46. Ibid., 77.

47. Ibid.

48. In particular, Vega cites Jill DeTemple, "Chains of Liberation: Poverty and Social Action in the Universal Church of the Kingdom of God," in *Latino Religious and Civic Activism in the United States*, ed. Gastón Espinosa, Virgil Elizonda, and Jesse Miranda (New York: Oxford University Press, 2005), 219–32.

49. Vega, *Latino Heartland*, 90.

50. Dias, "Evangélicos!," 24.

51. Johnson, "'The Quiet Revival,'" 244.

52. Dias, "Evangélicos!," 24.

53. Salguero is also president of the National Latino Evangelical Coalition and pastor of Iglesia El Calvario in Orlando, Florida.

54. Stephen Nessen, "Latinos Drawn to Evangelicalism Seem Immune to 'Francis Effect.'" *WNYC News*, July 9, 2015, accessed July 27, 2015, http://www.wnyc.org/story/new-yorks-lapsed-catholics-are-resisting-francis-effect/.

55. Vega, *Latino Heartland*, 88.

56. Ibid., 90.

57. DeTemple, "Chains of Liberation," 2005.

58. Vega, *Latino Heartland*, 90.

59. See Pew Research Center, "The Shifting Religious Identity of Latinos in the United States," May 7, 2014, 83: 61 percent of all Latinos attend congregations where "most/all" members are Latino while 16 percent attend where "few/none" are Latino.

60. Jane Juffer, "Hybrid Faiths: Latino Protestants Find a Home Among the Dutch Reformed in Iowa," *Latino Studies* 6 (2008): 290–312.

61. Laura López-Sanders, "Bible-Belt Immigrants: Latino Religious Incorporation in New Immigrant Destinations," *Latino Studies* 10 (2012): 128–54.

62. Juffer, "Hybrid Faiths," 302.

63. Ibid., 303.

64. López-Sanders, "Bible-Belt Immigrants," 136.

65. Ibid., 138.

66. Ibid.

6. LATINO PROTESTANTS AND THEIR POLITICAL AND SOCIAL ENGAGEMENT

1. It should be noted that "Latino" continues to be the subject of debate as to whether it is best understood as a racial or ethnic category. For insight into the debate, see Pew Research Center, "Is Being Hispanic a Matter of Race, Ethnicity, or Both?" Washington DC, June 15, 2015, accessed February 23, 2016, http://www.pewresearch.org/fact-tank/2015/06/15/is-being-hispanic-a-matter-of-race-ethnicity-or-both/. Also see a brief history on page 4 of David Rennie, "America's Hispanics: From Minor to Major," *Economist*, March 14, 2015, accessed February 22, 2016, http://www.economist.com/sites/default/files/20150314_sr_hispanics.pdf.

2. Rennie, "America's Hispanics," 1.

3. Pew Research Center, "Latino Voters and the 2014 Midterm Elections: Geography, Close Races, and Views of Social Issues," Washington, DC, October 16, 2014, accessed March 1, 2016, http://www.pewhispanic.org/2014/10/16/latino-voters-and-the-2014-midterm-elections/.

4. Rennie, "America's Hispanics," 2.

5. U.S. Census Bureau, "The Hispanic Population: 2010," May 2011, 2, accessed February 22, 2016, http://www.census.gov/prod/cen2010/briefs/c2010br-04.pdf.

6. Marta Tienda and Norma Fuentes, "Hispanics in Metropolitan America: New Realities and Old Debates," *Annual Review of Sociology* 40 (2014): 500.

7. See Jeremy Rehwaldt, "Responses by White Christians to Recent Latino Immigration in the Rural U.S. Midwest," *Religions* 6 (2015): 686–711.

8. Tienda and Fuentes, "Hispanics in Metropolitan America," 515.

9. See H. B. Marrow, *New Destination Dreaming: Immigration, Race, and Legal Status in the Rural American South* (Stanford, CA: Stanford University Press, 2011).

10. Idelisse Malavé and Esti Girodani, *Latino Stats: American Hispanics by the Numbers* (New York: The New Press, 2015), 58.

11. Ibid., 64.

12. Ibid., 65.

13. Ibid., 64.

14. Ibid., 38.

15. Ibid., 49.

16. Tienda and Fuentes, "Hispanics in Metropolitan America," 504.

17. Jessica Martínez, Edwin I. Hernández, Rebecca Burwell, Milagros Peña, and David Sikkink, "The Politics of the Latino Church: Understanding the Political Views and Behaviors of Latino Congregations in Chicago" (South Bend, IN: Center for the Study of Religion and Society, University of Notre Dame, September 14, 2012), accessed June 14, 2015, https://csrs.nd.edu/assets/81194/the_politics_of_the_latino_church_final.pdf.

18. Tienda and Fuentes, "Hispanics in Metropolitan America," 515.

19. Martínez et al., "The Politics of the Latino Church," p. 8.

20. See Gastón Espinsosa, "Latino Clergy and Churches in Faith-Based Political and Social Action in the United States," in *Latino Religions and Civic Activism in the United States*, ed. Gastón Espinosa, Virgilio Elizondo, and Jesse Miranda (New York: Oxford University Press, 2005). In particular, Espinosa reports on pp. 279–80 that "Latino Protestants were just as likely to be politically active as their white and black counterparts." He also cites a 1995 study that indicated that "Latino Protestants are more likely than Catholics to engage in skill-endowing activities that can be transferred into the political arena."

21. Paul A. Djupe and Jacob R. Neiheisel, "How Religious Communities Affect Political Participation among Latinos," *Social Science Quarterly* 93 (2012): 352.

22. Ibid., 349.

23. Norman Eli Ruano, "The Holy Ghost beyond the Church Walls: Latino Pentecostalism(s), Congregations, and Civic Engagement" (PhD diss., Loyola University Chicago, 2011), 276, accessed November 15, 2015, http://ecommons.luc.edu/luc_diss/267.

24. Ibid., 268.

25. Elizabeth Dias, "Evangélicos!" *Time*, April 15, 2013, 26.

26. The key issues that seem to drive Latino tendency to support the Democratic Party include education, jobs and the economy, health care, and immigration reform. For more detail, see Pew Research Center, "Latino Support for Democrats Falls, But Democratic Advantage Remains," Washington, DC, October 29, 2014, accessed July 15, 2015, http://www.pewhispanic.org/2014/10/29/latino-support-for-democrats-falls-but-democratic-advantage-remains/.

27. Pew Research Center, "Democrats Maintain Edge as Party 'More Concerned' for Latinos, but Views Similar to 2012," Washington, DC, October 11, 2016, accessed December 26, 2016, http://www.pewhispanic.org/2016/10/11/democrats-maintain-edge-as-party-more-concerned-for-latinos-but-views-similar-to-2012/. We also note that some research has indicated an interesting urban and rural divide among Latinos that manifested during the 2016 election that, again, reinforces our contention regarding heterogeneity *within* the Latino voting bloc. See Geraldo L. Cadava, "Rural Hispanic Voters—Like Rural White Voters—Shifted Toward Trump: Here's Why," *The Washington Post*, November 17, 2016, accessed December 26, 2016, https://www.washingtonpost.com/news/monkey-cage/wp/2016/11/17/rural-hispanic-voters-like-white-rural-voters-shifted-toward-trump-heres-why/?utm_term=.b0e6a53a81ae.

28. Pew Research Center, "Hillary Won Latino Vote but Fell Below 2012 Support for Obama," Washington, DC, November 29, 2016, accessed December 12, 2016, http://www.pewresearch.org/fact-tank/2016/11/29/hillary-clinton-wins-latino-vote-but-falls-below-2012-support-for-obama/.

29. Mary Jordan, "'He's Cuban. I'm Mexican.': Can Rubio and Cruz Connect with Latino Voters?" *Washington Post*, January 10, 2016, accessed March 31, 2016, https://www.washingtonpost.com/politics/2016/01/10/32d20f8e-b4bc-11e5-a842-0feb51d1d124_story.html.

30. John P. Bartkowski, Chris G. Ellison, Aida I. Ramos-Wada, and Gabriel A. Acevedo, "Faith, Race-Ethnicity, and Public Policy Preferences: Religious Schemas and Abortion Attitudes among U.S. Latinos." *Journal for the Scientific Study of Religion* 51 (2012): 356.

31. Russell Moore, "Evangelical Hispanics and the 2016 Vote: GOP Candidates Talking about Immigration Need to Take into Account This Growing Demographic," *Wall Street Journal*, May 7, 2015, accessed May 7, 2015, http://www.wsj.com/articles/evangelical-hispanics-and-the-2016-vote-1431040230.

32. See Louis DeSipio, "Power in the Pews? Religious Diversity and Latino Political Attitudes and Behaviors," in *From Pews to Polling Places: Faith and Politics in the American Religious Mosaic*, ed. J. M. Wilson (Washington, DC: Georgetown University Press, 2007): 161–84; and Jongho Lee and Harry P. Pachon, "Leading the Way: An Analysis of the Effect of Religion on the Latino Vote," *American Politics Research* 35 (2007): 252–72.

33. Ali Adam Valenzuela, "Tending the Flock: Latino Religious Commitments and Political Preferences." *Political Research Quarterly* 67 (2014): 936.

34. Valenzuela, "Tending the Flock."

35. Cadava, Geraldo L. "Rural Hispanic Voters—Like Rural White Voters—Shifted Toward Trump: Here's Why," *The Washington Post*, November 17, 2016. Accessed December 26, 2016. https://www.washingtonpost.com/news/monkey-cage/wp/2016/11/17/rural-hispanic-voters-like-white-rural-voters-shifted-toward-trump-heres-why/?utm_term=.b0e6a53a81ae.

36. Pew Research Center, "Latinos, Religion, and Campaign 2012: Catholics Favor Obama, Evangelicals Divided," Washington DC, October 18, 2012, accessed March 15, 2015, http://www.pewforum.org/2012/10/18/latinos-religion-and-campaign-2012/.

37. Pew Research Center, "The Shifting Religious Identity of Latinos in the United States: Nearly One in Four Are Former Catholics," Washington, DC, May 7, 2014, 128.

38. Ibid.

39. Pew Research Center, "Trends in Party Identification of Religious Groups," Washington, DC, February 2, 2012, accessed March 20, 2015, http://www.pewforum.org/2012/02/02/trends-in-party-identification-of-religious-groups/.

40. Malavé and Giordani, *Latino Stats*, 29.

41. Ibid., 30. The 36 percent figure is a slightly higher percentage than Pew finds.

42. Brian D. McKenzie and Stella M. Rouse, "Shades of Faith: Religious Foundations of Political Attitudes among African Americans, Latinos, and Whites," *American Journal of Political Science* 57 (2013): 219. This article stands as a significant discussion of religious impulses in political differences between different racial categories. However, McKenzie and Rouse do not filter for distinctions between Latino Catholics and Latino Protestants.

43. Ibid., 220.

44. Martínez et al., "The Politics of the Latino Church," 9–10.

45. Pew Research Center, "The Shifting Religious Identity of Latinos in the United States," 130.

46. James L. Guth, "Religion and American Public Attitudes on War and Peace," *Asian Journal of Peacebuilding* 1 (2013): 227–52.

47. Ibid., 236.

48. Ibid., 241.

49. Martínez et al., "The Politics of the Latino Church," 25.

50. Robert T. Jones, Daniel Cox, and Juhem Navarro, "2013 Hispanic Values Survey: How Shifting Religious Identities and Experiences Are Influencing Hispanic Approaches to Politics," Public Religion Research Institute, September 27, 2013, 14–15, accessed March 20, 2015, http://www.prri.org/research/hispanic-values-survey-2013/.

51. Pew Research Center, "Latino Support for Democrats Falls."

52. Jones et al., "2013 Hispanic Values Survey."

53. Ibid., p. 16.

54. Pew Research Center, "Changing Faiths: Latinos and the Transformation of American Religion," Washington, DC, April 25, 2007, 61–62.

55. Hernández et al., "The Politics of the Latino Church," 10.

56. Pew Research Center, "Changing Faiths," 60. It should be noted that 57 percent of Latino Catholics agreed with the statement as well.

57. Espinosa, "Latino Clergy and Churches," 300.

58. Hernández et al., "The Politics of the Latino Church," 17.

59. Ibid.

60. Ibid.

61. Pew Research Center, "Changing Faiths," 58.

62. See Christopher G. Ellison, Gabriel A. Acevedo, and Aida I. Ramos-Wada, "Religion and Attitudes toward Same-Sex Marriage among U.S. Latinos," *Social Science Quarterly* 92 (2011): 35–56.

63. Jones et al., "2013 Hispanic Values Survey," 3.

64. Quoted by Ellison et al., "Religion and Attitudes toward Same-Sex Marriage," 40.

65. See NHCLC, "Vision Statement," accessed June 3, 2015, https://nhclc.org/about-us/mission-vision-statement.

66. Ellison et al., "Religion and Attitudes toward Same-Sex Marriage," 42.

67. Regina Branton, Ana B. Franco, Jim Wenzel, and Robert D. Wrinkle, "Latino Attitudes toward Abortion and Marriage Equality: Examining the Influence of Religiosity, Acculturation, and Non-Response," *Journal of Religion and Society* 16 (2014): 11.

68. Ellison et al., "Religion and Attitudes toward Same-Sex Marriage," 47.

69. Ibid., 50.

70. Hernández et al., "The Politics of the Latino Church," 20.

71. Jones, Cox, and Navarro-Rivera found Latino Catholic support for same-sex marriage to even be a bit higher than did Pew: 62 percent. Jones at al., "2013 Hispanic Values Survey," 3.

72. Pew Research Center, "Latinos, Religion, and Campaign 2012," 7–8.

73. Christopher G. Ellison, Nicholas H. Wolfinger, and Aida I. Ramos-Wada, "Attitudes Toward Marriage, Divorce, Cohabitation, and Casual Sex Among Working-Age Latinos: Does Religion Matter?" *Journal of Family Issues* 34 (2012): 313.

74. Ibid., 301.

75. Branton et al., "Latino Attitudes toward Abortion and Marriage Equality," 15. These trends likely have been in place for awhile. A 2005 study that utilized data from 1990 also found that committed Latino Protestants, not Latino Catholics, represented the staunchest opponents of abortion within the U.S. Latino population. See Christopher G. Ellison, Samuel Echevarría, and Brad Smith, "Religion and Abortion Attitudes among U.S. Hispanics: Findings from the 1990 Latino National Political Survey." *Social Science Quarterly* 86 (2005): 192–208.

76. Pew Research Center, "The Shifting Religious Identity of Latinos in the United States," 120. Jones, Cox, and Navarro-Rivera report very similar numbers regarding attitudes toward abortion. A majority of Latino Catholics (52 percent say abortion should be legal in all cases—again, very comparable to Latino mainline Protestants. Nearly three-quarters of Latino evangelicals, on the other hand, say abortion should be illegal in all or most cases. See Jones at al., "2013 Hispanic Values Survey," 3–4.

77. Bartkowski et al., "Faith, Race-Ethnicity, and Public Policy Preferences," 343–58.

78. Ibid., 355.

79. Pew Research Center, "The Shifting Religious Identity of Latinos in the United States," 125.

80. Ibid., 126.

81. Ibid.

82. Ibid., 127.

83. Aida I Ramos, Christopher G. Ellison, and Walter Wilson, "Religion and Latino/a Attitudes toward the Poor and Government Assistance," unpublished manuscript.

84. Ibid., 15.

85. Pew Research Center, "Latinos, Religion, and Campaign 2012," 4.

86. Pew Research Center, "The Shifting Religious Identity of Latinos in the United States," 92.

87. Ibid. Also see Paul Barton, "Ya Basta! Latino/a Protestant Activism in the Chicano/a and Farm Workers Movements" in *Latino Religions and Civic Activism in the United States*, ed. Gastón Espinosa, Virgilio Elizondo, and Jesse Miranda (New York: Oxford University Press, 2005), 127–43. Barton discusses how Mexican American Protestants inherited from Anglo-American

missionaries "the idea that social reform was primarily a matter of evangelizing individuals so they could become productive and moral citizens."

88. Espinosa, 2005, 289. For instance, Latino Protestants are more likely than Latino Catholics to provide these types of services: gang outreach, immigrant support, day-care centers, ESL classes, citizenship classes, and after-school programs.

89. Pew Research Center, May 7, 2014, 50.

90. Espinosa, "Latino Clergy and Churches," 296.

91. See Jones at al., "2013 Hispanic Values Survey," 19.

92. Martínez et al., "The Politics of the Latino Church," 18.

93. Ibid., 22.

94. Gastón Espinosa, *Latino Pentecostals in America: Faith and Politics in Action* (Cambridge, MA: Harvard University Press, 2014).

95. Ibid., 322.

96. Ibid.

97. Ruano, "The Holy Ghost beyond the Church Walls," 16.

98. Kurt Streeter, "Spreading the Pentecostal Spirit." *Los Angeles Times*, February 2, 2014, accessed July 22, 2015, http://www.latimes.com/local/la-me-latino-pentecostal-20140202-story.html#page=1.

99. Edward Orozco Flores, *God's Gangs: Barrio Ministry, Masculinity, and Gang Recovery* (New York: New York University Press, 2014), 23.

100. Flores quotes Robert Brenneman, *Homies and Hermanos: God and Gangs in Central America* (New York: Oxford University Press, 2011), 164.

101. Luís León, "Born Again in East LA: The Congregation as Border Space," in *Gatherings in Diaspora: Religious Communities and the New Immigration*, ed. R. Stephen Warner and Judith G. Wittner (Philadelphia: Temple University Press, 1998), 163–96.

102. Flores, *God's Gangs*, 92.

103. Catherine E. Wilson, *The Politics of Latino Faith: Religion, Identity, and Urban Community* (New York: New York University Press, 2008), 3.

104. Ibid., 5.

105. Ibid., 93.

106. Ibid., 93.

107. Ibid., 116.

108. Ibid., 118.

109. Ibid., 134.

110. Ibid., 172.

111. Ibid., 138.

112. That type of strategic positioning has reaped dividends for Latino Protestant leaders: "Latino clergy and faith-based organizations are being courted by American presidents and political leaders to support their domestic policies

and political party platforms." See Gastón Espinosa, Virgilio Elizondo, and Jesse Miranda, "Conclusion: Assessing and Interpreting 150 Years of Latino Faith-Based Civic Activism," in *Latino Religions and Civic Activism in the United States*, ed. Gastón Espinosa, Virgilio Elizondo, and Jesse Miranda (New York: Oxford University Press, 2005), 310.

113. Wilson, *The Politics of Latino Faith*, 141.

114. Ibid.

115. Ibid., 158.

116. Ibid., 155.

117. Quoted in ibid., 140.

118. Ibid., 140

119. See NHCLC, "Vision Statement," accessed June 3, 2015, http://www.nhclc.org, accessed June 14, 2015.

120. Espinosa, *Latino Pentecostals in America*, 349.

121. See NHCLC, accessed June 14, 2015, http://www.nhclcorg.

122. See NHCLC, "Vision Statement," accessed June 19, 2015, https://nhclc.org/about-us/mission-vision-statement.

123. See James Oliphant, "Why Ted Cruz's Candidacy Isn't Catching Fire with U.S. Latinos," *Huffington Post*, accessed June 5, 2015, http://www.huffingtonpost.com/2015/06/05/ted-cruz-latinos_n_7517836.html.

124. Espinosa, *Latino Pentecostals in America*, 388.

125. Ibid., 395.

126. Tony Campolo and Shane Claiborne, "The Evangelicalism of Old White Men is Dead," *The New York Times*, November 29, 2016, accessed December 26, 2016, http://www.nytimes.com/2016/11/29/opinion/the-evangelicalism-of-old-white-men-is-dead.html?_r=0.

127. See NaLEC, "Categories Archives: Politics," accessed March 31, 2016, http://nalec.org/category/politics.

128. For more regarding Latino congregations and social capital, see the following case study from Immokalee, Florida: Philip J. Williams and Patricia Fortuny Loret de Mola, "Religion and Social Capital Among Mexican Immigrants in Southwest Florida," *Latino Studies* 5, no. 2 (207): 233–253.

7. LATINO PROTESTANTS AND THE FUTURE OF AMERICAN CHRISTIANITY

1. Anthony Daniel Perez and Charles Hirschman, "The Changing Racial and Ethnic Composition of the U.S. Population: Emerging American Identities," *Population and Development Review* 35 (2009): 1–51; Marta Tienda and Norma Fuentes, "Hispanics in Metropolitan America: New Realities and

Old Debates," *Annual Review of Sociology* 40 (2014): 499–520; U.S. Census Bureau, "The Hispanic Population: 2010," *2010 Census Briefs* (2011), accessed April 3 2015, http://www.census.gov/prod/cen2010/briefs/c2010br-04.pdf .

2. Pew Research Center, "Changing Faiths: Latinos and the Transformation of American Religion," April 25, 2007, Washington, DC, 7, accessed March 28, 2014, http://www.pewforum.org/files/2007/04/hispanics-religion-07-final-mar08.pdf.

3. Pew Research Center, "The Shifting Religious Identity of Latinos in the United States," Washington, DC, May 7, 2014, accessed May, 15, 2014, http://www.pewforum.org/2014/05/07/the-shifting-religious-identity-of-latinos-in-the-united-states/.

4. Gastón Espinosa, "The Pentecostalization of Latin American and U.S. Latino Christianity," *PNEUMA: The Journal of the Society for Pentecostal Studies* 26 (2004): 267; Andrew M. Greeley. "The Demography of American Catholics: 1965–1990," in *Religion and the Social Order: Vatican II and U.S. Catholicism*, ed. Helen Rose Ebaugh (Greenwich, CT: JAI Press, 1991); Larry Hunt, "The Spirit of Hispanic Protestantism in the United States: National Survey Comparisons of Catholics and non-Catholics," *Social Science Quarterly* 79 (1998): 828–45; Pew Research Center, "Religious Switching among Hispanics," Washington, DC, May 7, 2014, accessed April 3, 2015, http://www.pewforum.org/2014/05/07/hispanic-religious-switching/ .

5. Cecilia Menjívar, "Religion and Immigration in Comparative Perspective: Catholic and Evangelical Salvadorans in San Francisco, Washington, DC, and Phoenix," *Sociology of Religion: A Quarterly Review* 64 (2003): 21–45.

6. Frank Newport, "U.S. Catholic Population Less Religious, Shrinking," Gallup.com, February 25, 2013, accessed April 7, 2015, http://www.gallup.com/poll/160691/catholic-hispanic-population-less-religious-shrinking.aspx; Pew Research Center, "Changing Faiths"; Pew Research Center, "The Shifting Religious Identity of Latinos in the United States."

7. Robert Putnam and David Campbell, *American Grace : How Religion Divides and Unites Us* (New York: Simon & Schuster, 2010).

8. Frank Newport, *"Three-Quarters of Americans Identify as Christian,"* Gallup.com, December 24, 2014, accessed April 7, 2015, http://www.gallup.com/poll/180347/three-quarters-americans-identify-christian.aspx; Pew Research Center, "Changing Faiths."

9. R. Stephen Warner, "Immigration and Religious Communities in the United States," in *Gatherings in Diaspora: Religious Communities and the New Immigration*, eds. R. Stephen Warner and Judith Wittner (Philadelphia: Temple University Press, 1998).

10. For an analysis of contemporary racialized stereotypes in religion, see Gerardo Martí, *Worship across the Racial Divide: Religious Music and the*

Multiracial Congregation (New York: Oxford University Press, 2012), chaps 2 and 3; Gerardo Martí, "I Was a Muslim, But Now I Am a Christian: Preaching, Legitimation, and Identity Management in a Southern Evangelical Church," *Journal for the Scientific Study of Religion* 55 (2016): 250–70.

11. Juan Francisco Martínez, *Los Protestantes: An introduction to Latino Protestantism in the United States* (Westport, CT: Praeger, 2011), 100. See also Juan Francisco Martinez, *Walk with the People: Latino Ministry in the United States* (Nashville, TN: Abingdon Press, 2008), 58, and Daniel A. Rodriguez, *A Future for the Latino Church: Models for Multilingual, Multigenerational Hispanic Congregations* (Downers Grove, IL: IVP Academic, 2011), 57.

12. Martínez, *Los Protestantes*, 105. See also Pedrito Maynard-Reid, *Diverse Worship: African-American, Caribbean and Hispanic Perspectives* (Downers Grove, IL: IVP Academic, 2000), 161–86.

13. See Martí, *Worship across the Racial Divide*.

14. For example, see Martí, *Worship across the Racial Divide*.

15. See Gastón Espinosa, *Latino Pentecostals in America : Faith and Politics in Action* (Cambridge, MA: Harvard University Press, 2014); Felipe Hinojosa, *Latino Mennonites: Civil Rights, Faith, and Evangelical Culture* (Baltimore: Johns Hopkins University Press, 2014); Moises Sandoval, *On the Move: A History of the Hispanic Church in the United States*, 2nd ed. (Maryknoll, NY: Orbis Books, 2006).

16. For example, Harold J. Recinos, "Mainline Hispanic Protestantism and Latino Newcomers," in *Protestantes/Protestants: Hispanic Christianity within the Mainline Traditions*, ed. D. Maldonado Jr. (Nashville, TN: Abingdon Press, 1999); Teresa Chávez Sauceda, "Race, Religion, and la Raza: An Exploration of the Racialization of Latinos in the U.S. and the Role of the Protestant Church," in *Protestantes/Protestants: Hispanic Christianity within the Mainline Traditions*, ed. D. Maldonado Jr. (Nashville, TN: Abingdon Press, 1999); Kathleen Sullivan, "Iglesia de Dios," in *Religion and the New Immigrants*, eds. Helen Rose Ebaugh and Janet S. Chafetz (Walnut Creek, CA: AltaMira Press, 2000).

17. For example, Joshua A. Fishman, *Language in Sociocultural Change: Essays* (Stanford, CA: Stanford University Press, 1972), 57; Prema Kurien, "Decoupling Religion and Ethnicity: Second-Generation Indian American Christians," *Qualitative Sociology* 35 (2012): 447–68.

18. For example, Helen Rose Ebaugh and Janet S. Chafetz, eds., *Religion and the New Immigrants* (Walnut Creek, CA: AltaMira Press, 2000); Anthony M. Stevens-Arroyo, "The Emergence of a Social Identity among Latino Catholics: An Appraisal," in *Hispanic Catholic Culture in the U.S.: Issues and Concerns*, eds. J. P. Dolan and A. F. Deck (South Bend, IN: University of Notre Dame Press, 1994).

19. For example, Edward Flores, "'I Am Somebody': Barrio Pentecostalism and Gendered Acculturation among Chicano Ex-Gang Members," *Ethnic and Racial Studies* 32 (2009): 996–1016; Edward Flores, *God's Gangs : Barrio Ministry, Masculinity, and Gang Recovery* (New York: New York University Press, 2014); Luís León, "Born Again in East LA: The Congregation as Border Space," in *Gatherings in Diaspora: Religious Communities and the New Immigration*, eds. R. Stephen Warner and Judith G. Wittner (Philadelphia: Temple University Press, 1998).

20. For a congregationally based analysis, see Gerardo Martí, *A Mosaic of Believers: Diversity and Innovation in a Multiethnic Church* (Bloomington: Indiana University Press, 2005).

21. See Thierry Devos and Mahzarin R. Banaji, "American = White?" *Journal of Personality and Social Psychology* 88 (2005): 447–66; Que-Lam Huynh, Thierry Devos, and Laura Smalarz, "Perpetual Foreigner in One's Own Land: Potential Implications for Identity and Psychological Adjustment," *Journal of Social and Clinical Psychology* 30 (2011): 133–62; Tomás R. Jiménez, "Mexican Immigrant Replenishment and the Continuing Significance of Ethnicity and Race," *American Journal of Sociology* 113 (2008): 1527–67; Raymond Rocco, "Transforming Citizenship: Membership, Strategies of Containment, and the Public Sphere of Latino Communities," in *Latinos and Citizenship: The Dilemma of Belonging*, ed. Suzanne Oboler (New York: Palgrave, 2006).

22. Catherine E. Wilson, *The Politics of Latino Faith: Religion, Identity, and Urban Community* (New York: New York University Press, 2008).

23. Rubén Armendariz, "The Protestant Hispanic Congregation: Identity," in *Protestantes/Protestants: Hispanic Christianity within the Mainline Traditions*, ed. D Maldonado Jr. (Nashville, TN: Abingdon Press, 1999), 240.

24. Gastón Espinosa, Virgilio Elizondo, and Jesse Miranda, eds. *Latino Religion and Civic Activism in the United States* (New York: Oxford University Press, 2005).

25. On educational sorting, see Pedro Pedraza and Melissa Rivera, eds., *Latino Education: An Agenda for Community Action Research* (Mahwah, NJ: Lawrence Erlbaum Associates, 2008). On occupational sorting, see John D. Skrentny, *After Civil Rights: Racial Realism in the New American Workplace* (Princeton, NJ: Princeton University Press, 2014).

26. Melissa Guzman Garcia, "Spiritual Citizenship: Transcending the Boundaries of National Belonging," *International Migration Review* (forthcoming).

27. John P. Bartkowski, Aida I. Ramos-Wada, Christopher Ellison, and Gabriel A. Acevedo, "Faith, Race-Ethnicity, and Public Policy Preferences: Religious Schemas and Abortion Attitudes Among U.S. Latinos," *Journal for the Scientific Study of Religion* 51 (2012): 343–58.

28. Christopher G. Ellison, Gabriel A. Acevedo, and Aida I. Ramos-Wada, "Religion and Attitudes toward Same-Sex Marriage among U.S. Latinos," *Social Science Quarterly* 92 (2011): 35–56.

29. Ellison, Christopher G., Nicholas H. Wolfinger, and Aida I. Ramos-Wada, "Attitudes toward Marriage, Divorce, Cohabitation, and Casual Sex among Working-Age Latinos: Does Religion Matter?" *Journal of Family Issues* 34 (2013): 295–322.

30. For a notable example, see Jonathan E. Calvillo and Stanley R. Bailey, "Latino Religious Affiliation and Ethnic Identity," *Journal for the Scientific Study of Religion* 54 (2015): 57–78.

APPENDIX

1. Conceptual resources for approaching such observation include phenomenologists like Alfred Schutz, symbolic interactionists like Herbert Blumer, and qualitative researchers like Norman Denzin.

2. Howard S. Becker and Blanche Geer, "Participant Observation: The Analysis of Qualitative Field Data," in *Field Research: A Sourcebook and Field Manual*, ed. R. Burgess (London: Allen and Unwin, 1982), 239–50.

3. Danny L. Jorgensen, *Participant Observation: A Methodology for Human Studies, Applied Social Research Methods Series* (Newbury Park, CA: Sage, 1989), 21.

4. Sociologists Max Weber, Alfred Schutz, George Herbert Mead, and Peter Berger are among the theorists who forcefully demonstrate how the way in which people make sense of themselves and their worlds is critical to understanding the dynamics of any social setting.

5. Lewis Minkin, *Exits and Entrances: Political Research as a Creative Art* (Sheffield, UK: Sheffield Hallam University Press, 1997), 122.

BIBLIOGRAPHY

Abalos, David T. *Latinos in the United States: The Sacred and the Political*. South Bend, IN: University of Notre Dame Press, 2007.

Alcoff, Linda Martín. "Latino vs. Hispanic: The Politics of Ethnic Names." *Philosophy & Social Criticism* 31, no. 4 (2005): 395–407.

Alonzo, Armando. *Tejano Legacy: Rancheros and Settlers in South Texas, 1734–1900*. Albuquerque: University of New Mexico Press, 1998.

Armendáriz, Rubén. "The Protestant Hispanic Congregation: Identity." In *Protestantes/Protestants: Hispanic Christianity within the Mainline Traditions*, edited by D. Maldonado Jr., 239–54. Nashville, TN: Abingdon Press, 1999.

Barrett, David B., George T. Kurian, and Todd M. Johnson. *World Christian Encyclopedia*. New York: Oxford University Press, 1998.

———. *World Christian Encyclopedia: Religionists, Churches, Ministries: A Comparative Survey of Churches and Religions in the Modern World*. New York: Oxford University Press, 2001.

Bartkowski, John P., Aida I. Ramos-Wada, Christopher G. Ellison, and Gabriel A. Acevedo. "Faith, Race-Ethnicity, and Public Policy Preferences: Religious Schemas and Abortion Attitudes among U.S. Latinos." *Journal for the Scientific Study of Religion* 51, no 2 (2012): 343–58.

Barton, Paul. "*Ya Basta!* Latino/a Protestant Activism in the Chicago/a and Farm Workers Movements." In *Latino Religions and Civic Activism in the United States*, edited by Gastón Espinosa, Virgilio Elizondo, and Jesse Miranda, 127–43. New York: Oxford University Press, 2005.

———. *Hispanic Methodists, Presbyterians, and Baptists in Texas*. Austin: University of Texas Press, 2006.

Batalova, Jeanne and Jie Zong. Migration Policy Institute, "Central American Immigrants in the United States." Washington D.C., September 2, 2015. http://www.migrationpolicy.org/article/central-american-immigrants-united-states.

BibleGateway. "Holy Bible, New International Version." Accessed June 20, 2016. https://www.biblegateway.com/.

Bowler, Kate *Blessed: A History of the American Prosperity Gospel*. New York: Oxford University Press, 2013.

Branton, Regina, Ana B. Franco, Jim Wenzel, and Robert D. Wrinkle. "Latino Attitudes toward Abortion and Marriage Equality: Examining the Influence of Religiosity, Acculturation, and Non-Response." *Journal of Religion and Society* 16 (2014): 1–23.

Brenneman, Robert. *Homies and Hermanos: God and Gangs in Central America*. New York: Oxford University Press, 2011.

Brusco, Elizabeth E. *The Reformation of Machismo: Evangelical Conversion and Gender in Colombia*. Austin: University of Texas Press, 2011.

Butts, Michéle, "'I Could Realize What Sodom and Gomorrah Might Have Been': Image vs. Reality for Presbyterian Missionaries in New Mexico, 1872." *Journal of Presbyterian History* 774 (1997): 223–34.

Cadava, Geraldo L. "Rural Hispanic Voters—Like Rural White Voters—Shifted Toward Trump: Here's Why." *The Washington Post*, November 17, 2016. Accessed December 26, 2016. https://www.washingtonpost.com/news/monkey-cage/wp/2016/11/17/rural-hispanic-voters-like-white-rural-voters-shifted-toward-trump-heres-why/?utm_term=.b0e6a53a81ae.

Calvillo, Jonathan E. "The Living Borderlands: The Persistent Borderland Presence in Southern California Latino Protestant Congregations." In *Religion in Los Angeles*, edited by Richard Flory and Diane Winston. Berkeley: University of California Press, forthcoming.

Calvillo, Jonathan E., and Stanley R. Bailey. "Latino Religious Affiliation and Ethnic Identity." *Journal for the Scientific Study of Religion* 54, no. 1 (2015): 57–78.

Campo, Carlos. "What the New Majority-Minority Public Schools Mean for Christians." *Christianity Today*, August 22, 2014. Accessed February 20, 2016. http://www.christianitytoday.com/ct/2014/august-web-only/what-new-majority-minority-public-schools-mean-for-christia.html.

Campolo, Tony and Shane Claiborne. "The Evangelicalism of Old White Men is Dead." *The New York Times*, November 29, 2016. Accessed December 26, 2016. http://www.nytimes.com/2016/11/29/opinion/the-evangelicalism-of-old-white-men-is-dead.html?_r=0.

Cavalcanti, H. B., and Debra Schleef. "The Case for Secular Assimilation? The Latino Experience in Richmond, Virginia." *Journal for the Scientific Study of Religion* 44, no. 4 (2005): 473–83.

Chesnut, R Andrew. *Born Again in Brazil: The Pentecostal Boom and the Pathogens of Poverty*. New Brunswick, NJ: Rutgers University Press, 1997.

Creech, Joe. "Visions of Glory: The Place of the Azusa Street Revival in Pentecostal History." *Church History* 65, no. 3 (1996): 405–24.

Cruz, Samuel. *Masked Africanisms: Puerto Rican Pentecostalism*. Chicago, IL: Kendall/Hunt Publishing Company, 2005.

Darnell, Alfred, and Darren E Sherkat. "The Impact of Protestant Fundamentalism on Educational Attainment." *American Sociological Review* (1997): 306–15.

De León, Arnoldo. *They Called Them Greasers: Anglo Attitudes toward Mexicans in Texas, 1821–1900*. Austin: University of Texas Press, 2010.

DeSipio, Louis. "Power in the Pews? Religious Diversity and Latino Political Attitudes and Behaviors." In *From Pews to Polling Places: Faith and Politics in the American Religious Mosaic*, edited by J. M. Wilson, 161–184. Washington, DC: Georgetown University Press, 2007.

DeTemple, Jill. "Chains of Liberation: Poverty and Social Action in the Universal Church of the Kingdom of God." In *Latino Religious and Civic Activism in the United States*, edited by Gastón Espinosa, Virgil Elizonda, and Jesse Miranda, 219–32. New York: Oxford University Press, 2005.

Devos Thierry, and Mahzarin R. Banaji. "American = White?" *Journal of Personality and Social Psychology* 88, no. 3, (2005): 447–66.

Dias, Elizabeth. "Evangélicos!" *Time*, April 15, 2013.

Diaz-Stevens, Ana Maria, and Anthony M. Stevens-Arroyo. *Recognizing the Latino Resurgence in U.S. Religion: The Emmaus Paradigm*. Boulder, CO: Westview Press, 1997.

Djupe, Paul A., and Jacob R. Neiheisel. "How Religious Communities Affect Political Participation among Latinos." *Social Science Quarterly* 93, no. 2 (2012): 333–55.

Dowling, Julie A. *Mexican Americans and the Question of Race*. Austin: University of Texas Press, 2014.

Ebaugh, Helen Rose, and Janet Saltzman Chafetz. "Dilemmas of Language in Immigrant Congregations: The Tie That Binds or the Tower of Babel?" *Review of Religious Research* 41, no. 4 (2000): 432–52.

Elk, Lucila D. "Language and Literacy in the Pentecostal Church Public High School: A Case Study of a Mexican ESL Student." *The High School Journal* 92, no. 2 (2008): 1–13.

Ellison, Christopher G., Gabriel A. Acevedo, and Aida I. Ramos-Wada. "Religion and Attitudes Toward Same-Sex Marriage among U.S. Latinos." *Social Science Quarterly* 92, no. 1 (2011): 35–56.

Ellison, Christopher G., Samuel Echevarría, and Brad Smith. "Religion and Abortion Attitudes among U.S. Hispanics: Findings from the 1990 Latino National Political Survey." *Social Science Quarterly* 86, no. 1 (2005): 192–208.

Ellison, Christopher G., and Darren E. Sherkat. "The 'Semi-involuntary Institution' Revisited: Regional Variations in Church Participation among Black Americans." *Social Forces* 73, no. 4 (1995): 1415–37.

Ellison, Christopher G., Nicholas H. Wolfinger, and Aida I. Ramos-Wada. "Attitudes toward Marriage, Divorce, Cohabitation, and Casual Sex among Working-Age Latinos: Does Religion Matter?" *Journal of Family Issues* 34, no. 3 (2013): 295–322.

Espinosa, Gastón. "The Pentecostalization of Latin American and U.S. Latino Christianity." *PNEUMA: The Journal of the Society for Pentecostal Studies* 26, no. 2 (2004): 262–92.

———. "Latino Clergy and Churches in Faith-Based Political and Social Action in the United States." In *Latino Religions and Civic Activism in the United States*, edited by Gaston Espinosa, Virgilio Elizondo, and Jesse Miranda, 279–306. New York: Oxford University Press, 2005.

———. "'Today We Act, Tomorrow We Vote': Latino Religions, Politics, and Activism in Contemporary U.S. Civil Society." *Annals of the Academy of Political and Social Science* 612 (2007): 152–71.

———. "Separated Brothers: Latinos Are Changing the Nature of American Religion." *Economist*, July 16, 2009. Accessed February 19, 2016. http://www.economist.com/node/14034841.

———. *Latino Pentecostals in America: Faith and Politics in Action*. Cambridge, MA: Harvard University Press, 2014.

Espinosa, Gastón, Virgilio Elizondo, and Jesse Miranda, eds. *Latino Religion and Civic Activism in the United States*. New York: Oxford University Press, 2005.

Fishman, Joshua A. *Language in Sociocultural Change: Essays*. Stanford, CA: Stanford University Press, 1972.

Fitzgerald, Scott, and Jennifer Glass. "Conservative Religion, Early Transitions to Adulthood and the Intergenerational Transmission of Class." *Research in the Sociology of Work* 23 (2012): 49–72.

Fitzpatrick, James. *Puerto Rican Americans: The Migration to the Mainland*. Englewood Cliffs, NJ: Prentice-Hall, 1971.

Flores, Edward. "'I Am Somebody': Barrio Pentecostalism and Gendered Acculturation among Chicano Ex-Gang Members." *Ethnic and Racial Studies* 32, no.6 (2009): 996–1016.

———. *God's Gangs : Barrio Ministry, Masculinity, and Gang Recovery*. New York: New York University Press, 2014.

García, María Cristina. "Exiles, Immigrants, and Transnationals." In *The Columbia History of Latinos in the United States since 1960*, ed. David Gutiérrez. New York: Columbia University Press, 2004.

Garrard-Burnett, Virginia. *Protestantism in Guatemala: Living in the New Jerusalem*. Austin: University of Texas Press, 1998.

González, Justo, and Odina González. *Nuestra Fe: A Latin American Church History Sourcebook*. Nashville, TN: Abingdon Press, 2014.

Gonzales, Manuel G. *Mexicanos: A History of Mexicans in the United States*. Bloomington: Indiana University Press, 2009.

Granberg-Michaelson, Wes. "Think Christianity Is Dying? No, Christianity Is Shifting Dramatically." *Washington Post*, May 20, 2015. Accessed June 14, 2016. https://www.washingtonpost.com/news/acts-of-faith/wp/2015/05/20/think-christianity-is-dying-no-christianity-is-shifting-dramatically.

Greeley, Andrew M. "The Success and Assimilation of Irish Protestants and Irish Catholics in the United States." *Sociology and Social Research* 72, no. 4 (1988): 229–36.

———. "Defection among Hispanics." *America*, July 30, 1988: 61–62.

———. "The Demography of American Catholics: 1965–1990." In *Religion and the Social Order: Vatican II and U.S. Catholicism*, edited by H. R. Ebaugh, 37–56. Greenwich, CT: JAI Press, 1991.

Guerra, Gilbert, and Gilbert Orbea. "The Argument against the Use of the Term 'Latinx.'" *Phoenix*, November 19, 2015. Accessed August 25, 2015. http://swarthmorephoenix.com/2015/11/19/the-argument-against-the-use-of-the-term-latinx/.

Guth, James L. "Religion and American Public Attitudes on War and Peace." *Asian Journal of Peacebuilding* 1, no. 2 (2013): 227–52.

Gutiérrez, David G. "An Historic Overview of Latino Immigration and the Demographic Transformation of the United States." National Park Service U.S. Department of the Interior. Accessed April 10, 2016. https://www.nps.gov/heritageinitiatives/latino/latinothemestudy/immigration.htm.

Guzman Garcia, Melissa. "Spiritual Citizenship: Immigrant Religious Participation and the Management of Deportability." *International Migration Review* (forthcoming).

Harrison, Milmon F. *Righteous Riches: The Word of Faith Movement in Contemporary African American Religion*. New York: Oxford University Press, 2005.

Hernández, Edwin I., Milagros Peña, Kenneth G. Davis, and Elizabeth Station, eds. *Emerging Voices, Urgent Choices: Essays on Latino/a Religious Leadership*. Boston: Brill, 2006.

Hernández, Edwin I., Jeffrey Smith, Rebecca Burwell, Milagros Peña, and David Sikkink. "Healing Hands: The Health of Latino/a Churchgoers and Health Outreach among Latino Congregations in Chicago." South Bend, IN: Institute for Latino Studies and Center for the Study of Latino Religion, University of Notre Dame, 2010.

Hinojosa, Felipe. *Latino Mennonites: Civil Rights, Faith, and Evangelical Culture*. Baltimore: Johns Hopkins University Press, 2014.

Huffington Post. "Why Ted Cruz's Candidacy Isn't Catching Fire with U.S. Latinos." Accessed June 5, 2015. http://www.huffingtonpost.com/2015/06/05/ted-cruz-latinos_n_7517836.html.

Hunt, Larry L. "The Spirit of Hispanic Protestantism in the United States: National Survey Comparisons of Catholics and Non-Catholics." *Social Science Quarterly* 79, no. 4 (1998): 828–45.

———. "Hispanic Protestantism in the United States: Trends by Decade and Generation." *Social Forces* 77, no. 4 (1999):1601–24.

Huynh, Que-Lam, Thierry Devos, and Laura Smalarz. "Perpetual Foreigner in One's Own Land: Potential Implications for Identity and Psychological Adjustment." *Journal of Social and Clinical Psychology* 30, no. 2 (2011): 133–62.

Iannaccone, Laurence R. "Voodoo Economics? Reviewing the Rational Choice Approach to Religion." *Journal for the Scientific Study of Religion* 34, no. 1 (1995): 76–88.

Jackson, Robert H. *From Savages to Subjects: Missions in the History of the American Southwest*. New York: M.E. Sharpe, 2000.

Jiménez, Tomás R. "Mexican Immigrant Replenishment and the Continuing Significance of Ethnicity and Race." *American Journal of Sociology* 113, no. 6 (2008): 1527–67.

Jiménez, Tomás R., Corey D. Fields, and Ariela Schachter, "How Ethnoraciality Matters: Looking inside Ethnoracial 'Groups.'" *Social Currents* 2 (2015): 107–15.

Johnson, Marilynn. "'The Quiet Revival': New Immigrants and the Transformation of Christianity in Greater Boston." *Religion and American Culture: A Journal of Interpretation* 24, no. 2 (2014): 231–58.

Jones, Robert P., Daniel Cox, and Juhem Navarro-Rivera. "How Shifting Religious Identities and Experiences Are Influencing Hispanic Approaches to Politics." Public Religion Research Institute, September 27, 2013. Accessed March 29, 2016. http://publicreligion.org/site/wp-content/uploads/2013/09/2013_HVS_FINAL.pdf.

Jordan, Mary. "'He's Cuban. I'm Mexican.': Can Rubio and Cruz Connect with Latino Voters?" *Washington Post*, January 10, 2016. Accessed March 31, 2016. https://www.

washingtonpost.com/politics/2016/01/10/32d20f8e-b4bc–11e5-a842–0feb51d1d124_story. html.

Juffer, Jane. "Hybrid Faiths: Latino Protestants Find a Home among the Dutch Reformed in Iowa." *Latino Studies* 6, no. 3 (2008): 290–312.

Kaplowitz, Craig A. *LULAC, Mexican Americans, and National Policy*. College Station: Texas A&M University Press, 2005.

Keister, Lisa A. *Faith and Money: How Religion Contributes to Wealth and Poverty*. Cambridge, UK: Cambridge University Press, 2011.

———. "Religion and Wealth: The Role of Religious Affiliation and Participation in Early Adult Asset Accumulation." *Social Forces* 82, no. 1 (2013):175–207.

Keister, Lisa A., and E. Paige Borelli. "Religion and Wealth Mobility: The Case of American Latinos." In *Religion and Inequality in America: Research and Theory on Religion's Role in Stratification*, edited by Lisa A. Keister and Darren E. Sherkat, 119–45. New York: Cambridge University Press, 2014.

Keister, Lisa A, and Darren E. Sherkat. *Religion and Inequality in America: Research and Theory on Religion's Role in Stratification*. Cambridge, UK: Cambridge University Press, 2014.

Kessell, John L. *Spain in the Southwest: A Narrative History of Colonial New Mexico, Arizona, Texas, and California*. Norman: University of Oklahoma Press, 2002.

Korrol, Virginia Sanchez. *From Colonia to Community: The History of Puerto Ricans in New York City*. Berkeley: University of California Press, 1994.

Kurien, Prema. "Decoupling Religion and Ethnicity: Second-Generation Indian American Christians." *Qualitative Sociology* 35, no. 4 (2012): 447–68.

Leal, Fermin. "Templo Calvario Debuts New $11 Million Sanctuary." *Orange County Register*, July, 5, 2009. Accessed June 22, 2016. http://www.ocregister.com/articles/new–168362-church-sanctuary.html.

Lee, Jongho, and Harry P. Pachon. "Leading the Way: An Analysis of the Effect of Religion on the Latino Vote." *American Politics Research* 35, no. 2 (2007): 252–72.

León, Luís. "Born Again in East LA: The Congregation as Border Space." In *Gatherings in Diaspora: Religious Communities and the New Immigration*, edited by R. Stephen Warner and Judith G. Wittner, 163–96. Philadelphia: Temple University Press, 1998.

León, Luis D. *The Political Spirituality of Cesar Chavez: Crossing Religious Borders*. Berkeley: University of California Press, 2014.

Levitt, Peggy. *God Needs No Passport: Immigrants and the Changing Religious Landscape*. New York: The New Press, 2007.

Levy, Abe. "God Wants You to Graduate." *Christianity Today*, April 17, 2013. Accessed February 20, 2016. http://www.christianitytoday.com/ct/2013/april-web-only/god-wants-you-to-graduate.html.

Lindsay, Conrad Hackett, and D. Michael. "Measuring Evangelicalism: Consequences of Different Operationalization Strategies." *Journal for the Scientific Study of Religion* 47 (2008): 499–514.

López-Sanders, Laura. "Bible Belt Immigrants: Latino Religious Incorporation in New Immigrant Destinations." *Latino Studies* 10, nos. 1–2 (2012): 128–54.

Machado, Daisy L. *Of Borders and Margins: Hispanic Disciples in Texas, 1888–1945*. New York: Oxford University Press, 2003.

Maffly-Kipp, Laurie F. *Religion and Society in Frontier California*. New Haven, CT: Yale University Press, 1994.

Mahler, Sarah J., and Katrin Hansing. "Toward a Transnationalism of the Middle: How Transnational Religious Practices Help Bridge the Divides between Cuba and Miami." *Latin American Perspectives* 32, no. 1 (2005): 121–46.

Malavé, Idelissa, and Esti Giordani. *Latino Stats: American Hispanics by the Numbers*. New York: The New Press, 2015.

Marquardt, Marie Friedmann. "From Shame to Confidence: Gender, Religious Conversation and Civic Engagement of Mexicans in the U.S. South." *Latin American Perspectives*, 32, no. 1 (2005): 27–56.

Marrow, H. B. *New Destination Dreaming: Immigration, Race, and Legal Status in the Rural American South*. Stanford, CA: Stanford University Press, 2011.

Martí, Gerardo. *A Mosaic of Believers: Diversity and Innovation in a Multiethnic Church*. Bloomington: Indiana University Press, 2005.

———. 2008. *Hollywood Faith: Holiness, Prosperity, and Ambition in a Los Angeles Church*. New Brunswick, NJ: Rutgers University Press, 2008.

———. "The Diversity-Affirming Latino: Ethnic Options and the Ethnic Transcendent Expression of American Latino Religious Identity." In *Sustaining Faith Tradition: Race, Ethnicity, and Religion among the Latino and Asian American Second Generation*, edited by C. Chen and R. Jeung, 25–45. New York: New York University Press, 2012.

———. *Worship across the Racial Divide: Religious Music and the Multiracial Congregation*. New York: Oxford University Press, 2012.

———. "Latino Protestants and Their Churches: Establishing an Agenda for Sociological Research." *Sociology of Religion: A Quarterly Review* 76, no. 2 (2015): 145–54.

———. "I Was a Muslim, But Now I Am a Christian: Preaching, Legitimation, and Identity Management in a Southern Evangelical Church." *Scientific Study of Religion* 55, no. 2 (2016): 250–70.

Martin, David. *Tongues of Fire: The Explosion of Protestantism in Latin America*. Cambridge, MA: Blackwell Publishers, 1990.

Martínez, Jessica Hamar, Edwin I. Hernández, Rebecca Burwell, Milagros Peña, and David Sikkink. "The Politics of the Latino Church: Understanding the Political Views and Behaviors of Latino Congregations in Chicago." South Bend, IN: Center for the Study of Religion, University of Notre Dame, 2012.

Martínez, Juan Francisco. *Sea la Luz: The Making of Mexican Protestantism in the American Southwest, 1829–1900*. Denton: University of North Texas Press, 2006.

———. *Walk with the People: Latino Ministry in the United States*. Nashville, TN: Abingdon Press, 2008.

———. *Los Protestantes: An Introduction to Latino Protestantism in the United States*. Westport, CT: Praeger, 2011.

Massey, Douglas S. *Immigration and the Great Recession*. Stanford, CA: Stanford Center on Poverty and Inequality, 2012.

Matovina, Timothy. *Latino Catholicism: Transformation in America's Largest Church*. Princeton, NJ: Princeton University Press, 2012.

Maynard-Reid, Pedrito. *Diverse Worship: African-American, Caribbean and Hispanic Perspectives*. Downers Grove, IL: IVP Academic, 2000.

McKenzie, Brian D., and Stella M. Rouse. "Shades of Faith: Religious Foundations of Political Attitudes among African Americans, Latinos, and Whites." *American Journal of Political Science* 57, no. 1 (2013): 218–35.

Menchaca, Martha. *Recovering History, Constructing Race: The Indian, Black, and White Roots of Mexican Americans*. Austin: University of Texas Press, 2001.

———. *Naturalizing Mexican Immigrants: A Texas History*. Austin: University of Texas Press, 2011.

Menjívar, Cecilia. "Religion and Immigration in Comparative Perspective: Catholic and Evangelical Salvadorans in San Francisco, Washington, D.C., and Phoenix." *Sociology of Religion* 64, no. 1 (2003): 21–45.

Mintz, Sidney. *Worker in the Cane: A Puerto Rican Life Story*. New York: W.W. Norton, 1974.

Montejano, David. *Anglos and Mexicans in the Making of Texas, 1836–1986*. Austin: University of Texas Press, 2010.

Moore, Russell. "Evangelical Hispanics and the 2016 Vote: GOP Candidates Talking about Immigration Need to Take into Account This Growing Demographic." *Wall Street Journal*, May 7 2015. Accessed May 7, 2015. http://www.wsj.com/articles/evangelical-hispanics-and-the–2016-vote–1431040230.

———. "A White Church No More." *New York Times*, May 6, 2016. Accessed June 3, 2016. http://www.nytimes.com/2016/05/06/opinion/a-white-church-no-more.html?_r=0.

Mora, G. Cristina. "Cross-Field Effects and Ethnic Classification: The Institutionalization of Hispanic Panethnicity, 1965 to 1990." *American Sociological Review* 79, no. 2 (2014): 183–210.

———. *Making Hispanics: How Activists, Bureaucrats, and Media Constructed a New American.* Chicago: University of Chicago Press, 2014.

Morgan, Timothy. "Death Penalty Repeal Gains Support from Latino Evangelical Coalition." *Christianity Today*, March 31, 2015. Accessed February 20, 2016. http://www.christianitytoday.com/gleanings/2015/march/death-penalty-ban-gains-support-from-latino-evangelical-coa.html.

National Hispanic Christian Leadership Conference. Accessed June 14, 2015. https://nhclc.org/.

———. Mission Statement. Accessed June 3, 2015. https://nhclc.org/about-us/mission-vision-statement.

National Latino Evangelical Coalition. Accessed March 31, 2016. http://nalec.org/category/politics.

Navarro-Rivera, Juhem, Barry A. Kosmin, and Ariela Keysar, "U.S. Latino Religious Identification, 1990–2008: Growth, Diversity, and Transformation." Hartford, CT: Trinity College, 2008. Accessed March 29, 2016. http://commons.trincoll.edu/aris/files/2011/08/latinos2008.pdf.

Nessen, Stephen. "Latinos Drawn to Evangelicalism Seem Immune to 'Francis Effect.'" *WNYC News*, July 9, 2015. Accessed July 27, 2015. http://www.wnyc.org/story/new-yorks-lapsed-catholics-are-resisting-francis-effect/.

Newport, Frank. "Three-Quarters of Americans Identify as Christian." December 24, 2014. Accessed April 7, 2015. http://www.gallup.com/poll/180347/three-quarters-americans-identify-christian.aspx.

———. "U.S. Catholic Population Less Religious, Shrinking." February 25, 2013. Accessed April 7, 2015. http://www.gallup.com/poll/160691/catholic-hispanic-population-less-religious-shrinking.aspx.

Okamoto, Dina, and G. Cristina Mora. "Panethnicity." *Annual Review of Sociology* 40 (2014): 219–39.

Ortiz, Larry. "Latino Migration to Protestantism: A Historical, Socio-Cultural, Ecclesiastical Analysis." *Journal of Sociology and Social Welfare* 41, no. 3 (2014): 24–35.

Pedraza Pedro, and Melissa Rivera, eds. *Latino Education: An Agenda for Community Action Research.* Mahwah, NJ: Lawrence Erlbaum Associates, 2008.

Perez, Anthony Daniel, and Charles Hirschman. "The Changing Racial and Ethnic Composition of the U.S. Population: Emerging American Identities." *Population and Development Review* 35, no. 1 (2009): 1–51.

Pew Research Center. "Changing Faiths: Latinos and the Transformation of American Religion." Washington, DC, April 25, 2007. http://www.pewhispanic.org/2007/04/25/changing-faiths-latinos-and-the-transformation-of-american-religion/.

———. "U.S. Population Projections: 2005–2050." Washington, DC, February 11, 2008. Accessed March 28, 2016. http://www.pewhispanic.org/2008/02/11/us-population-projections–2005–2050/.

———. "Census History: Counting Hispanics," Washington, DC, March 3, 2010. Accessed February 5, 2016. http://www.pewsocialtrends.org/2010/03/03/census-history-counting-hispanics–2/.

———. "The 10 Largest Hispanic Origin Groups: Characteristics, Rankings, Top Counties." Washington, DC, June 27, 2012. Accessed April 26, 2016. http://www.pewhispanic.org/2012/06/27/the–10-largest-hispanic-origin-groups-characteristics-rankings-top-counties/.

———. "'Nones' on the Rise." Washington DC, October 9, 2012. Accessed August 23, 2016. http://www.pewforum.org/2012/10/09/nones-on-the-rise/.

———. "Latinos, Religion, and Campaign 2012: Catholics Favor Obama, Evangelicals Divided." Washington, DC, October 18, 2012. Accessed June 13, 2015. http://www.pewforum.org/2012/10/18/latinos-religion-and-campaign–2012/.

———. "A Milestone En Route to a Majority Minority Nation." Washington, DC, November 7, 2012. Accessed April 1, 2016. http://www.pewsocialtrends.org/2012/11/07/a-milestone-en-route-to-a-majority-minority-nation/.

———. "Hispanics of Puerto Rican Origin in the United States, 2011." Washington, DC, June 19, 2013. Accessed May 6, 2016. http://www.pewhispanic.org/2013/06/19/hispanics-of-puerto-rican-origin-in-the-united-states-2011/.

———. "Mapping the Latino Population, by State, County, and City." Washington, DC, August 29, 2013. Accessed June 22, 2016. http://www.pewhispanic.org/2013/08/29/mapping-the-latino-population-by-state-county-and-city/.

———. "Hispanic Nativity Shift." Washington, DC, April 29, 2014. Accessed February 22, 2016. http://www.pewhispanic.org/2014/04/29/hispanic-nativity-shift/.

———. "The Shifting Religious Identity of Latinos in the United States: Nearly One-in-Four Are Former Catholics." Washington, DC, May 7, 2014. Accessed May 15, 2014. http://www.pewforum.org/2014/05/07/the-shifting-religious-identity-of-latinos-in-the-united-states/.

———. "Religious Switching among Hispanics," May 7, 2014. Accessed April 3, 2015. http://www.pewforum.org/2014/05/07/hispanic-religious-switching/.

———. "Latino Voters and the 2014 Midterm Elections: Geography, Close Races, and Views of Social Issues," Washington, DC, October 16, 2014. Accessed March 1, 2016. http://www.pewhispanic.org/2014/10/16/latino-voters-and-the-2014-midterm-elections/.

———. "Latino Support for Democrats Falls, but Democratic Advantage Remains," Washington, DC, October 29, 2014. Accessed July 15, 2015. http://www.pewhispanic.org/2014/10/29/latino-support-for-democrats-falls-but-democratic-advantage-remains/.

———. "Religion in Latin America: Widespread Change in a Historically Catholic Region." Washington, DC, November 13, 2014. Accessed December 23, 2015. http://www.pewforum.org/2014/11/13/religion-in-latin-america/.

———. "A Majority of English-Speaking Hispanics in the U.S. Are Bilingual," Washington, DC, March 24, 2015. Accessed March 20, 2016. http://www.pewresearch.org/fact-tank/2015/03/24/a-majority-of-english-speaking-hispanics-in-the-u-s-are-bilingual/.

———. "Hispanic Population Reaches 55 Million, but Growth Has Cooled." Washington, DC, June 25, 2015. Accessed March 22, 2016. http://www.pewresearch.org/fact-tank/2015/06/25/u-s-hispanic-population-growth-surge-cools/.

———. "America's Changing Religious Landscape." Washington, DC, May 12, 2015. Accessed March 22, 2016. http://www.pewforum.org/2015/05/12/americas-changing-religious-landscape/.

———. "English Proficiency on the Rise Among Latinos: U.S. Born Are Driving Language Changes," Washington, DC, May 12, 2015. Accessed March 20, 2016. http://www.pewhispanic.org/2015/05/12/english-proficiency-on-the-rise-among-latinos/.

———. "Is Being Hispanic a Matter of Race, Ethnicity, or Both?" Washington, DC, June 15, 2015. Accessed February 23, 2016. http://www.pewresearch.org/fact-tank/2015/06/15/is-being-hispanic-a-matter-of-race-ethnicity-or-both/.

———. "The Impact of Slowing Immigration." Washington, DC, September 15, 2015. Accessed June 22, 2016. http://www.pewhispanic.org/2015/09/15/the-impact-of-slowing-immigration-foreign-born-share-falls-among-14-largest-us-hispanic-origin-groups/.

———. "The Unique Challenges of Surveying U.S. Latinos." Washington, DC, November 12, 2015. Accessed February, 12, 2016. http://www.pewresearch.org/2015/11/12/the-unique-challenges-of-surveying-u-s-latinos/.

———. "More Mexicans Leaving Than Coming to the U.S." Washington, DC, November 19, 2015. Accessed March 28, 2016. http://www.pewhispanic.org/2015/11/19/more-mexicans-leaving-than-coming-to-the-u-s/.

———. "With Fewer New Arrivals, Census Lowers Hispanic Population Projections," Washington, DC, December 16, 2015. Accessed April 2, 2016. http://www.pewresearch.org/fact-tank/2014/12/16/with-fewer-new-arrivals-census-lowers-hispanic-population-projections-2/.

———. "Is Speaking in Spanish Necessary to be Hispanic? Most Hispanics Say No." Washington, DC, February 19, 2016. Accessed February 22, 2016. http://www.pewresearch.

org/fact-tank/2016/02/19/is-speaking-spanish-necessary-to-be-hispanic-most-hispanics-say-no/.

———. "Democrats Maintain Edge as Party 'More Concerned' for Latinos, but Views Similar to 2012." Washington, DC, October 11, 2016. Accessed December 26, 2016. http://www.pewhispanic.org/2016/10/11/democrats-maintain-edge-as-party-more-concerned-for-latinos-but-views-similar-to-2012/.

———. "Hillary Won Latino Vote but Fell Below 2012 Support for Obama." Washington, DC, November 29, 2016. Accessed December 12, 2016. http://www.pewresearch.org/fact-tank/2016/11/29/hillary-clinton-wins-latino-vote-but-falls-below-2012-support-for-obama/.

Pineda, Luis Guillermo. "Parishes Fail to Market Catholicism to Hispanics," *National Catholic Reporter*, 43, no. 12 (2007). Accessed February 22, 2016. http://www.thefreelibrary.com/Parishes+fail+to+market+Catholicism+to+Hispanics.-a0158524887.

Pius XII. *Divino afflante spiritu*. Encyclical of Pope Pius XII on Promoting Biblical Studies, Commemorating the Fiftieth Anniversary of Providentissimus Deus. The Vatican, 1943.

Poblete, Renato, and Thomas O'Dea. "Anomie and the Quest for Community: The Formation of Sects among Puerto Ricans in New York," *American Catholic Sociological Review*, 27, no. 1 (1960): 18–36.

Putnam, Robert, and David Campbell. *American Grace: How Religion Divides and Unites Us*. New York: Simon & Schuster, 2010.

Ramirez, Daniel. *Migrating Faith: Pentecostalism in the United States and Mexico in the Twentieth Century*. Chapel Hill: University of North Carolina Press, 2015.

Ramos, Aida I. "Wounded to the Heart: Family, Identity Negotiation, and Racialization among Latino/a Converts." Paper Presented at the Annual Meetings of the Association for the Sociology of Religion (ASR) Chicago, IL, 2015.

Ramos, Aida I. "Understanding Reasons for Latino/a Catholic to Protestant Conversion." Unpublished manuscript, George Fox University, 2016.

Ramos, Aida I., Christopher G. Ellison, and Walter Wilson. "Religion and Latino/a Attitudes toward the Poor and Government Assistance." Unpublished manuscript, University of Texas at San Antonio, 2016.

Ramos, Aida I., Robert Woodberry, and Christopher Ellison, "The Contexts of Conversions among Latinos." Under review, George Fox University, 2016.

Recinos, Harold J. "Mainline Hispanic Protestantism and Latino Newcomers." *Protestantes/Protestants: Hispanic Christianity within the Mainline Traditions*, edited by D. Maldonado, Jr., 194–215. Nashville, TN: Abingdon Press, 1999.

Rehwaldt, Jeremy. "Responses by White Christians to Recent Latino Immigration in the Rural U.S. Midwest." *Religions 6* (2015): 686–711.

Rennie, David. "America's Hispanics: From Minor to Major." *Economist*, March 14, 2015. Accessed February 22, 2016. http://www.economist.com/sites/default/files/20150314_sr_hispanics.pdf.

Robeck, Cecil M. *The Azusa Street Mission and Revival*. Nashville, TN: Thomas Nelson, 2006.

Rocco, Raymond. "Transforming Citizenship: Membership, Strategies of Containment, and the Public Sphere of Latino Communities." In *Latinos and Citizenship: The Dilemma of Belonging*, edited by Suzanne Oboler, 301–38. New York: Palgrave, 2006.

Rodriguez, Daniel A. *A Future for the Latino Church: Models for Multilingual, Multigenerational Hispanic Congregations*. Downers Grove, IL: IVP Academic, 2011.

Rodríguez-Díaz, Daniel R., and David Cortés-Fuentes. *Hidden Stories: Unveiling the History of the Latino Church*. Orlando, FL: Asociación para la Educación Teológica Hispana (AETH), 1994.

Ruano, Norman Eli. "The Holy Ghost beyond the Church Walls: Latino Pentecostalism(s), Congregations, and Civic Engagement." PhD. Diss., 2011, Loyola University Chicago. http://ecommons.luc.edu/luc_diss/267.

Sáenz, Rogelio and Maria Cristina Morales. *Latinos in the United States: Diversity and Change*. Cambridge, MA: Polity Press, 2015.

Sanabria, Tomas V. "Personal and Religious Beliefs and Experiences." In *Pathways of Hope and Faith among Hispanic Teens: Pastoral Reflections and Strategies Inspired by the National Study of Youth and Religion*, edited by Ken Johnson-Mondragón, 41–79. Stockton, CA: Instituto Fe y Vida, 2007.

Sánchez, Esmeralda. "Latina, Pentecostal, and College-Bound." *Christianity Today*, December 2014. Accessed June 10, 2016. http://www.christianitytoday.com/women/2014/december/latina-pentecostal-and-college-bound.html.

Sandomirsky, Sharon, and John Wilson. "Processes of Disaffiliation: Religious Mobility among Men and Women." *Social Forces* 68, no. 4 (1990):1211–29.

Sandoval, Moises. *On the Move: A History of the Hispanic Church in the United States*, 2nd edition. Maryknoll, NY: Orbis Books, 2006.

Sauceda, Teresa Chávez. "Race, Religion, and la Raza: An Exploration of the Racialization of Latinos in the U.S. and the Role of the Protestant Church." In *Protestantes/Protestants: Hispanic Christianity within the Mainline Traditions*, edited by D. Maldonado Jr., 177–93. Nashville, TN: Abingdon Press, 1999.

Schaefer, Richard. *Encyclopedia of Race, Ethnicity, and Society*. Thousand Oaks, CA: Sage, 2008.

Shellnutt, Kate. "InterVarsity Names a Historic New President: Tom Lin's Appointment Is the Second Significant Position in Mission Leadership Gained by Asian Americans This Spring." *Christianity Today*, May 16, 2016.

Sherkat, Darren. "Embedding Religious Choices: Preferences and Social Constraints into Rational Choice Theories of Religious Behavior." In *Rational Choice Theory and Religion*, edited by Lawrence A. Young, 65–68. New York: Routledge, 1997.

Skirbekk, Vegard, Eric Kaufmann, and Anne Goujon. "Secularism, Fundamentalism, or Catholicism? The Religious Composition of the United States to 2043." *Journal for the Scientific Study of Religion* 49, no. 2 (2010): 293–310.

Skrentny, John D. *After Civil Rights: Racial Realism in the New American Workplace*. Princeton, NJ: Princeton University Press. 2014.

Smilde, David. *Reason to Believe: Cultural Agency in Latin American Evangelicalism*. Berkeley: University of California Press, 2007.

Smith, Christian, and Robert Faris. "Socioeconomic Inequality in the American Religious System: An Update and Assessment." *Journal for the Scientific Study of Religion* 44, no. 1 (2005): 95–104.

Stark, Rodney, and William Sims Bainbridge. *A Theory of Religion*. New York: Peter Lang, 1987.

Steigenga, Timothy J., and Edward L. Cleary. *Conversion of a Continent: Contemporary Religious Change in Latin America*. New Brunswick, NJ: Rutgers University Press, 2007.

Stevens-Arroyo, Anthony M. "The Emergence of a Social Identity among Latino Catholics: An Appraisal." In *Hispanic Catholic Culture in the U.S.: Issues and Concerns*, edited by J. P. Dolan and A. F. Deck, 77–130. South Bend, IN: University of Notre Dame Press, 1994.

Streeter, Kurt. "Spreading the Pentecostal Spirit." *Los Angeles Times*, February 2, 2014. Accessed July, 22, 2015. http://www.latimes.com/local/la-me-latino-pentecostal-20140202-story.html#page=1.

Sullivan, Kathleen. "Iglesia de Dios." In *Religion and the New Immigrants*, edited by H. R. Ebaugh and J. S. Chafetz, 141–51. Walnut Creek, CA: AltaMira Press, 2000.

Telles, Edward E., and Vilma Ortiz, *Generations of Exclusion: Mexican Americans, Assimilation, and Race*. New York: Russell Sage Foundation, 2008.

Thomas, Lorrin. *Puerto Rican Citizen: History and Political Identity in Twentieth-Century New York City*. Chicago: University of Chicago Press, 2010.

Tienda, Marta, and Norma Fuentes. "Hispanics in Metropolitan America: New Realities and Old Debates." *Annual Review of Sociology* 40 (2014): 499–520.

U.S. Census Bureau. "Facts for Features: Hispanic Heritage Month 2014: Sept. 15–Oct. 15." September 8, 2014. Accessed April 3, 2015. http://www.census.gov/newsroom/facts-for-features/2014/cb14-ff22.html.

———. "The Hispanic Population: 2010." May 2011. Accessed April 3 2015. http://www.census.gov/prod/cen2010/briefs/c2010br-04.pdf .

Valenzuela, Ali Adam. "Tending the Flock: Latino Religious Commitments and Political Preferences." *Political Research Quarterly* 67, no. 4 (2014): 930–42.

Vasquez, Manuel A. "Pentecostalism, Collective Identity, and Transnationalism among Salvadorans and Peruvians in the U.S." *Journal of the Academy of Religion* 67, no. 3 (1999): 617–36.

Vega, Sujey. *Latino Heartland: Of Borders and Belonging in the Midwest.* New York: New York University Press, 2015.

Villarreal, Andrés. "Explaining the Decline in Mexico-US Migration: The Effect of the Great Recession." *Demography* 51, no. 6 (2014): 2203–28.

Walker, Randi Jones. *Protestantism in the Sangre de Cristos, 1850–1920.* Albuquerque: University of New Mexico Press, 1991.

Wasem, Ruth E. *Cuban Migration to the United States: Policy and Trends.* Washington DC: Library of Congress Congressional Research Service, 2009. Accessed May 1, 2016. http://fpc.state.gov/documents/organization/125936.pdf.

Westoff, Charles F., and Emily A. Marshall, "Hispanic Fertility, Religion, and Religiousness in the U.S." *Population Policy Research Review* 29, no. 4: 441–52.

Williams, Norma. *The Mexican American Family: Tradition and Change.* Lanham, MD: AltaMira Press, 1990.

Williams, Philip J. and Patricia Fortuny Loret de Mola, "Religion and Social Capital Among Mexican Immigrants in Southwest Florida." *Latino Studies* 5, no. 2 (207): 233–253.

Wilson, Catherine E. *The Politics of Latino Faith: Religion, Identity, and Urban Community.* New York: New York University Press, 2008.

Wind, James P., and James W. Lewis, eds. *American Congregations, Volume 1: Portraits of Twelve Religious Communities.* Chicago: University of Chicago Press, 1994.

Woodberry, Robert. "The Missionary Roots of Liberal Democracy." *American Political Science Review* 106, no. 2 (2012): 244–274.

Wright, Stuart A. "Reconceptualizing Cult Coercion and Withdrawal: A Comparative Analysis of Divorce and Apostasy." *Social Forces* 70, no. 1 (1991): 125–45.

Yohn, Susan Mitchell. *A Contest of Faiths: Missionary Women and Pluralism in the American Southwest.* Ithaca, NY: Cornell University Press, 1995.

INDEX

ABOUT THE AUTHORS

Mark T. Mulder's scholarship focuses on urban congregations and changing racial-ethnic demographics. Mulder is professor of sociology at Calvin College. He is the author of *Shades of White Flight: Evangelical Congregations and Urban Departure*. In addition, Mulder has published numerous peer-reviewed articles in academic journals, including *Social Problems* and the *Journal of Urban History*. He has also published pieces for church audiences and won awards from the Evangelical Press Association and the Associated Church Press for his writing.

Aida I. Ramos is assistant professor of sociology at George Fox University and a research fellow with the Latino Protestant Congregations Project, a three-year ethnographic study seeking to gain a social scientific understanding of Latino Protestant congregational life and practice. She has published in several peer-reviewed journals, including the *Social Science Quarterly*, the *Journal for the Scientific Study of Religion*, and the *Journal of Family Issues*. Ramos was raised in the border city of El Paso, Texas—a social context that has influenced her research interests in how social institutions like churches help to structure the well-being of Latino in ways that stratify, but also promote, resilience.

Gerardo Martí is L. Richardson King Associate Professor of Sociology at Davidson College. He is author of *A Mosaic of Believers: Diversity and Innovation in a Multiethnic Church, Hollywood Faith: Holiness, Prosperity, and Ambition in a Los Angeles Church, Worship across the Racial Divide: Religious Music and the Multiracial Congregation*, and

The Deconstructed Church: Understanding Emerging Christianity. Among several research collaborations and professional roles, he currently serves as the editor in chief of the peer-reviewed journal *Sociology of Religion: A Quarterly Review.*